My GPO in London: Tril(

The GPO in London (2016)

The Post Office in London, GPO North, South, East, and West
And the Savings Bank in which, your money to invest.

The Post Office Tower's tinted glass glistening in the sun
With the restaurant revolving and people having fun.

Parcels at Mount Pleasant stacked up very high
While underground on its railway the trains do shuttle by.

On the Euston postal, the Great Train Robbery took place
And mail vans along the crowded streets do race.

Switchboard operators plugging cords all day
Making the connections across all of the UK.

Dorothy Annan's murals depicting telecom themes
London telephone exchanges bursting at the seams!

Telegrams and telex, other messages daily fleeting
While in a Confravision studio important clients are meeting.

Front cover photo: A panel from Dorothy Annan's mural depicting 'Radio communications and television' (see Fleet Building)
© J. Chenery (2016)

Rear cover photo: Penny Veck driving Mail Rail ride at Mount Pleasant.
© J. Chenery (2017) (See Mail Rail)

The Seven Ages of Man totem pole at BT's Baynard House, London

"This Sculpture commissioned by Post Office Telecommunications and created by Richard Kindersley after inspiration from Shakespeare's seven ages of man was unveiled by Lord Miles of Blackfriars on 23 April 1980." © J. Chenery (2015)

My GPO in London: Trilogy Edition

John Chenery

Faraday Building, London
© J. Chenery (2016)

A Light Straw Presentation 2019

Quote from *Job in a Million* (1936): *"On your faithful performance of a public service will depend the future greatness of the Post Office. It's a vast organization, and you as a small part of that will be called upon to put public service before anything else."*

Important Note(s)

The thoughts and explanations expressed in this book are solely those of the author and contributors. They are not intended to imply any endorsement from trading units of Royal Mail Plc., Post Office Ltd., British Telecommunications Plc., Openreach Ltd., NS & I, or any of their associated companies.

Copyright © 2018 John Chenery
ISBN 978-0-244-14069-4

All rights reserved. This book or any portion thereof may not be reproduced or used in any manner whatsoever without the express written permission of the publisher except for the use of brief quotations in a book review or scholarly journal.

First edition February 2019.

A Light Straw Presentation formatted at Fynevue in England.

www.lightstraw.co.uk/mygpofamily

My GPO in London is the SECOND in a planned trilogy of books unravelling the history of the General Post Office, and its successors.

This tome is my own perspective of the GPO organisation, as it evolved, in London. Dates and events are quoted to aid comprehension and rekindle memories. Scholars and researchers are requested to make their own independent enquiries to verify the accuracy of the material herein.

Dedication

This book is dedicated to:

- All GPO, Post Office and BT staff, past and present.

> Memorandum 10/6/2019
>
> To *My GPO Family* Member:
>
> The Beaumont Family
>
> Remembering the days of Deryck and Ann.
>
> FROM: John

To Mum

Hope you like the trip down memory lane

Jane and Kristan
X e Sam xx

Contents

Acknowledgements viii
Preface xiii
Introduction 1
Establishing the GPO Timeline 3
Outlet 1: The GPO in London 13
Outlet 2: GPO East 49
Outlet 3: GPO West 61
Outlet 4: Roman Bath Street 67
Outlet 5: Electric Telegraph Company 81
Outlet 6: Tube Service (TS) 87
Outlet 7: GPO North 101
Outlet 8: GPO Time Services 111
Outlet 9: Master Clocks 123
Outlet 10: Rugby Radio 149
Outlet 11: Speaking Clock 155
Outlet 12: King Edward Building 163
Outlet 13: On the Grid 181
Outlet 14: Mail Rail 193
Outlet 15: The Postal Museum 203
Outlet 16: Telegraphs and Telegrams 213
Outlet 17: Electra House 231
Outlet 18: Fleet Building 235

Outlet 19: At Doctors' Commons 255
Outlet 20: Post Office Savings Bank 267
Outlet 21: GPO South 291
Outlet 22: Trunks and Tolls 305
Outlet 23: Trunk Mechanisation 323
Outlet 24: Bloomsbury and Fitzrovia 335
Outlet 25: On His Majesty's Service 351

Inspiring book list:

Between the Lines by Robert C. Morris

Built for Service:
Post Office Architecture by Julian Osley

Hold the Line Please:
The Story of the Hello Girls by Sally Southall

Post Office/British Telecom Factories 1870-1994
by Ken Govier, David Proctor, John Spanton, Charles Reynolds

The History of Rugby Radio Station
by Malcolm Hancock

Transmitting Signals:
The early and working life of R. Neil M. Alston

Acknowledgements

BT Heritage and Archives

Special thanks to *BT Heritage and Archives* (David Hay and his team) for easy access to their records and for allowing publication of photographs from www.bt.com/btdigitalarchives.

Page/Title	Finding Number
21 Wren House (1938)	TCB 417/E10734
35 Dollis Hill (1933)	POST 121/348
37 Wood Street (1948)	TCB 417/E15529
39 Studd Street (1950)	TCB 417/E16725
43 2-12 Gresham Street (1959)	TCB 417/E26664
48 RTC Paul Street (1966)	TCB 417/E33128
51 GPO East (1860)	TCB 473/P07064
61 Central Telegraph Office (1941)	TCB 417/E11766
79 Clerkenwell School of Telephony (1924)	TCB 417/E03010
90 CTO Street Tubes (1934)	TCB 473/P00277
95 Baudot Operator at CTO (1934)	TCB 473/P00362
96 Pneumatic Tubes at CTO (1912)	TCB 475/YB04
98 Central Hall CTO (1929)	TCB 417/E06312
99 Phonograms at CTO (1935)	TCB 473/P00610
121 Time Service in GPO West (1928)	TCB 417/E05273
141 The Chronopher (time carrier) (1912)	TCB 475/YB23
143 Clock No. 24 (1922)	TCB 417/E02684
144 Clock No. 30 (1932)	TCB 417/E07821
156 Speaking Clock at Holborn (1950)	TCB 473/P04728
159 Speaking Clock Mk. III (c1962)	TCE 361/ARC00844
169 Inspection of Messengers (1917)	TCB 417/E01930
170 Public Counter at KEB (1962)	TCB 473/P07988
171 National Postal Museum	TCB 473/P10484

232 Electra House (1950)   TCB 473/P04705
243 CTO Printergram Positions (1962)   TCB 417/E27625
244 CTO Combined Working (1962)   TCB 417/E27626
248 CTO Telex Switchboards (1961)   TCB 417/E28071
255 Doctors' Commons   TCB 473/P03672
260 Bakehouse Court (1939)   TCB 417/E11308
261 Faraday SE Block (1939)   TCB 417/E11306
268 POSB HQ QVS (c1880)   TCB 475/ZE18
282 POSB Blythe House (1946)   TCB 417/E14042
283 POSB Blythe House (1946)   TCB 417/E14039
295 Faraday North Block (1931)   TCB 417/E07232
320 Faraday Citadel (1945)   TCB 417/E13765
325 Holborn Tandem (1927)   TCB 417/E05131
346 Post Office Tower (1971)   TCB 346/T841

Geograph (www.geograph.org.uk)
Page 44: Camelford House, Albert Embankment © Stephen Richards (2011) See www.geograph.org.uk/photo/2615410

Page 285: Charles House, West Kensington © Ruth Sharville (2010) See www.geograph.org.uk/photo/1700695

Page 288: Manor Gardens © Julian Osley (2014) See www.geograph.org.uk/photo/3959536

Copyright Google (2018)
Page 349: Post Office Central Headquarters, 23 Howland St., London W1P 6HQ (01-631 2345). Street view image capture July 2015.

Copyright London Metropolitan Archives, City of London
Page 265: The Bell, 6 Addle Hill (1982) [Used under licence.]
https://collage.cityoflondon.gov.uk/

Copyright Royal Mail courtesy of The Postal Museum (2018)
Page 26: Plan circa 1890 shewing Post Office properties.
[Ref: POST 21/59 used under licence.]

Page 165: Royal Mail vans in The Yard at King Edward Building (1931) [Ref: POST 118/5089 used under licence.]

Page 176: Remains of Roman Wall within the Yard at KEB (1936) [Ref: POST 118/498 used under licence.]

All other photos and diagrams are credited on the individual pages.

Other Thanks

Thanks to *The Postal Museum*, and the *Great Britain Philatelic Society* (www.gbps.org.uk) for making access to historical Post Office documents possible. Chris Hogan of the *Post Office Vehicle Club* for help with the GPO/Post Office/RM, and BT timelines.

Merrill Lynch (Robert Ayling, Steven J. Clark, George Russel, Martin Barrow) and the *Museum of London* (Jackie Keily) for Roman Wall access and history.

Barbara Mower for Post Office Tower revolving platform story and photo.

TfL Corporate Archives; *TfL/TSBA Group* for allowing use of 'underground symbol' on London diagram(s).

Also: Andrew Emmerson, Malcolm Knight, Adam Oliver, Richard Truscott, John Tythe, Dan Glover, Simon Chappell, Neil Johannessen, David Cott, and *Telecommunications Heritage Group* for inspiration, fact-checking and support.

For an ongoing historical review of *The Company* see also my *Light Straw* website: www.lightstraw.co.uk

Books by the Author:

My GPO Family: Supplied for the Public Service (2017)
My GPO Family: Trilogy (abridged) *Edition* Part 1 (2018)
My GPO in London: Trilogy Edition Part 2 (2019)
London's Trunks, Tolls and Telex (2020)
My GPO Legacy: Trilogy Edition Part 3 (2021)

Companion Photobooks to *My GPO in London*

Mail Rail at Mount Pleasant (2018)
Roman Wall at Merrill Lynch (2018)
Dorothy Annan Murals (2018)

See www.mygpofamily.com for more details.

A modern-day postman wheeling an HCT (high-capacity trolley) past Blythe House © J. Chenery (2010)

Abbreviations

BIS Brought into service (date)
RFS Ready for service (date)
TE/ATE Telephone Exchange/Automatic Telephone Exchange

E-in-C (Engineer-in-Chief's) Reports
PMG (Postmaster-General) Reports
POEEJ Post Office Electrical Engineers' Journal
POTJ Post Office Telecommunications Journal

Preface

In book one of *My GPO Family: Supplied for the Public Service (and Trilogy Edition)*, I described how the General Post Office (GPO) had influenced my life as I was growing up, and throughout my working career. The Post Office never failed to enthral me with its innovative ideas for change and its steadfast products and services which have endured the test of time! At its peak, the Post Office employed over 358,000 people to operate both the Postal and Telecommunications businesses of the UK. Today, Post Office Ltd., which operates the counters business, is the only part still owned by the Government. Privatised companies, Royal Mail and British Telecommunications run what remains of the once public, national postal and telecoms infrastructures, respectively.

Massive changes have occurred since the original GPO ran everything, but the core products of providing essential communications remain true. Under the new regimes, each company strives for an ever more modern approach to meet the needs of its customers whilst remaining competitive within the current regulatory climate(s).

The Post Office has always been good at re-organising and reinventing itself to ensure its continued serviceability and none more so than in London, where projects on a large scale have often been both essential and unusually complex.

This book explores the GPO's origins and activities in London, as its headquarters and the delivery of its services became centred upon the St. Paul's Cathedral area of the City. The progression and expansion of its services relied upon suitable accommodation as the requirements for equipment and staff increased with demand. Throughout, the administration of the company changed as it developed and finally evolved, almost beyond recognition, into separate public limited companies of British Telecommunications (1984), and Royal Mail Group (2002).

Recounting the beginnings of the GPO estate in London, with studies of the important buildings, some already swept away by 20th century redevelopment, will perhaps evoke memories of the reader's own period with, or knowledge of the company.

The aim is to give a 'flavour' of bygone times, rather than being a definitive tome, for which time and research is beyond the scope of this current publication. Readers are invited to pursue further information for topics within, that particularly interest them. I have attempted to produce this 'compendium of the GPO in London' in an easily flowing progression of factual events, well-illustrated with historical photographs from BT Heritage and Archive's extensive collection and supplemented by my own modern-day snaps to complete the story.

This second volume in the *My GPO* trilogy takes us from the very early beginnings of the Post Office right up to the era of the Post Office Tower in the mid-1960s. Note: Several chapters have been written as 'stand-alone' stories, therefore there is some overlap of information between topics.

Inevitably, an organisation as vast as the Post Office is too big to adequately discuss fully in just one London volume, therefore the evolution of telephone switching (through the 60s and 70s) will be explored in more detail in a later book entitled *London's Trunks, Tolls, and Telex*.

John Chenery
December 2018

Introduction

A Long History

As part of the Civil Service, the organisation of the GPO (General Post Office) was renowned for a long history of stability, with methods of operation meticulously recorded and subject only to gradual change. With some exceptions, improvements in technology always had to be tried and tested before implementation. The well-ordered hierarchy was slow to react to increased demand for its services and significant progress was only hastened by legislation, which eventually moved virtually all aspects of the business into the private sector.

My impressionable era of the Post Office was the late 1960s and early 1970s when many of its more modern showcase buildings and major projects were nearing completion. These new purpose-built structures served their functions well until, in a comparatively short period, the technology and the equipment within became outdated. Such specialist designs, often built on constricted sites, didn't lend themselves to other uses and thus many were demolished only 40 years after their construction. Older, bigger, more traditional buildings of brick and ornate stonework continued to survive past this period as they were more suitable for conversion into luxury flats or office spaces.

The GPO had some truly unique buildings in its empire across London as postal, telegraph and telephone services had developed over many, many decades. The pace of life, and the evolution of the equipment needed to supply these services, continued ever faster as the organisation re-invented itself to meet these challenges.

My GPO in London: Trilogy Edition

What follows, is a glimpse of the GPO's London networks, organisation, buildings, services, and people. This is my personal 'take' on how the GPO operated as it provided jobs and services for everyone.

Showcase to the World

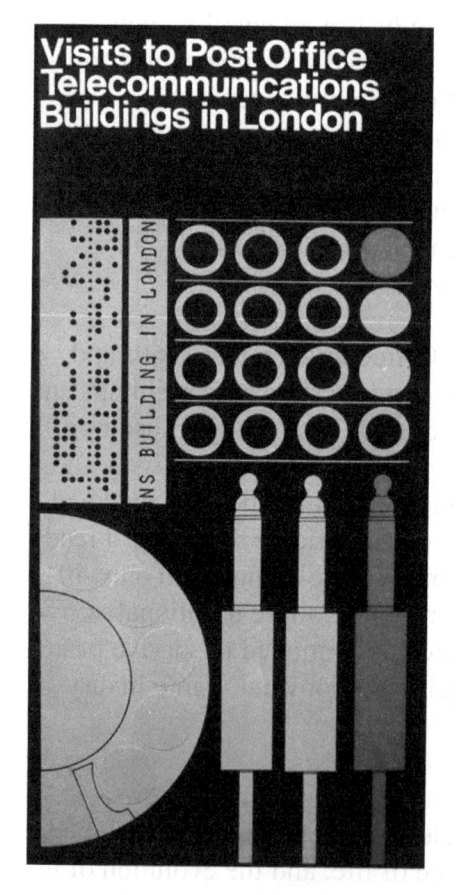

'*Members of the public are invited to visit a number of Post Office Telecommunications buildings either in parties, small groups or on their own. In most cases, conducted tours can be arranged if applications are made in advance, preferably three weeks before the date of the proposed visit.*'

Buildings included were, the Post Office Tower, Faraday Building, Fleet Building and Electra House.

Leaflet PH 1623 (TCB 318/PH 1623)
Visits to Post Office Telecommunications Buildings in London (c.1969)

Timeline

Establishing the GPO Timeline

The early history of the General Post Office (GPO) in London is couched in the terms of old English, the ramblings of parliamentary proceedings, the familiarities of improper street names, and the relentless redevelopment of the City. Notwithstanding, the entrepreneurship and artfulness of the government and businesses alike, each wanting the best outcomes.

The GPO had its beginnings with Royal Mail as the UK postal service was established...

Royal Mail 1516

Royal Mail's origin can be traced back to 1516 with the appointment of a Master of the Posts, Brian Tuke.

In the beginnings of a public postal network (c.1600s), post houses on post roads, inns, and taverns all competed for carriage of the mail at varying rates and commissions. Inland and foreign mail 'letter offices' operated in an uncoordinated manner.

Thomas Witherings 1635

'Proposition for settling staffets or packet post betwixt London and all parts of His Majesties dominions for the carrying and recarrying of His subjects' letters.' (June 1635)

With authority to regularise the situation, Witherings set up the first official Letter Office in his own home in Sherborne Lane (EC2).

[Reference: *Masters of the Post* by James Duncan Campbell 2011.]

My GPO in London: Trilogy Edition

There is much conjecture with conflicting reports of where these early 'letter/receiving offices' were located, or indeed what constituted a 'post office' in the modern sense.

General Letter Office (1653-1666) Threadneedle Street

In 1653 previous agreements were revoked and, as Postmaster-General, John Manley administered inland and foreign post.

1653 is the earliest date given for a Post House in Threadneedle St. [Reference: *Masters of the Post* by Duncan Campbell-Smith 2011.]

> Near this spot the
> General Letter Office
> stood in Post House Yard
> 1653-1666
> Here were struck in 1661
> the first postmarks in
> the world

Blue plaque, Prince's Street EC2.
© J. Chenery (2017)

These were not insubstantial premises as staff lived on site. The combined staff of the Inland and Foreign Letter Office was a total of 45, [Reference: GPO by E.T. Crutchley 1938.] employed thus:

Timeline

Staff of the Inland and Foreign Letter Office

- 8 clerks of the road: controlling dispatches and assessing postage
- 3 foreign office clerks
- 2 receivers of letters at the window
- 1 general accountant
- 1 sub accountant
- 1 letter marker, or stamper
- 1 agent 'to ryde the several rodes and find out abuse'
- 28 letter carriers or porters

Settling the Post 1657

This postal service was formalised with Oliver Cromwell's parliament establishing the 1657 *'Act for the Setling of the Postage of England, Scotland and Ireland'*.

'From henceforth there be one General Office, to be called and known by the name of the Post Office of England...And one officer.... under the name of Post Master General.'

General Post Office (GPO) 1660

However, Charles II disputed Cromwell's laws and so the Post Office act of 1660 was passed to legally recognise the formation of the organisation:

'An Act for Erecting and Establishing a Post Office.'

My GPO in London: Trilogy Edition

Thus, the *General Letter Office*, subsequently known as the *General Post Office*, was formalised in London. Henry Bishop was appointed Postmaster-General in 1660, and in 1661 the first British postmark was introduced.

Threadneedle Street Post House (1666)

Leake's survey map of December 1666 after the Great Fire clearly shows a Post House marked on Threadneedle Street.

'In the early hours of Monday morning the resident staff began to leave the General Letter Office, a huge building at the lower end of Threadneedle Street, opposite the Stocks Market at the junction of Poultry, Cornhill and Lombard Streets. They followed the not entirely courageous lead of Sir Philip Frowde, a senior official who lived at the Letter Office; he and his wife had fled to safety around midnight, while the flames were still several streets away. James Hickes, the senior clerk, held on for another hour.'

[Reference: *By Permission of Heaven: The Story of the Great Fire of London* by Adrian Tinniswood 2004.]

After the Great Fire of London

'The general Post-office is for the present held at the two Black Pillars in Bridges Street, over against the Fleece-Tavern, Covent Garden, till a more convenient place can be found in London.'

[Reference: *London Gazette* No.85 3-10 September 1666 www.thegazette.co.uk/London/issue/85/]

Many other locations are mentioned, in papers, but not confirmed until...

Timeline

Bishopsgate Street (1676)

Ogilby and Morgan's Large-Scale Map of the City as Rebuilt by 1676. The map is endorsed, *Post Office, General, Bishopsgate Street Within, B59.*

[www.british-history.ac.uk/no-series/london-map-ogilby-morgan/1676/]

GPO Post Office Court EC3 (1678-1829)

Located between King William Street, and Lombard Street.

Post Office Court tablet
© J. Chenery (2017)

The General Post Office moved from Bishopsgate Street to a building on this site on Lady Day 1678 and remained here until the opening of St. Martins-le-Grand on the 23rd September 1829.

The premises off Lombard Street had been home to Sir Robert Viner (City banker and Lord Mayor in 1674).

My GPO in London: Trilogy Edition

'The first Entrance out of Lombard Street into this House is through a large Gate and broad Entry, which leadeth into a handsome Court neatly paved with Free Stone, enclosed in with the Buildings belonging unto it; and behind the House is a Yard for Stabling and Coaches, where there is a back Gate into Sherborn Lane: This House is very convenient for the Management of this great Business of the General Post-Office.'

[Reference: John Strype's *A Survey of the Cities of London and Westminster* 1720.]

The postal service carried mail, inland and abroad, but it wasn't until 1680 that a local (London) *Penny Post* was established by merchant William Docwra. The scheme, which eventually had hundreds of *receiving-houses* (shops, inns and coffee houses), was adopted by the Post Office in November 1682. *Letter-carriers* transported the mail (up to as many as twelve times a day) to and from the *receiving-houses* and the General Letter Office, where the mail was sorted, taxed and stamped.

Throughout its history in London, the ever-growing Post Office was frequently faced with the need to acquire larger and more appropriate accommodation in the provision of its services.

'In 1765 four houses in Abchurch Lane were taken, and additional offices erected; and from time to time other additions were made, until the whole became a cumbrous and inconvenient mass of buildings, ill adapted to the great increase which had taken place in the business of the Post Office.'

[Reference: *London Vol 3*. (1842) Edited by Charles Knight.]

Timeline

Uniforms

In 1793 London's General Post letter-carriers were issued with uniforms.

A *Letter to the Treasury* of 21 March 1814 expressed concerns about the suitability of the GPO premises...

'There is great insecurity from the various offices being in different streets. Some are in Lombard Street, some in Abchurch Lane, some in Sherborne Lane. The mail coaches cannot take up the mail at the General Post-Office; the street will not admit of it.'

The security of the mail relied upon the integrity of its staff. This paragraph is included as a curiosity, to illustrate the locations and postal terms of the day...

Mail Theft (1819)

Extract from: Old Bailey Proceedings Online (www.oldbaileyonline.org, version 7.2, 13 December 2017), April 1819, trial of THOMAS JEFFCOTT (t18190421-54).

JOHN PRICE MADDER. *"I am in the employ of the Post-office, it is part of my duty to receive the bags from the receiving-houses. On the 10th of September I did not receive the Princes-street bag."*

JOHN TULLIDER. *"I am a messenger. On the 10th of September I received the Princes-street bags - they were sealed and unbroken. I took them into the Post-office."*

Cross-examined by MR. JARVIS.

Q. *"Are you a bellman?"*

My GPO in London: Trilogy Edition

A. *"No. I did not fetch it from Princes-street, I received it at the Post-office in Lombard-street; they are put through the window in the Paid Letter-office, where I stand, and open the paid bags."*

Q. *"Are the paid bags brought to you by the bellman or by a messenger?"*
A. *"There are messengers in the Post-office, whose duty it is to collect the bags from the districts."*

COURT. Q. *"Have you any doubt that you received the paid letter bag that day?"*
A. *"I have not."*

The solution towards accommodating a growing postal service was to commission architect Sir Robert Smirke to design new premises.

St. Martin's-le-Grand (1829)

The new General Post Office building was in the design of a palatial museum. By 1818 a two-acre site had been secured and thus work began in 1824 on a grand neo-classical styled building with a cavernous central hall, and Ionic columns, the whole clad in Portland stone.

'This splendid edifice was opened in the presence of a great concourse of people, for the commencement of the business of the Post-office department, a short time before five o'clock yesterday morning' [Reference: The *Morning Post* 24 September 1929, p.3.]

[See ***GPO East*** chapter for more detail.]

Timeline

Postal Reform (1840) under Rowland Hill

Postage had always been payable upon delivery, but the introduction of a national minimum postage of one penny, on 10 January 1840, stipulated prepayment. This was facilitated by the launch of the first adhesive postage stamp, the *Penny Black* in May 1840. However, by 1841, this was replaced by the *Penny Red*, to allow the more secure black cancel marks to be applied.

Later postal history is continued through individual chapters.

Telecommunications Timeline

1846 The Electric Telegraph Company

The Electric Telegraph Company, from which BT is ultimately descended, was established on 18 June 1846. The company built an extensive telegraph network throughout the UK.

The Telegraph Acts of 1868-70

These gave Her Majesty's Postmaster-General the right to acquire and operate the existing inland telegraph systems in the UK.

1876 First Telephone Call

On 10 March 1876 Alexander Graham Bell spoke, *"Mr. Watson. Come here. I want to see you."*

The 1880 Ruling

A court judgement on 20 December 1880 ruled in favour of the Post Office by stating that a telephone was a telegraph and a telephone conversation was a telegram under the Telegraph Act,

My GPO in London: Trilogy Edition

1869. Thereafter, the Postmaster-General issued operating licenses to allow competing telephone companies to trade.

1912 Post Office Telephones

From 1 January 1912 the General Post Office became the monopoly supplier of telephone services with the exception of the remaining municipal services in Hull, Portsmouth and Guernsey.

1969 Post Office Corporation

On 1 October 1969 the Post Office became a Public Corporation no longer under direct control of HM Government.

1975 Post Office Telecommunications

The telephone part of the service was rebranded to become Post Office Telecommunications.

1980 British Telecom – part of the Post Office

In May 1980 British Telecom was revealed as the new name for the telephone side of the business, although it was still 'part of the Post Office'.

1981 British Telecom

After Vesting Day on 1 October 1981, British Telecom was the trading name of the British Telecommunications corporation, entirely separate from the Post Office.

1984 British Telecommunications plc

On 6 August 1984, British Telecommunications became a public limited company. British Telecom was the first in a series of state-owned utility privatisations as HM Government initially offered 50.2% of its shares to the public and employees.

Outlet 1: The GPO in London

The General Post Office's estate evolved out of a necessity to be able to provide the services that the Post Office offered, and which the public demanded. Grand, bold, new buildings were designed to be attractive and functional; the showcase of a proud public service. In later years, function dictated the ultimate form, in the pre-digital age as demand exceeded capacity, but regardless, the designs were innovative, if not sometimes controversial by their perceived ugliness!

The Ministry of Works

As part of the government and crown, many GPO buildings were designed by architects from the Ministry of Works. Notable architects were Eric Bedford who designed the Post Office Tower and Faraday Building extension, in the 1960s. And Henry Tanner, the extensive Post Office Savings Bank HQ, Blythe House. Not forgetting, Albert Robert Myers (H M Office of Works in Westminster and London from 1899) for Faraday Building (1933).

The Office of Works existed as long ago as 1378 with a duty for the Royal Estate, buildings and residences of the king. From about 1851 the Office was responsible to Parliament. World War II established an urgent need for new government, office and utility buildings and so the Ministry of Works and Buildings was formed in 1940. The department went through many changes of title as its remit altered over the years:

My GPO in London: Trilogy Edition

- 1940 to 1942 Ministry of Works and Buildings
- 1942 to 1943 Ministry of Works and Planning
- 1943 to 1962 Ministry of Works
- 1962 to 1970 Ministry of Public Building and Works
- 1970 became part of the Department of the Environment
- 1972 most functions transferred to PSA (Property Services Agency)
- Early 1990s splitting up of PSA and privatisation of services

The following is a summary of sites for *My GPO in London*. The GPO estate was a vast sprawling empire of postal, clerical, engineering, management, and support services. All are worthy of inclusion, but the featured buildings are particularly relevant to the storyline.

GPO Sites

In retrospect, the GPO had some fine buildings in its empire across London as postal, telegraph and telephone services continued to develop. To distinguish the growing number of main sites the (new) *General Post Office*, in St. Martin's le Grand, became *GPO East*, and subsequent sites were thus *GPO West, North, and South*.

There follows:

1. An extract from the Post Office Guide of 1911 listing key departments
2. A composite *diagram* of main GPO buildings (across the decades) centred around St. Paul's

GPO in London

CENTRAL DEPARTMENTS OF THE POST OFFICE

The **Postmaster-General**, the **Secretary** and **Solicitor** to the Post Office and the **Comptroller and Accountant-General**, have their offices at the General Post Office North, St. Martin's le Grand, E.C.

The **Central Post Office Savings Bank** is at Blythe Road, West Kensington, W.; address "The Controller."

The **Money Order and Postal Order Department** is at 144A, Queen Victoria Street, E.C., but will shortly be removed to Manor Gardens, Holloway, N.; address "The Controller, Money Order Department, London."

The Office of the **Engineer-in-Chief** is at the General Post Office West, St. Martin's le Grand, E.C.

The office of the **Controller of the London Postal Service** is at the General Post Office, King Edward Street, E.C.

The **Central Telegraph Office** is at the General Post Office West, St. Martin's le Grand, E.C.; address "The Controller."

The Office of the **General Manager of the Post Office London Telephone system** is at the General Post Office South, Carter Lane, E.C.

The Office of the **Controller of Stores** is at 17-19, Bedford Street, W.C.

The **Returned Letter Office** is at Mount Pleasant, E.C.

[Extract from Post Office Guide 1911]

My GPO in London: Trilogy Edition

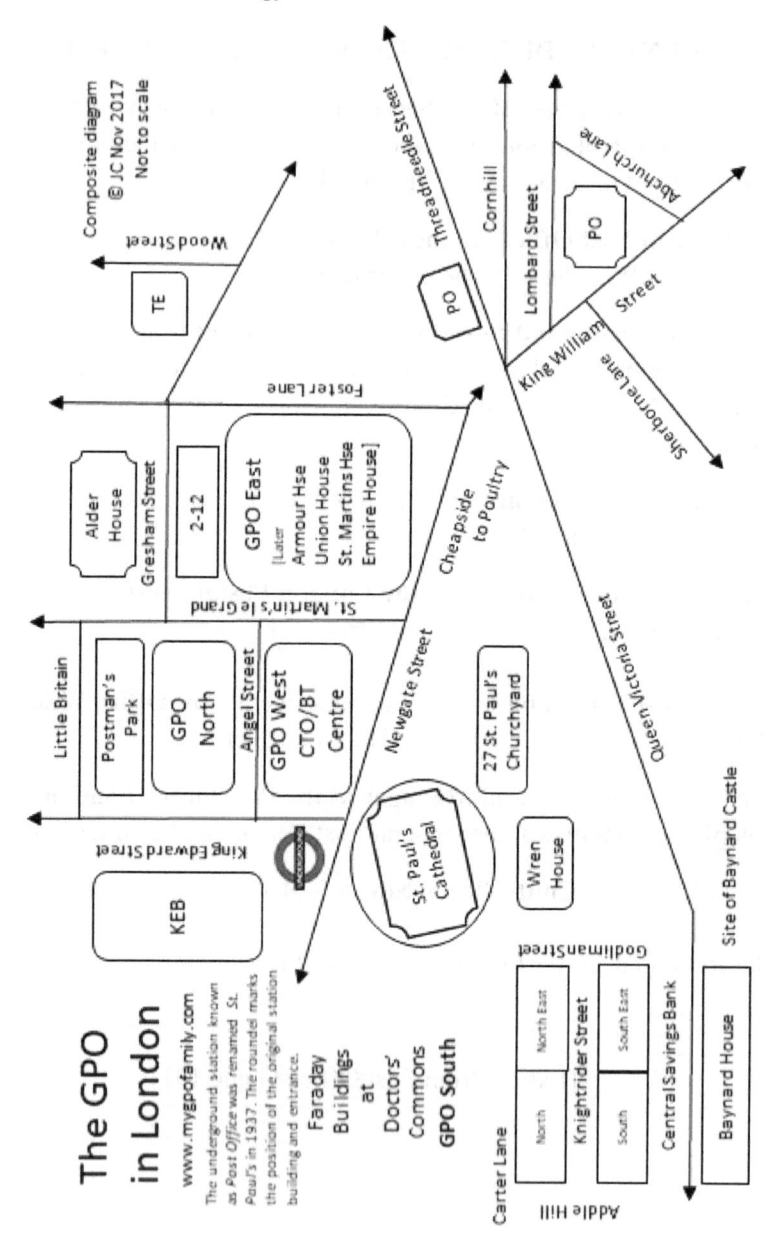

GPO in London

From early days, Central London, close to St. Paul's Cathedral became the very heart of the GPO's organisation. Operator centres, HQ buildings, both postal and telecom all developed in the shadow of the cathedral. As business grew, the buildings became ever grander, and extensive. This trend continued right up to the dawn of the digital era, after which a contracting of operations and slimming down of a once phenomenal organisation began...

BT Centre may have been the last of the grand London sites to be commissioned.

Post Office Works (2017)

The Post Office did its work on a major scale
And there was often some prestige it had to avail

Public service buildings grand
For a long time they had to stand

Functional and utilitarian too
The Tower it had a special view

Later ones were brutally bold
As well the Cold War may have foretold

Many designed by the Office of Works
Architects and Civil Service clerks

Few remain unto this present day
Vast complexes simply swept away!

My GPO in London: Trilogy Edition

Chasing Growth

The GPO's London organisation of its estate, was constantly changing to try and keep pace with the demand for its services. This imperative was forever present as the media of communications evolved through the decades, in line with contemporary trends. The letter post gave way to the telegram as a means of urgent communication, which in turn was usurped by the telephone. The letter and parcel post grew too, alongside international communications and telex services, culminating in e-mail and the internet, which was another revolution in the making.

Many interim services were offered and supplied over the years, such as Intelfax, radiopaging, carphones, telemessaging, telemetry – all of which competed for office, staff, and equipment accommodation. Specialist telephone and telex equipment needed custom-designed buildings, and postal areas needed ample space for both manual, and later machine sorting.

In the 1880s this turmoil of postal, banking, telegraph, and telephone growth, gave the greatest impetus to the sourcing of additional sites to meet public demand. Even then, new buildings were quickly outgrown and ever more premises were sought. Tracking the department designations for each building is almost impossible, even for those who worked there, as traditionally, employees concentrated upon their own work areas, almost exclusively. The GPO was a business, not an archival system, although its often meticulous, record-keeping is fascinating to study.

GPO in London

Wartime severely restricted expansion and consequently it wasn't until the 1960s and 70s that another frenzied era of building relieved the post-war boom, both for local and international growth.

There follows a chronological summary of important buildings in the GPO estate...

GPO East (1829-1910)
St. Martin's-le-Grand/Gresham Street/Foster Lane

GPO East was the first of the grandiose headquarters buildings in the City. By 1844 the main work areas were:

- The Inland Office
- The Newspaper Office
- Foreign and Ship Letter Departments
- The Railway Room
- The Letter-Carriers' Office
- The Money Order Office
- The Secret Office *

* Where letters were opened under authority of the Secretary of State (Home Office).

The work of *GPO East* eventually outgrew the site, despite partial rebuilding and numerous extensions.

GPO East closed in 1910 and was demolished 1912/13.

[See **GPO East** chapter for more details.]

My GPO in London: Trilogy Edition

Place/Year	1800s	1870	1880	1890	1900	1910	1920	1930	1940	1950	1960	1970	1980	1990	2000	2010
GPO East	1829 Postal															
GPO West		1874 Telegraphs and telegrams				1910										
BT Centre											1962					
GPO South					1902 Telephone service								1985 THQ			
GPO North				1895 GPO HQ												
King Edward Building						1910 Postal HQ and Sorting office							1984			
Post Office Railway								1927 Underground mail service						1996		2003
Mount Pleasant			1888 Postal sorting									1977				
PO Savings Bank			1880 Bank 1903													
QVS					1903 POSB HQ											
Blythe House																

GPO Timelines: Building Occupancy Dates.

GPO in London

London was crammed with warehouses trading all types of goods. Some sites were gradually developed into grander more permanent buildings...

27 St. Paul's Churchyard (1863)

This little-known key site was first occupied by the Post Office Savings Bank until its move to Queen Victoria Street in 1880.

Wren House (1938)
© *BT Heritage and Archives TCB 417/E10734*

In the 1930s the premises were redeveloped into *Wren House*, encompassing 27-30 St. Paul's Churchyard. During the war the

My GPO in London: Trilogy Edition

19th City of London (2nd GPO) Battalion Home Guard was based there. By 1947 it was a *Trunk Training School* for telephonists, and the *Long-Distance Area* HQ. *Wren House* was demolished during road widening and the creation of *Carter Lane Gardens* in the early 1960s. [See also later entry for (new) Wren House 1964.]

**GPO West (1874-1962)
Newgate Street/St. Martin's-le-Grand**

GPO West was intended as a new headquarters building to relieve the overcrowded *GPO East*, but due to the rapid growth and popularity of the Telegram Service, it soon became the Central Telegraph Office (CTO) for London.

It too was extended with extra storeys, but was devastated by bombing in WWII. A partial-rebuild after the war kept it in business until alternative accommodation and re-routing of circuits was completed. The run-down of the pneumatic tube systems as the telephone gained prominence, and the decentralisation of London switching ensured its fate.

GPO West closed in 1962 and was demolished in 1967. The buildings on the western side of the site (Roman Bath Street) continued in use until the early 1970s. Clearance of the whole area allowed the Museum of London to carry out archaeological excavations during 1975-1979, until work commenced in 1980 on a new HQ building that was to become British Telecom Centre (BTC).

[See chapter *Tube Service* for more details of *GPO West.*]

Post Office Factories (1870)

In 1870 the General Post Office, by act of Parliament, gained control of the Telegraph Service in the UK. Two telegraph repair factories, one in Holloway (London) and the other in Bolton, formed the beginnings of the Post Office's manufacturing and supply work. In 1967 Factories became a Division of the Purchasing and Supply Department. Hence, the name of *Fac. D.*

London-based factories: Perivale in Ealing; Bovay Place, Holloway, and Crayford Stores Depot. MNDXs (Mobile Non-Director Exchanges) were assembled at Bilton Way, Enfield. Studd Street in Islington was originally the HQ of the GPO stores department.

Birmingham-based factories: Jubilee Works in Sherlock Street, Highgate; Garrison Lane and Fordrough Lane, in Bordesley Green.

Other factories were located in Edinburgh, and Cwmcarn, South Wales. Cwmcarn notably produced the Slimtel (one-piece) telephone.

During WWII, workers at Garrison Lane unknowingly assembled racking and wired-up components for the code-breaking Colossus computers, which utilised many standard GPO parts. Post Office factories were renowned for producing both new and refurbished equipment to an extremely high quality which ensured longevity in use. After privatisation, the terms of British Telecom's licence, stipulated that any part of the company which manufactured telecommunications equipment was required to be transferred to a subsidiary company no later than July 1986. Thus in 1985, *BT*

My GPO in London: Trilogy Edition

Factories was reorganised into two subsidiaries, *BT Fulcrum Communications* and *BT Consumer Electronics*.

BT's evolving strategy in the competitive marketplace was to dispose of parts of its business that were outside of its core growth area. With the rental base declining as customers chose to buy their own phones, there was no requirement to retain a (costly) telephone manufacturing division, and even less need for a fully-fledged repair facility. In 1990 Standard Telephones and Cables (STC) bought British Telecom's Cwmcarn based manufacturing business. Under this agreement, STC ran the final production line of the Vanguard telephone. In April 1991, the remaining 25% of BT's telephone refurbishing business was sold to Fulcrum Communications Limited. Finally, after 120 years (1870 to 1991) the Post Office/BT involvement in the direct manufacture and refurbishment of telegraph and telephone equipment, had ended.

In 2003 at BT's Ashford warehouse, the *Connected Earth* auction sold off decades of accumulated historical telephony artefacts as BT began to rationalise its huge property estate.

References: *Post Office/British Telecom Factories 1870-1994* by Ken Govier, David Proctor, John Spanton, Charles Reynolds.
Post Office Factories 100 Years of Service (THQ: ICU 231/71)

Post Office Savings Bank (1880)

The HQ of the Post Office Savings Bank (POSB) was built at 144 Queen Victoria Street, circa 1880. It was demolished in 1929 in favour of the International Exchange (*Faraday Building*) which opened in 1933. The extensions (mid-1880s) of the POSB, along Carter Lane became *GPO South*, and subsequently formed the

GPO in London

North Block of Faraday Buildings. [See chapters *Doctors' Commons* and *POSB* for more details.]

Christ's Hospital Site(s)
The Post Office had ambitious land-purchase plans which it co-ordinated in order to secure the required accommodation for its central London operations. The extensive land bordering properties owned by Christ's Hospital were of major interest.

For the new building of *GPO North*, the site was to encompass the Queen's Hotel (formerly the *Bull and Mouth Inn*), the former Angel Inn, houses in Bull and Mouth Street and Magpie Court. Bull and Mouth Street was to become part of Postman's Park.

'In view of the need for improved accommodation for sorting work at the General Post Office East, arrangements have been made to acquire nearly the whole of the site (or about 3.5 acres) formerly occupied by Christ's Hospital.' [PMG report 1904.]

Subsequently the *King Edward Building* was to feature a large *Sorting Block* adjacent to the main premises.

Site Map circa 1890s
The map (next page) shows the extent of the Post Office's proposed land acquisitions.

Christ's Hospital land - between Giltspur Street (on the far left) and King Edward Street (middle) which was destined to be the *King Edward Building* and yard.

My GPO in London: Trilogy Edition

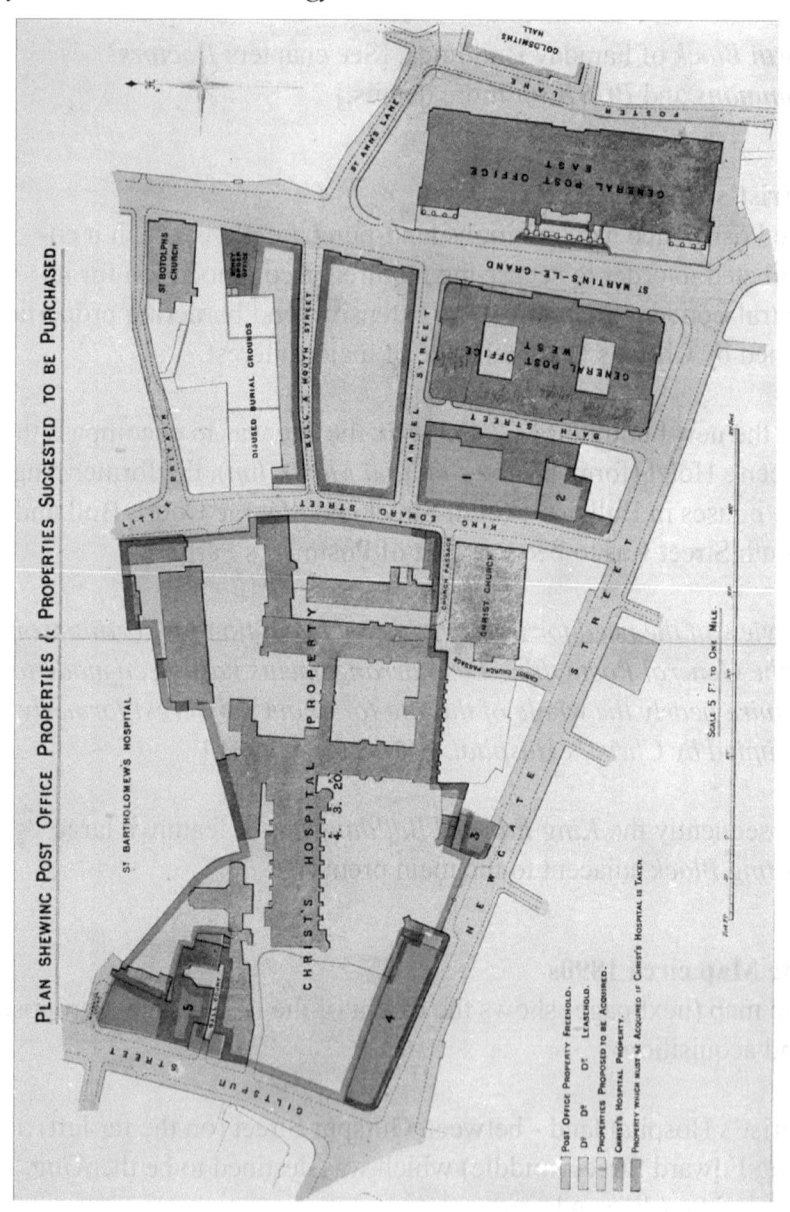

© *Royal Mail Group Ltd, Courtesy of The Postal Museum, 2018.*

GPO in London

Christ's Hospital sculpture on Newgate Street.
© J. Chenery (2018)

Christ's Hospital

Founded near this site by King Edward VI - 1552
To house, feed and educate needy children.

Incorporating the Royal Mathematical School,
founded by King Charles II – 1673.

The School moved to Horsham, West Sussex – 1902
where its historic mission continues.

Sculpted by Andrew F Brown

My GPO in London: Trilogy Edition

GPO South (1880-2005)

Originated as the Post Office Savings Bank HQ, but was subsequently re-developed into a large telecommunications centre, as national and international telephone calls were switched through London. The *North Block* was demolished in 2005, excepting the entrance porticos, which were incorporated into a new hotel.

At GPO South: Faraday North Block, viewed from Knightrider Street
© J. Chenery (2001)

GPO in London

GPO North (1895-1984)

*GPO North with BT Centre (right).
Viewed from King Edward Street
© J. Chenery (2017)*

GPO North was built as the principal administration headquarters of the Post Office and was sited between King Edward Street and St. Martin's-le-Grand, Angel Street and Little Britain.

It was sold in 1986, as by then Posts and Telecommunications had distinctly separate London HQs.

[See chapter *GPO North* for more details.]

My GPO in London: Trilogy Edition

Mount Pleasant (1888)
Henry Tanner/Albert Myers (*Office of Works*)

Mount Pleasant © J. Chenery (2017)

Parcel sorting moved into the *Cold Bath Fields* prison site from about 1888. New blocks were constructed between 1925 and the official opening in 1934. The separate Post Office (counters) block opened on 18 June 1937. Wartime bomb damage on 18 June 1943 destroyed the (1890) London Parcel Section block. Letter sorting transferred in stages from *GPO East,* and later the *King Edward Building*, making *The Mount* the principal sorting office in London.

GPO in London

NTC's Telephone House 2-4 Temple Avenue, Embankment, EC4
© J. Chenery (2018)

My GPO in London: Trilogy Edition

*NTC's Telephone House 2-4 Temple Avenue, Embankment, EC4
Photo: Mercury the winged messenger © J. Chenery (2018)*

GPO in London

NTC (1881-1911)

Amidst the GPO's London developments, the National Telephone Company had some impressive buildings and extensive manual switchboards, before its empire was subsumed into the 1912 nationalisation.

'The organised tuition of telephone operators was commenced in London in 1899, when the first operating school in the world was opened.' [NTC Journal issue 70.]

The NTC telephone school moved from Telephone House to Salisbury House in 1906.

'The Metropolitan offices of the National Telephone Company occupy a large amount of space in one of the palatial modern City office buildings, Salisbury House, London Wall. Just across the street is the London Wall Exchange, one of the largest [10,000 mult. capacity] and busiest of the London exchanges, as it furnishes the telephone service for the half square mile which contains the world's financial centre.' [NTC Journal issue 6, 1906.]

NTC's Telephone House EC4 (1899)

In the 1990s, Prestel HQ, and BT Archives were located in the former NTC building in Temple Avenue. The ornate and lofty Grade II listed building still occupies a large site on the corner of Temple Avenue and Victoria Embankment. BT Archives moved to Holborn in 1997.

My GPO in London: Trilogy Edition

King Edward Building (1905)

Had the longest Post Office counter in the UK and sorted mail for London EC and Foreign Section (overseas). [See separate chapter.]
Rowland Hill - Postal reformer. Statue outside KEB.

Blythe House (1899) Henry Tanner

Blythe House was built between 1899 and 1903 as the headquarters of the Post Office Savings Bank in West Kensington. In its heyday it employed approximately 4000 staff. [See *POSB* chapter.]

Post Office Tube (1900)
The public underground station that was later re-named St. Pauls. [See *On the Grid* chapter for its history.]

Post Office Railway (1927)
The Post Office (underground) Railway ran exclusively to carry letters and parcels between GPO sorting offices (and selected mainline stations), in a fast, efficient manner. [See *Mail Rail* chapter.]

Circuit Laboratory and Training School (1924)

In the King Edward Building, the Circuit Laboratory was introduced on 1 October to aid testing of new automatic telephone equipment. Next to the Circuit Lab., the Automatic Training School, later known as the Central Training School (CTS) was set up as a necessary means of training staff in the supervision and maintenance of the growing number of Strowger automatic telephone exchanges. The CTS was transferred to *Dollis Hill* in

GPO in London

1930 and then to Stone in Staffordshire after World War II.

PO Research Station Dollis Hill (1930)

Dollis Hill (1933)
© BT Heritage and Archives POST 121/348

A letter to the *Engineer-in-Chief* dated 1914 set out the restrictions imposed upon the Research Department by lack of suitable accommodation at which time it was based in Telephone House, Victoria Embankment, and *GPO West*. It cited the current urban environment as being unsuitable in which to set up testing of heavy or bulky telephone exchange equipment, as well as:

Telegraph motor generators; wireless telegraph generators; heavy lead-covered cables, on drums, or laid out straight; cables submerged in water tanks or troughs; experimental aerial lines;

My GPO in London: Trilogy Edition

power plant for testing fuses or insulators; protection of lines from power plant and lightning.

By 1920 an 8-acre site within easy travelling distance of the City had been secured at Dollis Hill in Willesden. The Research Department restated its case for extensive accommodation quoting that it was then attempting to carry out experiments in the following inadequate buildings:

General Post Office West; King Edward Building; 43-45 Newgate Street; Post Office Superintending Engineer's Office, Denman Street, SE.; Norwich Street, EC.; New Barnet Telephone Exchange; and Threadneedle Street Telegraph Office, EC.

Dollis Hill was developed gradually during the 1920s with wooden huts until the permanent buildings were authorised and the site was officially opened 23 November 1933 by Prime Minister Ramsay MacDonald.

Engineers at Dollis Hill developed the wartime code-breaking computer, Colossus which was used at Bletchley Park. The Premium Bond random number generator, ERNIE was devised by the same team.

By 1975 Martlesham Heath in Suffolk had become the new centre for Post Office research and development. In 1999 the site name was changed to *Adastral Park*, after the RAF motto *Per Ardua Ad Astra* (through adversity to the stars).

GPO in London

Electra House (1933)

Home of the Overseas Telegraphs was at Temple Place on Victoria Embankment, WC2. [See also chapter **Electra House**.]

Wood Street (1929)

Wood Street exchange complex (1948)
© BT Heritage and Archives TCB 417/E15529

The first multi-unit *Director* automatic exchanges *Metropolitan and National* opened in the newly constructed six-storey Wood

My GPO in London: Trilogy Edition

Street building during 1929. It was planned to ultimately accommodate three, 10,000-line units. When *London Wall* subsequently followed circa 1936, there was a total of 16,500 working lines, as well as 87 auto-manual 'A' positions, and 52 toll positions. The third unit was originally planned to be *Empire*, but that name was not adopted.

The whole building was gutted by fire after being bombed on 29 December 1940. Lines were diverted to nearby exchange units (e.g. *Avenue*, and *City* in *Faraday!*) to restore service until rebuilding was possible. An intermediate frame in *Salisbury House*, served *London Wall* subscribers (possibly a legacy from the NTC exchange era?).

Thus, *Monarch TE* was BIS 13 Sept 1947 into the rebuilt Wood Street. Provision was also made for *Metropolitan* and *Headquarters TEs*, as well as capacity to relieve *Faraday International* (switchboards) The practice of relocating and renaming exchange units was well-established to meet the ever-changing needs of the London telephone` service.

Circa 1966 a large extension adjacent to Wood Street included an international switching centre (ISC) and new operator centre (ICC) to be BIS in the early 1970s.

Faraday Building (1933)

Was built to house the International Exchange and the growth in the inland automatic telephone switching network.
[See **GPO South** chapter.]

GPO in London

Post Office Supplies

In 1937 Engineering stores were at Studd Street, Islington; Postal stores at Mount Pleasant, Clerkenwell; Stamps, stamped stationery and postal orders at Somerset House; Repair factory at Holloway. By 1998 BT's 'supply-chain' stock was held in a vast national distribution warehouse at the 500-acre Magna Park site in Lutterworth, Leicestershire.

Studd Street

Studd Street (1950)
© BT Heritage and Archives TCB 417/E16725

My GPO in London: Trilogy Edition

John Tythe writes, *"The building, now known as 8 Esther Anne Place, was an engineering building, which housed the Engineer-in-Chief's Office; London Test Section and London Materials Section, and the main GPO Stores prior to its move to the Crayford depot, and also the GPO Factories division until that part and those based in Bovay Place, Holloway, transferred to Bilton Way, Enfield."*

Charles House (1948-2010)

Home of the Kensington Computer Centre, and later the London HQ of Post Office Savings Bank. [See chapter **POSB**.]

Fleet Building (1959-2015)

A vast telecommunications centre, designed by W.S. Frost under guidance from chief architect Eric Bedford, of the Ministry of Works. The new Central Telegraph Office, Inland and International Telex. [See chapter **Fleet Building**.]

Engineer-in-Chief's Office

The Engineer-in-Chief's office was originally located in *GPO West* but was displaced by the growth of the telegraph services and moved into Alder House circa 1925. The burgeoning state of accommodation is discussed in the chapter **Roman Bath Street**.

GPO in London

THE POST OFFICE
ENGINEERING DEPARTMENT
offers interesting careers to
UNIVERSITY GRADUATES
of British Nationality who obtain an Honours Degree.

Posts are available in the following grades:-

EXECUTIVE ENGINEER for male Honours Graduates in ENGINEERING or PHYSICS on work associated with the Design or development of Electronic and Electro-Mechanical Telephone Systems Radio and Television installations, Radio Propagation, Mechanisation of Postal Services, Ancillary Power Plant.

SCIENTIFIC OFFICER for male or female Honours Graduates in ENGINEERING, PHYSICS or MATHEMATICS, on works of a basic research nature in the fields of Telecommunications, including Electronics, Electronic circuitry, Physics of magnetic materials, Physical Metallurgy, Digital Computers, Mathematics and development of semi-conductors.

My GPO in London: Trilogy Edition

All the posts are permanent and pensionable and applicants will be interviewed in London by the Civil Service Commission. Most of the posts are in London, but a limited number of Provincial vacancies exist. Applications for interview, informal discussion or further information, should be addressed to THE STAFF CONTROLLER, ENGINEER-IN-CHIEF'S OFFICE, GENERAL POST OFFICE, ALDER HOUSE, ALDERSGATE STREET, LONDON, E.C.1.

2-12 Gresham Street (1958)

In the late 1950s a vast new rented building was commissioned, and thus from 1958 *2-12 Gresham Street* became the main home of the engineering department. It was from here that the *Post Office Electrical Engineers Journals* (POEEJs) were published. From Oct 1996 the Journals moved to *8-10 Gresham Street*, and thence to *The Angel Centre* from Aug 1998, until early 2003.

2-12 Gresham Street became Standard Life's building, which was then demolished in 2000. Cantillon Ltd was commissioned to strip out the asbestos before the new building, renamed *10 Gresham Street* was constructed. Cantillon worked on other ex-Post Office sites; *Armour and Union House*, Aldgate (1995) and RM sorting office at *148 Old Street* (2015).

GPO in London

2-12 Gresham Street (1959)
© *BT Heritage and Archives TCB 417/E26664*

Camelford House (1962)

At 87-90 Albert Embankment.
Architect: TP Bennett & Sons.

In Albert Embankment conservation area. Was the London Telecommunications Regional HQ - a 16-storey tower and a 12-storey curving wing.

My GPO in London: Trilogy Edition

*Camelford House, Albert Embankment (2011) © Stephen Richards
See geograph.org.uk/photo/2615410 for copyright terms.*

Proctor House (1962) at 100-110 High Holborn WC1

Procter House was constructed in the 1960s with 126,806 square feet of office space and 22 retail units.

'Accommodation in this newly constructed building became available in the latter part of 1963 and staff were transferred there from Alder House, 2-12 Gresham Street and State House in a series of moves spread over several week-ends.' [E-in-C's report 1963.]

Procter House (South entrance) © J. Chenery (2000)

Nigel Pope: '*Procter House was the home of the TXE4 development team throughout the 1970s and 80s.*'

'*Surprisingly, there was no equipment there at all. If you wanted to work on TXE4 kit you either had to go to the STC factory in New Southgate or to one of a growing number of exchange sites.*'

Procter House was originally let to British Telecom until 24th March 1998 at a rent of £3,740,000 per annum.

My GPO in London: Trilogy Edition

Bee Bee Developments Ltd totally refurbished the building(s) in 2001.

Wren House at 15 Carter Lane

Foundation stone laid 2 November 1933 by Ralph Montagu Cook JP. Rebuilt 1989.

Continental Switchrooms (1964)

Wren House, Carter Lane © J. Chenery (2012)

The GPO renamed this building when they moved from 27 St. Paul's Churchyard. An overspill centre for international calls was officially opened by the Postmaster-General, the Rt. Honourable

Anthony Wedgwood Benn on 29 June 1964. Wren's corded switchboards connected inter-continental calls until 1988, when newer centres such as Kelvin House IDQ opened.

Post Office Tower (1965)

Eric Bedford's unique design allowed for microwave signals carrying radio, TV and telephone channels to be transmitted across the UK. The *White Heat of (60s) Technology* at its best.
[See chapter ***Bloomsbury and Fitzrovia***.]

References:

The Utilization of Large Telecommunications Buildings – IPOEE Red Paper No. 228 by TJ Morgan (1967).

POEEJs
Vol 27 1934 *The Engineer-in-Chief's Training School.*
Vol 24 1931 *Engineering Research in the Post Office.*

BT Digital Archives www.bt.com/btdigitalarchives

London RTC Paul Street (1960s)

LTR's Regional Training Centre in Telephone House, 69-77 Paul Street, EC2.

Paul Street at Shoreditch was equipped for training all aspects of telecommunications from cable jointing, plumbing, Strowger switching, Director maintenance, through to PMBX installations,

My GPO in London: Trilogy Edition

and Sub's appts. Lecture rooms, power and metal workshops, a library, together with an O/H pole park provided a comprehensive range of training methods.

RTC Paul Street (1966)
© *BT Heritage and Archives TCB 417/E33128*

In Detail

In the following chapters, key buildings are studied in greater detail, particularly those in the area once known as the *Post Office District* (close to St. Paul's Cathedral). Other buildings detailed follow the progression of the GPO's services as they evolved. The GPO's estate encompassed thousands of premises, too numerous to mention more than a selected few within these pages!

Outlet 2: GPO East

GPO East (1829-1910)
St. Martin's-le-Grand/Gresham Street/Foster Lane

An impractical conglomeration of buildings at Lombard Street gave way to a new *General Post Office*; a Grecian-style elevation of grand pillars fronted on to the east side of St. Martin's-Le-Grand, with the rear of the building backing onto Foster Lane.

Architect, Sir Robert Smirke, designer of sections of the British Museum, was commissioned to devise the new postal and sorting office and HQ. The scheme was made possible by an act of parliament.

City of London and Westminster Streets and Post Office Act 1815 55 Geo 3 c.91 (Local Act)

'An Act for enlarging and improving the West End of Cheapside in the City of London, also Saint Martin's-le-Grand, Aldershot Street, Saint Anne's Lane, and Foster Lane; and for providing a Site for a new Post Office between Saint Martin's-le-Grand and Foster Lane aforesaid.'

In clearing space for the new headquarters over 130 houses were demolished and 1,000 inhabitants displaced; such were the powers of government when planning for essential public services. In more recent times, the Post Office, as a government department, relied upon the 1969 act to ensure that its work was not unduly hindered.

My GPO in London: Trilogy Edition

Post Office Act 1969

'The Minister may authorise the Post Office to purchase compulsorily any land in Great Britain which is required by it for, or in connection with, the exercise of its powers or as to which it can reasonably be foreseen that it will be so required.'

Additionally, a common occurrence, in London, was the choosing of sites which had once been burial grounds; this was almost certain, for so many had died in the Great Plague. In this particular instance, skulls were dug up during excavations for utilities, because the area had once been a burial ground for St. Vedast Church. The remains were re-interred.

John Mallcott

The first stone of the new *General Post Office* building was laid in May 1824. In 1926 stonemason John Mallcott gave testimony in the Old Bailey to theft of his property from the work site. The report substantiates the scale of the new build.

JAMES LARTER was indicted for stealing, on the 6th of February 1826, 3 stone saws, value 10s., the goods of John Mallcott.

"JOHN MALLCOTT. I am contractor for the stone work of the Post Office and have about one hundred men employed there; I believe these three saws to be mine. (Property produced and sworn to.)"

[Old Bailey Proceedings Online (www.oldbaileyonline.org, version 8.0, 04 September 2018), February 1826, trial of JAMES LARTER (t18260216-3).]

GPO East

The new General Post Office

GPO East (1860)
© BT Heritage and Archives TCB 473/P07064

The sending of a letter in the nineteenth century was as special then as it is becoming rare today. The opening of the new General Post Office HQ would have been a wonderment of its time.

The Standard (London) reported on 12 August 1829:

"During nearly the whole of yesterday, crowds of persons were assembled in the neighbourhood of the new post office, under the expectation that this splendid building would be exposed fully to public view by the removal of the paling which surrounds it."

This was perhaps one of many GPO buildings for which the RFS (Ready for Service) date slipped! The gathering of mail coaches

My GPO in London: Trilogy Edition

and the illumination of the building was a fascination. A public utility such as the GPO was highly regarded.

After the official opening (23 September 1829), the *Morning Post* (newspaper) of 24 September reported:

'A large concourse of people, said to amount to 10,000, assembled last night to witness the first departure of the Mails.'

GPO East was about 400 feet long, 130 wide, and 64 feet high. The site extended from St. Martin's-Le-Grand with Gresham Street to the south, and part way along Gresham Street.

The Inland Department occupied half of the building near Aldersgate Street, while the Foreign Department was allocated the remainder towards Cheapside. The Sorters' Room had 150 gas burners (lights) to aid working. The basement of the building held the mail-guards' rooms, armoury and servants' quarters. An iron railing encompassed the site which, at night, was illuminated by 1000 gas burners! At the old site, the Comptroller's offices were set to become a receiving office for foreign and inland letters.

The Inland Department was a hive of activity as thousands of letters and newspapers were received, sorted, postmarked, and made up into leather mail bags ready for despatch at 8 pm to destinations throughout the UK. The scale, organisation and importance of the work would take another chapter to describe sufficiently!

Between eight and twenty-eight mail coaches took up position, at the appointed hour, in single file, to be loaded with mail bags. At the final slamming of each boot lid, the drivers wasted no time in departure towards the Great North Road. A flick of the whip, and a

GPO East

pull on the reigns set horses in motion, as coach after coach sped off, carrying the mail, along the cobbled streets and out of town.

GPO London Town (2017)

At the General Post Office in London town
The sightseers nightly gather round.

Horses and coaches assemble in order
Stabled at inns overnight they boarder.

The inland post, its volumes sorted
Mail bags packed, it won't be thwarted.

More than twenty mail coaches lined-up outside
Each destination displayed on the side.

A flick of the whip and a pull on the reigns
The carriages a purchase on the cobbles gain.

The departures a wonderment as each coach leaves
Under gaslight thousands of eyes perceive.

For each driver, the mail must go through
A guard with pistols, and a blunderbuss too!

Up the Great North Road they rattle apace
The schedule's tight, so they must race!

A blow on the post horn, at the toll-gate approach
Nothing must stop the Royal Mail, or encroach!

My GPO in London: Trilogy Edition

The daily gathering of crowds at the General Post Office included news vendors, hawkers, and sightseers, some of whom arrived by hackney carriage. As the volume of post handled at St. Martin's-le-Grand continued to increase, the local situation was encumbering the ability to efficiently despatch the mail.

Post Office (Offences) Act 1837

'... *to prevent Obstructions opposite the General Post Office in London, be it enacted, that no Hackney Carriage shall stand or ply for Hire opposite the General Post Office in Saint Martin's-le-Grand, London.*'

'...*and every Hawker, News vender, or idle or disorderly Person, who shall stop or loiter on the Flagway or Pavement opposite the General Post Office in Saint Martin's-le-Grand, or any Part thereof respectively, shall forfeit for every such Offence Five Pounds.*'

Mail Coaches

Coach livery was a black upper, with maroon doors and lower panels, and red wheels. Mail coaches were staffed by contractors. The guard was a Post Office employee, armed with two pistols and a blunderbuss. His uniform included a black hat with a gold band, and a scarlet coat with blue lapels and gold braid. The sound of the post horn warned other road users to make way for the Royal Mail, as well as alerting toll-gate keepers to open the gate! Timekeeping was important; mail bags were thrown out from the coach to the Letter Receiver or Postmaster, whilst still on the move, unless the town was a scheduled stop. The run wasn't for the faint-hearted!

GPO East

Mail coach no.105 Bristol to London, on display at The Postal Museum (TPM) © J. Chenery (2017)

Inns and Coaching Houses

Mail coaches and horses for London were stabled at local inns, close to the GPO. Of note was the *Bull and Mouth* inn, which in 1830 was replaced by the Queen's Hotel. This in turn was demolished in 1887, and then became the site of *GPO North*, in 1890.

My GPO in London: Trilogy Edition

Blue plaque © J. Chenery (2010)

In its prime the 'Bull and Mouth' sent forth the Edinburgh and Aberdeen Royal Mail by York; the Edinburgh, Glasgow, and Aberdeen coach by Ferry-bridge to Newcastle, where the Glasgow passengers changed; the Glasgow and Carlisle Royal Mail; the Newcastle 'Wellington'; Shrewsbury and Holyhead 'Union' and 'Oxonian'; Birmingham 'Old Post Coach' and 'Aurora'; Leeds Royal Mail and 'Express'; and Leicester 'Union Post Coach.'

[Extract from *The Great North Road: London to York* by Charles G. Harper 1901.]

GPO East

The 'Bull in Mouth' was commemorated by a terracotta memorial on the façade of the Queen's Hotel. The sign is currently displayed in the lower garden enclosure of the Museum of London, London Wall.
Inscription: 'Milo the Cretonian an ox slew with his fist and ate it up at one meal, ye gods what a glorious twist.' © J. Chenery (2018)

My GPO in London: Trilogy Edition

Another very popular and busy inn was *The Swan with Two Necks*, in Lad Lane (which became Gresham Street). By 1835 its coaching business deployed 1200 horses. The last regular London-based coach service was London to Norwich, via Newmarket 6 Jan 1846 - long-distance mail had switched to rail transport.

Mail by Rail

Euston Grove station opened 20 July 1837, thus the *London and Birmingham Railway Post Office (RPO)* service from Euston, commenced on 22 May 1838, and by 1 October a TPO (Travelling Post Office) ran through to Preston. By 1847, the Euston to Carlisle (via Birmingham) TPO was the North Western Night Down. The history of TPOs is complex, because carriages could be added at intermediate stations, and the designation of the train changed en route.

Mail by Rail was a mix of *stowage vans* (carriages) purely to transport the mail, and/or *sorting vans*, in which Post Office staff sorted the letters and packets into pigeonholes, while the train was moving. Hence the name *Travelling Post Offices*. Mail coaching stock was originally run together with passenger carriages, but in later years, solely as Postal Special trains. Carriage of mail by the railways was ensured by…

Conveyance of Mails Act 1838

'…*it shall be lawful for the Postmaster-General, by Notice in Writing under his Hand delivered to the Company of Proprietors of any such Railway, to require that the Mails or Post Letter Bags shall…*'

GPO East

'...be conveyed and forwarded by such Company on their Railway, either by the ordinary Trains of Carriages, or by special Trains, as Need may be, at such Hours or Times in the Day or Night as the Postmaster-General shall direct.'

Expansion and Closure

The postal reform in 1840 made the mail service affordable to many. Two extra storeys were added to the *General Post Office* building, following the huge growth in mail volumes, but this was still not sufficient to cope with the demand.

In 1869 a new headquarters building (*GPO West*) was started on the western side of St. Martin's-le-Grand, but the accommodation intended for the postal business was soon given over to the new telegraph service. To distinguish sites, the existing *General Post Office* building was renamed *GPO East*.

Further expansion in the volumes of mail dictated that the London letter post was transferred to *Mount Pleasant* from about 1900. In 1905 the foundation stone was laid for another postal building in the City, but the new *King Edward Building* was not to be ready until 1911.

GPO East closed in 1910 and was demolished 1912/13. An Ionic cap from the right-hand corner of the main portico, a five-ton relic, was presented to the Walthamstow Urban Council and can be seen today at Church End, London, E17. Additionally, an engraved foundation stone is preserved next to a section of London Wall which stands in the basement of Merrill Lynch's HQ.

[See chapter **King Edward Building** for more information.]

My GPO in London: Trilogy Edition

Inscribed stone block from GPO East 1826.
© J. Chenery (2018)

'*THIS STONE was laid 25th August [1826] in the 6th year of the Reign of GEORGE IV. JOHN MALLCOTT Mason.*'

References

www.british-history.ac.uk/old-new-london/vol2/pp208-228#p1
britishpostofficearchitects.weebly.com
www.gbps.org.uk
The Postal Museum Info sheets
An Illustrated History of the Travelling Post Office by Peter Johnson (2009).

Outlet 3: GPO West

GPO West (1874-1962) Newgate Street/St. Martin's-le-Grand

An area close to St. Paul's was to become the very centre of GPO operations for generations to come. Started in 1869, *GPO West* was a four-storey construction of granite and Portland stone, constructed on a plot to the west of the *General Post Office (GPO East)*. The Office of Works architect was James Williams.

Central Telegraph Office: GPO West (1941)
© BT Heritage and Archives TCB 417/E11766

My GPO in London: Trilogy Edition

The houses on the east side of (Roman) Bath Street, which ran parallel to King Edward Street, were demolished to make way for *GPO West*. As a proposed HQ, this was quite a grand building. The design included two light wells – a clever feature for allowing natural lighting of large offices.

'The building is rectangular, having frontages of 286 feet to St. Martin's-le-Grand and Bath Street, and frontages of 144 feet to Newgate Street and Angel Street, and is 84 feet in height from the paving line. The central hall is intended for the staff of the Accountant-General. In the north court there are placed four steam-engines, each of 50 horse power, for working the pneumatic tubes.'

Citation: Walter Thornbury, 'Aldersgate Street and St. Martin-le-Grand', in Old and New London: Volume 2 (London, 1878), pp. 208-228. British History Online http://www.british-history.ac.uk/old-new-london/vol2/pp208-228 [accessed 9 October 2018].

Telegraphs

The GPO assumed responsibility for the telegraph service from 1870, and so the Electric Telegraph Company's (ETC) pneumatic tube systems were arranged to be re-terminated into *GPO West* in Jan 1874, and thus the GPO's own Central Telegraph Office (CTO) was established.

Telephones

In 1884, liberalisation of the emerging telephone networks allowed for the provision of Call Offices in shops, post offices, railway stations, etc., to allow the public access to the telephone service.

A London to Paris submarine cable, terminating in *GPO West*, was

GPO West

brought into service on 1 April 1891 with a charge of 8 shillings [40p] for a three-minute conversation. Public Call Offices were typically within: General Post Office (West), Bath Street, E.C. (always open), Threadneedle Street Branch Post Office, near the Royal Exchange (open from 8.0 a.m. to 8.0 p.m.), and the Telegraph Office, West Strand (always open). In the days long before coinbox mechanisms, an attendant would supervise the call and collect the monies due. The first of the GPO's standard kiosks did not appear until the 1920s.

Telephone trunk (long distance) service which had first been connected via *GPO West* in 1895, was displaced in 1904 to *GPO South* as the popularity of the telephone grew, and telegram service in the *CTO* expanded.

Floor Designations

'In order to meet the requirements of the Telegraph Service it has been necessary to add an additional storey [fourth floor] to the General Post Office building on the west side of Saint Martin's-le-Grand, as well as to acquire other premises in Bath Street for dining rooms, etc.' [PMG Report 1884.]

By 1891, the allocation of workspaces was:

- Basement: Boiler and well pumps *, pneumatic engines, battery, gas meter and test rooms. Porters and secretaries' kitchens. Registry, secretaries' and telegraph messengers.

- Ground: Public entrance. Clerk of Works, Postmaster-General, Private Secretary, Engineer-in-Chief, Engineers' branch and messengers. Telegraph delivery messengers. Cashiers, ledgers, bookkeeping and accounts. Tube room.

My GPO in London: Trilogy Edition

- First: Upper part of Tube room. Secretaries, Correspondence, Solicitors and Clerks. Foreign and Colonial Branch.

- Second: Registry, Controller Central Telegraph Station, Constables room, Cable room and Paris switch. Medical Officers, Library, and Appointment Branch.

- Third: Retiring Room, Kitchen, Lavatories, Workshop, Batteries, Test Boxes, Superintendent, Racing and Special Events, News, IRISH, Stationery. Telegraph instrument room.

- Fourth: Metropolitan and Suburban Telegraph Room, Upper part of instrument room.

[Extracted from *The Engineer* 18 Dec 1891.]

* An Artesian well filled two 6,000-gallon tanks that supplied water for the steam engines which provided pneumatic suction, to operate the street tubes. Electric motors operated the tubes, in lieu of steam engines, once the generation of electricity was more commonplace.

In 1927 preparations were made to expand onto a fifth floor!

'The strengthening of the walls, precedent to the erection of a fifth floor at the CTO has been completed. Extensive shifts of tubes, telegraphs, telephones and common services have been involved, in order to make space for thickened walls, stanchions, etc. The opportunity has been taken to straighten out the routes of the tubes, and brass has replaced lead in several instances.'
[POEEJ April 1927 Vol 20 Pt1 Page 77.]

GPO West

Further Expansion

Overflow accommodation was added at the rear of GPO West (see *Roman Bath Street* chapter for details), and the buildings were connected by overhead bridges (walkways) at second floor level.

Wartime

Damage to the building was sustained in both WWI and II, finally resulting in partial demolition and a rebuild between 1941 and 1943, and reinstatement of tube working by 1947. War had a profound effect upon the development and locations of future telecommunications services within London; specifically, the automatic switching of telegraph/teleprinter traffic was delayed.

Closure

'Because of inevitable changes in techniques the building has outlived its original purpose as a central office.'

In its heyday: *'The galleries were lofty, with good light from spacious windows. The instrument tables had none of the sleek anonymity of the modern hammer-grey metal cover; every set was individual and very impressive with a prodigious amount of lacquered brass. Sounders, keys, standard relays and indicating needles in elegant Gothic cases contributed to the variety of apparatus.'*
[*The Closing of the CTO* – POEEJ Oct 1961 Vol 54 Pt 3 page 186.]

From 1960, cable and radio circuits were transferred to Electra House. The automatic Telex service in Fleet Building superseded manual connections, and the Telegram service moved to the new CTO, also in Fleet.

My GPO in London: Trilogy Edition

GPO West closed in 1962 and was demolished in 1967. The pneumatic tube system was abandoned and left for the scrap man. *'Brass tubing, painted regulation cream, is being pulled like a stream of giant spaghetti out of the old central telegraph office just to the north of St. Paul's Cathedral...Battleship Grey electric motors that had driven compressors... The tubes under the streets of London are encased in lead and will remain, as far as we know. It's too costly a job to get them up.'* [The Observer – 17 Feb 1963.]

BT Centre

The site remained vacant until the building of *BTC* (British Telecom Centre) from August 1980. Planned in 1978, with the authority of the Post Office Board, the new HQ was designed with the brief…

'the building had to reflect a commercially orientated and cost-conscious public body… an efficient and economic building.'
[The BT Centre Site – An Historical Summary.]

BTC opened in 1985 as the corporate HQ of the newly privatised British Telecommunications Plc., with the main entrance at 81 Newgate Street.

In May 2018 *The Telegraph* reported, *"BT will exit the St. Paul's headquarters and find a new London building that offers open plan working."*

The quest to match evolving working practices with suitable accommodation at sustainable rates is ever ongoing!

Outlet 4: Roman Bath Street

Roman Bath Street was subsumed within the redevelopment of the site of *GPO West* during the building of BT Centre in 1980.

BT Centre (St. Martin's-le-Grand) in the shadow of St. Paul's Cathedral.
© J. Chenery (2010)

My GPO in London: Trilogy Edition

Roman Bath Street (Earlier Times)

Roman Bath Street was located between King Edward Street and St. Martin's-le-Grand. Roman Bath Street contained the overflow buildings for departments which could not be housed in the Central Telegraph Office (*GPO West*) due to lack of space.

Roman Bath Street originally appears to have been a cul de sac off Newgate Street, until the roads and frontages were altered for the building of *GPO West*. Properties in the vicinity were acquired over many years with the assistance of various site acts:

'*Under the Post Office Sites Act 1865, Section 10, the Postmaster-General was required at the expense of the Post Office to continue Roman Bath Street until it formed a junction with Angel Street.*

'*...It would seem that Roman Bath Street was at that time a cul de sac and that the Postmaster-General provided the land for continuing it to Angel Street.*'

[Extract from PO Solicitor's letter 1934.]

Properties on the corner of King Edward Street and Angel Street were under consideration from the late 1890s onwards. [Diagram next page.]

'*...the premises at the corner of Angel Street and King Edward Street, E.C. have been purchased by the Department for the enlargement of the Central Telegraph Office Cloak Rooms and Refreshment Rooms.*'

[Solicitor's letter 1898.]

Roman Bath Street

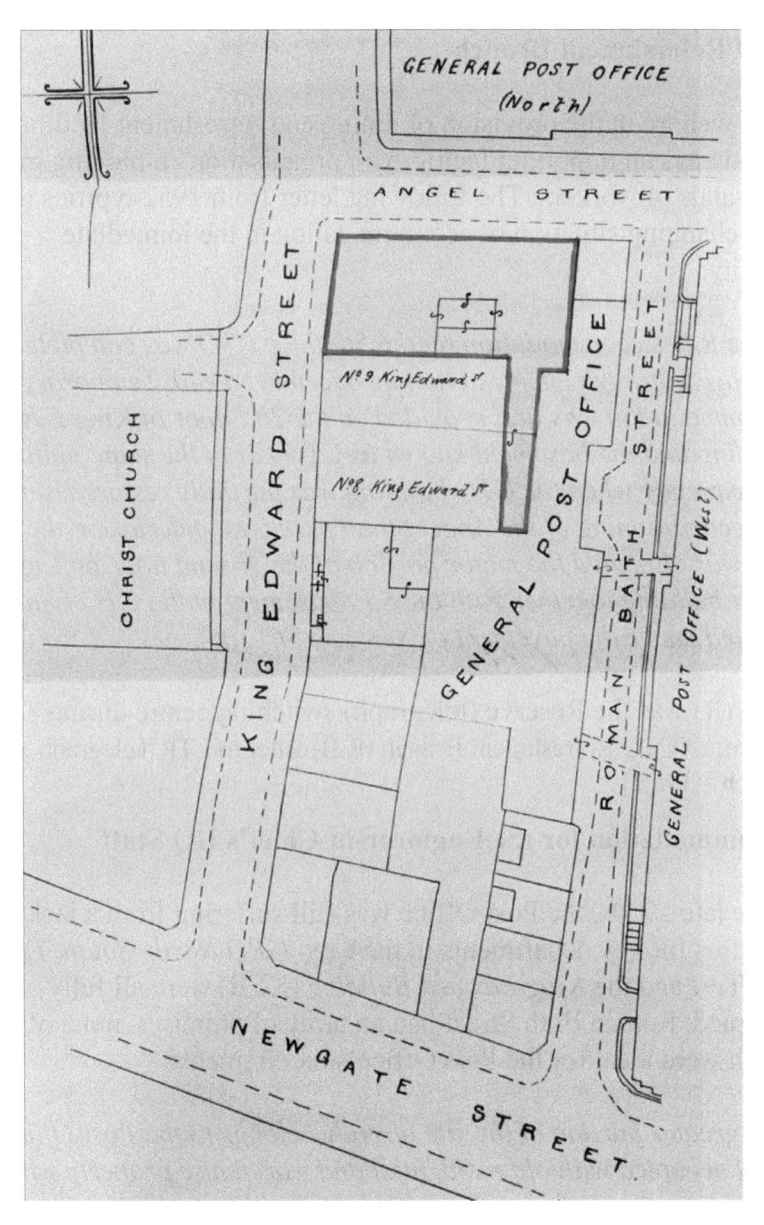

Properties under consideration for purchase (Circa 1890)

My GPO in London: Trilogy Edition

CTO Refreshment Branch

Staff welfare in the provision of dining and refreshment facilities was always an important factor in an organisation employing many thousands of workers. The following letter from 1952 typifies the ever-changing situation of accommodation in the immediate vicinity.

'...the R.B. accommodation on the 5th floor CTO was completely destroyed through enemy action in December 1940. Temporary accommodation was first provided on the 2nd floor of King Edward Building and the basement known as CTO (R) in the same building. Subsequently when the CTO building was partially restored, and the reconditioning of the Angel Street premises undertaken, the R.B. was allocated the major portion of the ground floor of Angel Street building together with the S.E. basement buffet CTO (vaults situated under the pavement of Newgate Street).'

CTO (R) was the Reserve (telegraph) switching centre during wartime. [CTO Refreshment Branch (R.B) letter to LTR Telegraph Branch – 1952.]

Accommodation for the Engineer-in-Chief's HQ Staff

In the late 1920s, the Post Office was still suffering from a lack of premises for key departments in the City. *GPO North, South, East and West* and the *King Edward Building* (KEB) were all fully occupied. Roman Bath Street had an array of premises, none of which were ideal for the Post Office's requirements.

'The greater portion of the site already belongs to the Post Office but is occupied with old residential and warehouse property which is quite unsuitable for modern requirements.'

Roman Bath Street

The Post Office was well-versed in dealing with property acquisitions, although the *Office of Works'* tendency to investigate multiple solutions for each site inevitably led to lengthy delays in resolution. In part, this approach was most likely to appease the Treasury that its public money was going to be judiciously spent on the final scheme adopted. Additionally, for planning consents to proceed, the solutions submitted had to satisfy Post Office requirements, as well as those of the local council/corporation, public utilities, highway authorities, and sometimes the public too!

A new building for Roman Bath Street was the subject of many letters between the Government, the Office of Works and Post Office representatives.

Letter to the Engineer-in-Chief [15th August 1932]

'The chief obstacle in the way of the provision of a new building to house the whole of your Head Quarter Staff is the extreme reluctance of the Treasury to sanction the capital outlay involved. A further complication was introduced by the proposal of the Office of Works to build over K.E.B. yard instead of on the Roman Bath Street site. Much time has been spent in the examination and discussion of the relative merits and demerits, financial and practical, of the rival schemes. When the case was submitted to Sir Evelyn Murray in 1928, both he and the then Postmaster-General favoured the provision of a building on part only of the Roman Bath Street site, and authority to proceed with this scheme was sought from the Treasury. The Treasury, however, did not look with favour on this particular scheme; and further time was occupied in considering the several alternatives. It was not until July 1931 that Sir Evelyn Murray authorized a semi-official approach to the Treasury in favour of the full Roman Bath Street scheme; and he

My GPO in London: Trilogy Edition

indicated then that he was not prepared to press the Treasury at that time if they demurred on the ground of expense.

A semi-official letter was sent to the Treasury on 11 August 1931- on the eve of the Financial Crisis. That crisis, and several changes of personnel at the Treasury, prevented further discussion until February of this year. At the discussion which took place at the Treasury in February last, the Treasury representatives seemed fairly well disposed towards the full Roman Bath Street scheme but wished for further information on traffic in K.E.B. Yard of the obstructions which would be necessary if a building were erected over the yard. They also indicated that they did not look with favour on the proposal to spend money in the near future on the acquisition of that part of the Roman Bath Street block not already in the possession of the Postmaster-General.

It was accordingly arranged that Mr. Myers should develop the K.E.B. Scheme to the extent of determining the exact positions and dimensions of the stanchions which would be required in the yard, and then erect obstacles in those positions in order that the effect on the yard traffic might be studied. Those obstacles have just been erected, and Mr. Myers has produced a rough outline plan of a building which includes a basement garage for L.P.S. [London Postal Service] vans. It has been agreed that a building on these lines would meet the convenience of the L.P.S. and that stanchions as indicated would not unduly obstruct the flow of vehicular traffic in the yard. But, Mr. Myers had explained that a building with stanchions in these positions (roughly at 43 foot centres) would involve a cost of £15,000 to £20,000 more than a building with stanchions at (roughly) 30 foot centres; and it has been agreed that the plan shall be developed a stage further in order to shew the number and position of stanchions with the shorter spans. Mr. Myers will put this work in hand at once; but he says that on

Roman Bath Street

account of the amount of detailed calculation of stresses involved, he cannot promise to report for another 2 or 3 months.

The next stage will be another conference with the Treasury to decide between the Roman Bath Street scheme and the K.E.B. scheme. It will be seen that the difficulties so far experienced have been of a kind which could not readily be surmounted by the appointment of a Committee such as you suggest; but when a definite decision is reached in favour of one or other of the schemes under consideration it will no doubt be desirable to set up such a Committee to deal with the plans and numerous points of detail which will arise.'

A (draft) letter to the Treasury in 1933 highlighted the ongoing problems:

'I am directed by the Postmaster-General to advert to Post Office letter dated 31st July 1928, relative to the acquisition of certain property in Roman Bath Street for the purpose of providing permanent accommodation for the Post Office Engineer-in-Chief's Headquarters staff, and to submit the following considerations in support of the adoption of the larger scheme referred to in paragraph 6 (ii) of that letter.

The Engineer-in-Chief's Headquarters staff in July 1928, numbered 670, plus 62 employed in the Automatic Training School and Circuit Laboratory in the King Edward Building. Since that date two changes affecting the composition of the Engineering Headquarters staff have taken place, viz.:

(i) the Automatic Training School has been removed to Dollis Hill (Treasury letter E.18016/2 dated 9th July 1930) and
(ii) the Mechanical Transport Section has been transferred from

My GPO in London: Trilogy Edition

the Stores Department to the Engineer-in-Chief (Treasury letter E.25857 dated the 29th May 1931).'

'At the present time, the Engineering Headquarters staff comprises 1056 persons (excluding the Dollis Hill Research Station). Spread over eight separate buildings, and occupying a total floor space of about 93,000 sq. ft. of which some 7,000 sq. ft. is for storage etc.

The occupation appears somewhat extravagant on an ordinary clerical basis, but this is explained by the large proportion of drawing work, the space required for photographic and other copying work, the Circuit Laboratory, and the presses or 'museum' cases for apparatus patterns.

In order to provide for the continually growing work it has been necessary to rent all the available space in Alder House, and also to spend a good deal on making a considerable part of the existing Roman Bath Street premises tolerably suitable for office use.

Continued experience of the working of the Engineer-in-Chief's Office split up between so many separate buildings, most of which are 200 or 300 yards distant from Alder House, confirms the great inconvenience involved, and reveals a serious weakening of the system of personal contact which is so necessary not only between the heads of sections and Engineer-in-Chief, but also between the many officers of various ranks throughout the office.

...it is impossible to foresee any diminution in the rate of growth of the headquarters staff, particularly in view of present indications of improving trade and a prosperous telephone system.'

The letter was quantified by figures of staff numbers and building allocations, which were spread over eight main sites:

Engineer-in-Chief's Office HQ Accommodation [circa 1933]

1. **Alder House**
   Engineer in Chief's HQ
2. **Metropolitan TE (Silver Street)**
   4th and 5th floors Contracts Section
   5th Floor Telephone Section (TI Group)
   1st and 4th floors Radio Section (Wood Street)
3. **Empire House (St. Martin's-le-Grand)**
   3rd Floor Test Section
4. **GPO (West) EC1**
   Ground floor Telegraph Section
5. **Roman Bath Street EC1**
   4th Floor Designs Section (Photocopying)
   Ground floor Editorial Section (Rotaprint)
6. **Angel Street EC1**
   1st and 2nd floors MT Section
   3rd floor Telegraph Section PW Group
7. **8 King Edward Street EC1**
   1st, 2nd and 3rd floors Equipment Section (Accommodation Group)
   3rd floor Accounts Section (Valuation Group)
8. **KEB Sorting Office Block EC1**
   2nd floor Construction Section
   2nd floor Power Section
   2nd floor Telephone Section (Circuit Laboratory)

There were further letters in this correspondence adding to the case of a new, larger building in Roman Bath Street, because the Engineer-in-Chief's department was still growing. The *KEB*

My GPO in London: Trilogy Edition

scheme to excavate a (garage) basement and build over the *Yard* was rejected as the building height would have exceeded that specified in the London Building Act. Although Crown exemption could have been used, the RBS scheme was preferable.

Another act of parliament allowed the project to proceed...

Post Office (Sites) Act 1934

'An Act to enable the Postmaster-General, for the purpose of the Post Office, to acquire lands in London, and for purposes connected therewith.' [22nd June 1934.]

The incorporation of street/area improvements were very often a condition of granting permission as this article in *The Times* reports.

Street Widening in The City

'Arrangements are being made between the Postmaster-General and the City Corporation for the closure of Roman Bath Street. The Postmaster-General is surrendering portions of 76 to 80 Newgate Street, and 1 to 3, and 7 to 10, King Edward Street in order that Newgate Street may be widened to 60ft. and King Edward Street to 40ft. at that point. Consequential works in connexion with sewers, etc., and paving are to cost the City over £5,000.'

[The Times newspaper 21/03/1934.]

E-in-C Annual Report to 31st March 1934

'The proposed new Headquarters Building on the Roman Bath Street site has now reached the planning stage and several

Roman Bath Street

discussions have taken place between this Department and the Office of Works. It is hoped that the existing block will be demolished during 1935-36.'

Plans for a subway connecting the new building to the King Edward Building were also drawn up, though without further research it is unclear of the final outcome. It appears that the new project was then commonly known as the *Angel Street* building.

Angel Street

Jim (Dusty) Miller, who was a Messenger/Young Postman at the Central Telegraph Office (CTO) between 1946-1950 recalled...

"Just across the road from the CTO was another building. This building was almost as big as the CTO and was known as Angel Street. This building was connected to the CTO by a bridge built at the second-floor level. The function of this building was to provide rest rooms, locker rooms and a restaurant for the many staff employed at the CTO."
[From Postal Heritage www.postalmuseum.org/]

Post Office Training

The 1920s saw the formalisation of training in all departments of the Post Office.

My GPO in London: Trilogy Edition

LPS Counter School (1920)

'The scheme of training here described has been developed at the London Postal Service Counter School situated in Roman Bath Street, E.C.1, and it applies to the counter clerks and telegraphists in the London Postal Service.'

The senior class syllabus covered the following topics:

- Inland Revenue and other Stamp business
- Postal Orders Issue
- Postal Orders Payment
- Postal Drafts
- Money Orders Issue and Payment (ordinary)
- Money Orders (transfer of payment etc.)
- National Savings Certificates
- Postage Franking Meters
- Stamping of Documents
- Prepayment of postage in money
- Telephone accounts
- Telegraph Money Orders (inland and imperial and foreign)
- Pensions and Allowances
- Savings Bank business
- Licences
- Balance at counter

[London Counter School by G.C. Wickins from PO Green Paper No.16 Staff Training in London 1935.]

Roman Bath Street

Telephone Schools

Clerkenwell School of Telephony (1924)
© BT Heritage and Archives TCB 417/E03010

The *Clerkenwell School of Telephony* opened in *Clerkenwell TE* in 1923. This was for learning manual exchange systems.

For auto-manual training, i.e. assistance calls for automatic exchanges, the training was initially carried out on adapted positions at the AMCs, but in October 1931 the London automatic school opened in *Terminus* TE.

[London Telephone Schools by J.D. Pettigrew from PO Green Paper No.16 Staff Training in London 1935.]

My GPO in London: Trilogy Edition

By 1946 telephonist recruitment was at Waterloo Bridge House, SE1. In the 1960s LTR's Camelford House had this role.

Engineering Schools:

Engineer-in-Chief's School

During the period from 1924 to 1930 the Engineer-in-Chief's Training School was housed in King Edward Building, adjacent to the Circuit Lab and the cooperation between the two was mutually advantageous. In 1930 when the School was transferred to Dollis Hill, the partnership was dissolved.

Circuit Lab

The Telephone Branch Circuit Laboratory was established in King Edward Building EC1 in 1924. The Circuit Lab moved to Armour House, St. Martin's-le-Grand in October 1953 as accommodation changes continued.

Regional Training Centres (RTCs)

From about 1947 RTCs such as Bletchley Park ran residential schools for clerical and engineering departments of the Post Office. Bletchley's code-breaking outstation at Drayton Parslow was also used by the GPO after the war. Shirley, West Midlands served those from Birmingham and Manchester, although many engineers attended the Central Training School (CTS) at Yarnfield, Stone in Staffordshire.

[See also *Telephone House, Paul Street*, on page 48.]

Outlet 5: Electric Telegraph Company

Early telecommunication services were established in the lucrative financial district of London, close to the Bank of England. Of these businesses the Electric Telegraph Company was to be the most influential in the development of pneumatic tube systems, the despatch of telegrams, and the regulation of UK time-keeping.

1 Founders' Court
In 1846, the (private) Electric Telegraph Company (ETC) was established by an Act of Parliament. William Fothergill Cooke and Joseph Lewis Ricardo secured Cooke and Charles Wheatstone's patents to allow full use of the current technology, and thus discourage competition in their operating systems. At 1 Founders' Court, Lothbury, in 1848, the company set up its first Central Telegraph Station (CTS), in the heart of London. Initial business was the provision of railway circuits linking London to Birmingham and Manchester.

12-14 Telegraph Street
By 1859 the ETC had outgrown Founders' Court, so it transferred its main network and CTS to the northern side of Great Bell Alley. Such was the proliferation of telegraph activity in the area, that the City Corporation subsequently renamed the alley to Telegraph Street. As a consequence, the telegraphic call-sign became TS.

36 Coleman Street
Notably, The Telephone Company Limited (Bell's Patents) set up the first public telephone exchange at 36 Coleman Street in August 1879.

My GPO in London: Trilogy Edition

The Electric Telegraph Company &
The Telephone Company Limited (Bell's Patents) – London Sites

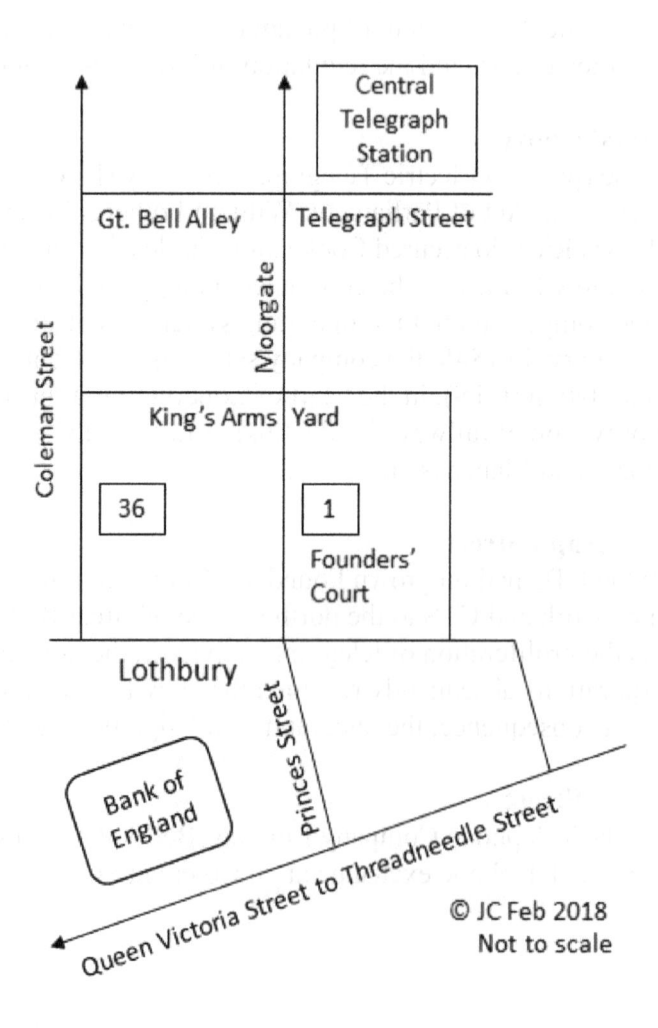

Central Telegraph Station

Gt. Bell Alley | Telegraph Street

Moorgate

Coleman Street

King's Arms Yard

36 | 1

Founders' Court

Lothbury

Princes Street

Bank of England

Queen Victoria Street to Threadneedle Street

© JC Feb 2018
Not to scale

ETC

The Electric Telegraph Company also leased premises in the Strand, Charring Cross; a clock department at 142 Strand and a more prestigious building at 448 Strand, which had once been the GWR's stylish ticket office.

From 1848, lead-sheathed, tar-insulated copper lines radiated from the CTS at Founders' Court through cast-iron pipes under the pavements across London. Circuits linked railway stations at London Bridge, Waterloo Bridge, Paddington, Willesden Junction and northward to connect lines to Birmingham, and beyond.

Connections were made to a new telegraph station in the General Post Office (*GPO East*) in St Martin's-le-Grand. At this time, the GPO otherwise had no direct involvement with the provision or running of the telegraph service.

Greenwich Connections

In October 1851, George Airy, Astronomer Royal, commenced his plans for the distribution of Greenwich Mean Time (GMT) via new ETC lines from the Royal Observatory to Lewisham Station and thence over the railway telegraphs to London Bridge terminus and connection to ETC HQ in Lothbury. The ETC could then send GMT clock synchronisation signals over its networks throughout the UK. [See chapter ***GPO Time Services*** for more details.]

CF Varley and J Latimer Clark

Key appointments to the company were that of Josiah Latimer Clark, consultant engineer, and Cromwell Fleetwood Varley, consultant electrician. Together with William Fothergill Cooke, these were the innovators of their time, at the forefront of the adoption of new technology and practical business applications.

Pneumatic Tubes (1853)

If merchants trading on the Stock Exchange were delayed from receiving important telegrams which had arrived at ETC's Central Telegraph Station, both parties' financial business might have suffered. To ensure speedy despatch of messages, CF Varley set up a pneumatic tube system between the two sites. This established a precedent for the future delivery of telegraph messages in London. [See chapter *Tube Service* for more details.]

Houses of Parliament

In 1853 ETC also installed a telegraph station in the lobby of the Houses of Parliament which included a large electric clock over the entrance. Additionally, a system for alerting members, throughout the Palace, to a *division vote* in the House, was provided by the fitting of 30 electric bells, which could simultaneously be activated from the division lobby. A century later, operated by the GPO, the provision of external private circuits and division bells to honourable members' (nearby) homes was still a valued service.

EITC

The ETC merged with its subsidiary, the International Telegraph Company, in 1855 to form the Electric and International Telegraph Company. An underwater cable from East Anglia to Holland linked UK circuits to the continent. Associations with rival companies produced an extensive network over which telegraphs could be transmitted.

ETC

Central Telegraph Station

The new CTS, in Telegraph Street (1859), was an extensive operation. Continental lines, domestic lines, and local relays were all powered by direct current from a central source of 750 battery boxes each of 10 or 12 cells.

A journalist visiting the battery cellar in the basement remarked

"Arranged side by side upon shelves, like the coffins in some ancient catacombs, are a multitude of wooden boxes from which the proceeds the life of the electric wire."

[http://distantwriting.co.uk/electrictelegraphcompany.html]

Up to 800 wires connected the battery supplies to the telegraph instruments, and lines, with a common earth attached to the gas and water mains.

Six main circuit routes were diverted from the Lothbury premises to Telegraph Street:

1. West to Paddington railway station by way of Gresham Street, Holborn and Oxford Street

2. South-west to Westminster and Parliament by Fleet Street and the Strand

3. South to the Borough (Union Street, Southwark) via London Bridge railway station

4. North to the Angel, Islington along the City Road, past Euston Square and King's Cross railway stations

5. From Finsbury Square eastwards to Shoreditch railway station

My GPO in London: Trilogy Edition

6. South from the Strand to the Waterloo Bridge railway station

Telegraph Act 1869

Endowed the Post Office with a monopoly on telegraphic communication in the UK with effect from 1 January 1870.

"More than 1,300 new telegraph offices were opened during the year; making the whole number at the end of 1871 upwards of 5,000. Messages transmitted increased by about 25 percent; the whole number during the year having been nearly 12,000,000. Besides these messages there were about 700,000 sent on behalf of the newspaper press." [PMG Report 1872.]

Central Telegraph Office (CTO)

The GPO operated ETC's established CTS in Telegraph Street until its own CTO (*GPO West*) was ready, and all lines were finally transferred to the new premises on 17 January 1874.
[PMG Report 1874 page 11.]

The ETC is considered to be the founder of British Telecom.

References

BT Archives: Info Sheets.
PMG reports: 1872, 1874.

Outlet 6: Tube Service (TS)

Pneumatic Tube Systems

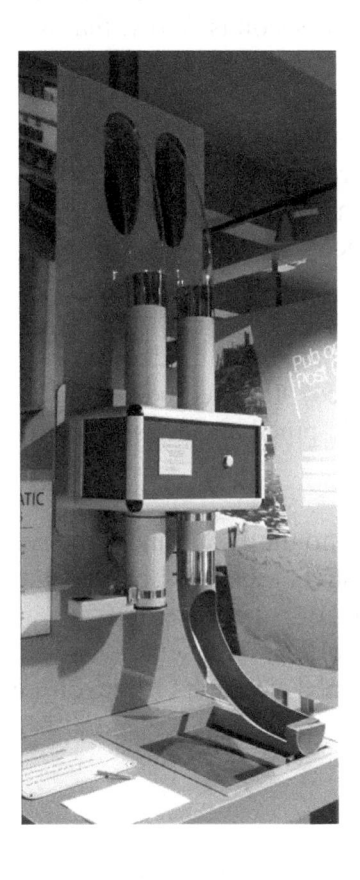

'Did you know there was once a forty-mile network of pneumatic tubes under London?

They connected the Central Telegraph Office near St. Paul's Cathedral directly with Parliament, the Stock Exchange, and other important places.

Messages travelled by air pressure to their destination – try out the system here.'

Demo tube system and notice at The Postal Museum 2017

At a visit to the newly opened Postal Museum (TPM) in July 2017, the pneumatic tube system attracted my attention. The rather bulky and transparent tubes running across the ceiling were intended to be obtrusive, and the empty pods next to the pipe terminal were obviously destined to be used. I stuffed one of the pods into the

My GPO in London: Trilogy Edition

tube and closed the end stop, being careful not to trap my fingers. Immediately the pod went whizzing-along inside the tube at a speed almost too fast to notice its progress! I was surprised that it travelled so quickly and was dropping into the receiving box at the other side of the gallery, within just a few seconds. Wow, that was fun!

I'd seen older, metal-tube systems operating in large department stores and shoe shops, in the 1960s, to return change (coins and notes) to the customer, but I'd forgotten how efficiently they worked! In *Faraday Building*, tubes once sent telephone (charge) tickets from the switchboard to the Ticket Cab (pricing room).

Those in-house systems were long gone, although modern-day supermarkets (e.g. J Sainsbury, and Tesco) still used pods to transport cash from the tills, via a plastic-piped airflow system, to a safe collection point.

Surprisingly, pneumatic tubes date back to the 1850s and there was once an extensive external network of street tubes, in London and other major cities. In London, thousands of paper telegram messages were conveyed between post offices, financial institutions and Parliament, to the Central Telegraph Office, of the Post Office.

History

In 1853 J. Latimer Clark, a consultant engineer of the Electric Telegraph Company (ETC), installed a 220-yard pneumatic tube system between the Stock Exchange in Threadneedle Street and the ETC's Central Telegraph Station (CTS) in Lothbury. The system only allowed transmission of the carriers (pods) in one direction, as they were sucked through the pipes by a partial vacuum. The

Tube Service

carriers had to be returned to their origin by messenger boy. In 1858, CF Varley, consultant electrician of the ETC devised the addition of a *plenum chamber* which, using compressed air, forced the carriers in the opposite direction, making bothway-working a practical proposition. Typically, this allowed despatch from a central station equipped with air pumps, and a return from a distant office having no special equipment.

Later appointments were Richard Spelman Culley, who took over from Latimer Clark; assistant engineer W H Winter; and a notable civil engineer Robert Sabine. All of them later transferred to *Post Office Telegraphs* as the Telegraph Acts of 1868-70 gave Her Majesty's Postmaster-General the right to acquire and operate the existing inland telegraph systems.

On 29 January 1870, RS Culley became the first Engineer-in-Chief of the Post Office. Sabine had an in-depth understanding of physics:

"The problem of a successful pneumatic system is simply...to make a given quantity of air expand from one pressure to another in such a way as to return a fair equivalent of the work expended in compressing it."

Together, the two engineers made the Post Office tube system an efficient platform for the speedy despatch of telegrams.

Extent of the Network
Historically, most telegraph offices had been established at railway stations, which weren't necessarily close to towns, whereas the business of the Post Office was predominantly urban. Thus, in early 1870, the network was re-aligned, and 740 miles of new wire was laid under London's streets.

My GPO in London: Trilogy Edition

At Telegraph Street

ETC's existing Central Telegraph Station (premises) boasted a configuration of 7 air-circuits to: Fenchurch Street, 980 yards; Leadenhall Street, 670 yards; Gresham House, 588 yards; Cornhill, 490 yards; Old Broad Street, for the British Indian Submarine Telegraph Company, 370 yards; the Stock Exchange, 324 yards and Founders' Court, 223 yards.

GPO West (CTO)

The Post Office re-terminated all of the telegraph plant to its newly opened Central Telegraph Office (CTO) on St. Martin's-le-Grand, at the corner of Newgate Street, by 17 January 1874.

A typical array of a street tubes terminal in the CTO (1934)
© *BT Heritage and Archives TCB 473/P00277*

Tube Service

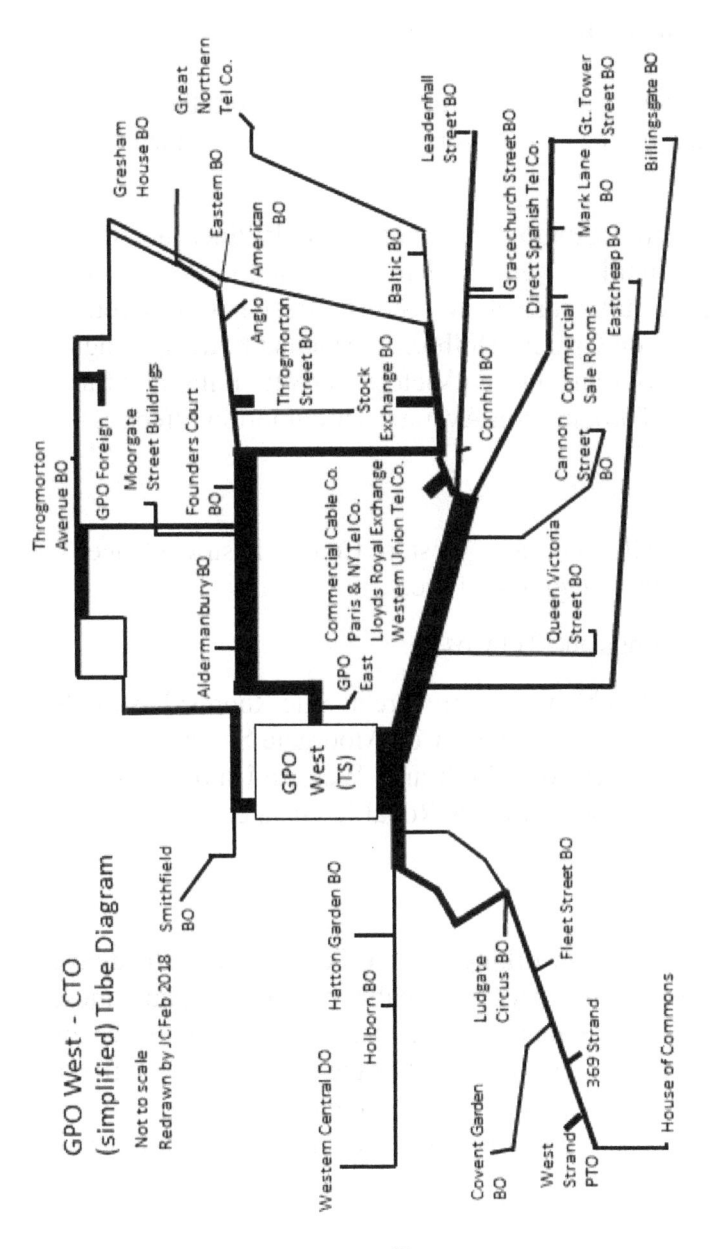

My GPO in London: Trilogy Edition

CTO – Pneumatic Tube Routes

The network of pneumatic tubes radiating from the Central Telegraph Office (CTO) were routed to many Branch Offices (BOs):

Aldermanbury; Anglo American; Baltic; Billingsgate; Cannon Street; Cornhill; Covent Garden; Eastcheap; Eastern; Fleet Street; Founders Court; Gracechurch Street; Great Tower Street; Gresham House; Hatton Garden; Holborn; Leadenhall Street; Ludgate Circus; Mark Lane; Queen Victoria Street; Smithfield; Stock Exchange; Throgmorton Avenue; Throgmorton Street.

And other offices:

GPO East; GPO Foreign; Western Central District Office; West Strand Postal Telegraph Office.

Other buildings and Tel Cos.:

Commercial Cable Co.; Commercial Sale Rooms; District Spanish Tel Co.; Great Northern Tel Co.; Moorgate Street Buildings; Paris & New York Tel Co.; 339 Strand; Western Union Tel Co.; House of Commons; Lloyds Royal Exchange.

Tube Service

Postal messengers working in the CTO referred to the delivery of telegrams as Tube Service, probably because the paper messages originated by pneumatic tube, either from a distant office, or within GPO West; such was the extent of the tube network. Officially the work was the Telegram Service, but the TS initials on the messengers' caps could be interpreted to a number of meanings, even Telegraph Street.

Tube Service

TECHNICAL INSTRUCTION X
PNEUMATIC TUBES
ENGINEER-IN-CHIEF'S OFFICE
G.P.O. WEST, LONDON,
December 1920.

1.   The **pneumatic services** of the Department are in general made use of as a means of conveying **telegraphic messages**.

2.   In practically every office where important telegraph traffic is dealt with and where the **Counter, Delivery, and Instrument Rooms are not adjacent**, some form or other of pneumatic despatch is used for connecting up the points, and in many large towns tubes are laid in the street for **connecting the Head Office with other buildings**.

3.   Tubes are, therefore, divided into two classes, known as **House** and **Street Tubes**.

4.   The tubes may be **hand or power worked**. In the former case a reciprocating air-pump operated by hand through a lever is generally used, and in the latter case reciprocating pumps or rotary air blowers operated by electrical or mechanical power are employed.

5.   In most cases **compressed air** is used for **sending** carriers from, and **rarefied air** for **drawing** carriers to, a central station from which the tubes radiate and are worked. In house installations where short power-worked tubes are

used it is often found preferable to loop the tubes and make use of one of these methods of working only.

6. For **house tube** installations the principle connections are between the Instrument Room and
(1) The Counter
(2) The Delivery Room
(3) The Telephone Room
In the case of (1) and (2) the loaded carriers practically all flow in one direction, but in the case of (3) the telegraphic work is in both directions.

7. The authorised practice is to return empty carriers by hand for hand-operated installations, and by tube when power is used.

8. **Street tubes** are worked up, down, and in both directions. If the traffic between two offices is sufficiently large, two tubes are installed to deal with the up and down work respectively. Where the traffic is smaller the work is carried by one tube worked alternately up and down. Where the traffic is in one direction only, and the power provided can only deal with carriers moving in that direction, the empty carriers are returned in batches by hand.

At its peak more than 5000 staff were employed in *GPO West*. Telegraph instruments, the circuits and signalling evolved over the years as transmission technology improved. Thus, a full range of systems included: Morse, Wheatstone automatic, Baudot, Creed, Murray, and Hughes. Consequently, the working galleries were rearranged, refurbished, and re-equipped as practices changed.

Tube Service

Baudot instrument operator at CTO (1934)
© BT Heritage and Archives TCB 473/P00362

If one imagines the scene of telegraphic halls furnished with long desks, filled with clerks operating morse equipment, or in later days, teleprinters; side galleries of additional transmitting and receiving equipment; telephones ringing; messenger boys rushing about, and the sounds of message pods flying through the tubes, vibrating and clunking throughout the day. The CTO was such a busy place!

To a new observer of a modern-day call centre, with its rows and rows of desks, call turrets and computers, the scene would probably be an awe-inspiring sight, combined with one of amazement at the organised pace of activity! The *CTO*, in its day, would have been its equal - modern technology handling the latest media innovation;

My GPO in London: Trilogy Edition

in this case the transmission of morse or baudot-coded messages by wire and tubes.

Pneumatic Tubes in the CTO (1912)
© *BT Heritage and Archives TCB 475/YB04*

Tube Service

At the CTO (2018)

The scene is set at the CTO
A building where Baudot-coded messages go!

By teleprinter, (pneumatic) tube or telephone
The telegram's headed into the zone.

Rows and rows of benches placed
Where clerks and teleprinters race.

Receiving a message or relaying it fast
It's modern technology of the past.

A whoosh as a message-carrier's sucked away
The tubes vibrate throughout the day.

Another clunk at the (carrier) buffer stop
A post boy then departs with the telegram to drop.

G. Stow Probationer (Learner) Telegraphist (1927)

In 1982 George aged 72 recalled his work: *"Huge clocks, noises of all descriptions. The tic-toc of the Baudot cadences, the chatter of sounders, the high-speed whirring of slip printers and perforators. Everywhere, there were rapid movements of staff, as speed was of the essence and I was soon to be found, with others, rushing around, collecting and distributing messages, between the instrument positions and a divisional sorting point, which was presided over by a dragon-like lady, who would rap on the boxes with a pencil if we dared to linger for a moment. Delay was simply not tolerated, and so many messages were of vital importance."*

My GPO in London: Trilogy Edition

The Central Hall CTO (1929)
© *BT Heritage and Archives TCB 417/E06312*

Tube Service

CTO Fourth-floor Phonograms (1935)
© *BT Heritage & Archives TCB 473/P00610*

My GPO in London: Trilogy Edition

Phonogram Working

By the mid-1930s the whole of the fourth floor West Gallery, and part of the North Gallery in the CTO had possibly the world's largest installation of phonogram, and telephone-telegram equipment, for this method of working - 50,000 messages a day were handled.

- Phonogram: 12 suites of sixteen positions
- Telephone-telegram: 6 suites of sixteen positions

'...and provided a central point for the dictation of telegrams by and to telephone subscribers over the telephone network.'

[POEEJ Vol 30 1937 Pt1: The CTO Inland Phonogram and Telephone-Telegram Installation.]

End of Tube Service

GPO West was virtually destroyed in WWII (December 1940). Temporary tube service continued at the protected installation (*CTO R*) in *King Edward Building* by November 1941, until service was transferred back to the partially rebuilt *GPO West* in 1947.

With more use being made of the telephone service, the liability and practicality of maintaining a tube service ultimately led to its obsolescence.

A new *CTO* in *Fleet Building* was operational from 1962; no provision was made for the continuance of pneumatic delivery tubes.

Outlet 7: GPO North

GPO North- Angel Street/St. Martin's-le-Grand
© J. Chenery (2017)

My GPO in London: Trilogy Edition

GPO North (1895-1984)
King Edward Street/St. Martin's-le-Grand/Angel Street.

GPO North was built as the principal administration headquarters of the Post Office, and was the third GPO building in the area, after *GPO East* and *GPO West*. The architect was Henry Tanner from the *Office of Works*.

> THIS STONE WAS LAID
> BY THE
> RIGHT HONOURABLE HENRY CECIL RAIKES.M.P.
> HER MAJESTY'S POSTMASTER GENERAL.
> ON THE 20 TH OF NOVEMBER. 1890.
> THE JUBILEE YEAR OF
> UNIFORM INLAND PENNY POSTAGE

[The uniform inland Penny Post had been introduced on 10 January 1840. In 1890, special commemorative postal stationery was issued to mark this anniversary, and exhibitions were held at the Guildhall and South Kensington Museum.]

The *Morning Post* reported (25/12/1894): *'The irregular piece of land is bounded by St. Martin's-le-Grand on the east, St. Botolph's-churchyard on the north, King Edward-street on the west, and Angel street on the south. The eastern frontage is wider than the rest, and on the northern side the site curves inwards in a manner exasperating to an architect, but by narrowing the courtyard, which runs the whole length of the building from St. Martin's-le-Grand to King Edward-street, Mr. Tanner has been*

GPO North

enabled to get similar accommodation in the north and south wings.'

The state of affairs of the existing GPO sites was made clear…

'GPO North is to be devoted exclusively to the administrative as distinguished from the executive branch. Letters and parcels are confined to the old building [GPO East], and have been for years. Telegraphs, telephones, engineering, and administration are crowded together in GPO West.'

'The Western office was opened in 1873, and years ago it had stretched out its arms - there are footbridges across the road, to be precise - and had embraced another huge block on the other side of Roman Bath-street, its western boundary.'

GPO North was connected to *GPO West* by

'a handsome covered-in gangway across Angel-street, at the height of the second floor.'

Ornamental keystones:

'The features of Mr. Raikes look east and those of Mr. Arnold Morley west- two Postmaster-Generals. Inside the courtyard the arches are surmounted with the faces of Mr. Plunket and Mr. Shaw-Lefevre - two First Commissioners.'

Accommodation for the Post Office was a burgeoning issue. A fourth floor had been added to *GPO West* in 1884, and the growing popularity of the telephone had yet to be compounded. The Post Office Savings Bank was flourishing, and at *GPO East* the volume of letters to be sorted was ever-increasing!

My GPO in London: Trilogy Edition

GPO North from Postman's Park © J. Chenery (2017)

GPO North

Postman's Park

The garden was opened in 1880, and is made up of the churchyards of St. Leonards, Foster Lane, St. Botolph, Aldersgate and the graveyard of Christchurch, Newgate Street. It is home to the famous Watts memorial*, built in 1900 as a tribute to heroic men and women.

* A series of ceramic tiles on which are remembered long ago acts of heroic self-sacrifice by ordinary men, women and children.

The End

After Vesting Day in April 1984, British Telecommunications Plc was no longer 'part of the Post Office' and a new HQ (*BT Centre*) was in the process of being built on the former *GPO West* site. *GPO North* was purchased on behalf of Nomura International Plc in 1986. The interior of the building was gutted and rebuilt within the remaining exterior. Nomura House is at 1 St. Martin's-le-Grand.
In 2010 Nomura moved to a brand-new building (*Watermark Place*) at 1 Angel Lane, former site of BT's *Mondial House*. Nomura sold *GPO North* in 2014 for £171 million.

London Landmarks Half Marathon (LLHM) 2018

On 25 March 2018 the first LLHM brought history back to *GPO North* as the route through Angel Street took in views of two ex-postal vehicles, exhibited by the Post Office Vehicle Club. David Cott's Land Rover Defender *Postbus*, and Jim Cawte's *Royal Mail* Morris (van) were splendid restoration examples of modern postal history. Out of shot, other visitors to the area were dressed in period costumes which had been lent by *The Postal Museum*. The green Penfold letter box completed the scene.

My GPO in London: Trilogy Edition

GPO North from Angel Street © D.A. Cott (2018)

GPO North

The Penfold Postbox designed by John Penfold in 1866.

This postbox was unveiled by
Their Royal Highnesses
The Prince of Wales and The Duchess of Cornwall
on 6th September 2016.

It commemorates 500 years since the knighting of
Brian Tuke, the first Master of the Posts
by King Henry VIII in 1516.

This act was the catalyst for the creation of the Royal Mail we know today. Tuke had the influence and authority to establish key post towns across the country and build out a formal postal network.

The building that this postbox is now situated outside was the General Post Office (GPO) Headquarters from 1894-1984. The earlier GPO building was located opposite this site
from 1829-1912.

Other HQ Buildings

The extent of the Post Office's activities led to a sprawl of departments and staff across London, often with no easily defined centre. Posts and Telecoms were part of the same business, so hierarchies and functions could be mixed, even within the same building. The distinction between central functions, the company's official HQ, and the operational postal or telecommunications regions, changed as the businesses re-organised and finally began the split on the way to privatisation. A full study of the GPO's hierarchy is beyond the scope of this current tome.

My GPO in London: Trilogy Edition

*Penfold postbox (green replica) outside BT Centre
St. Martin's-le-Grand © J. Chenery (2018)*

GPO North

HQ Terms

Post Office – The name of the combined business(es) operating, telephones, post offices (counters), and mail handling, at the start of the study.

CHQ – Central Headquarters meaning the HQ of centralised functions of both sides of the business. [See **Bloomsbury and Fitzrovia** chapter.]

PHQ - Post Office Headquarters meaning the HQ of the whole business; usually the administrative centre.

PHQ – Postal Headquarters referring to the postal side of the business.

THQ – Telecommunications Headquarters referring to the telephone side of the business.

RHQ – Regional Headquarters of either business.

HQ Overview

The administrative HQ of the Post Office was run from *GPO North* until July 1984 when it moved, due to lack of staff restaurant facilities, to 33 Grosvenor Place (the old British Steel building). British Telecom moved into BT Centre in 1985 at privatisation of the telephone business.

Numerous functions and departments were housed in all manner of buildings across London, not limited to: Castle House, Empire House, Euston Towers, 100-110 High Holborn, Leith House, London House, Procter House, River Plate House, State House, 90-91 Wood Street, and others.

My GPO in London: Trilogy Edition

RHQ of the postal (mail handling) and counters business operated in various premises between 148 and 166 Old Street EC1 from the 1950s onwards. This was the operational base of the London Postal Region (LPR). In 1986 Post Office Counters was formed and became a wholly owned subsidiary of the Post Office corporation in August 1987.

The regional base of the telephones business, London Telecommunications Region (LTR) was located at Camelford House from 1962 onwards. The Engineering Department (THQ) had been located in Alder House, and spread over many sites, but moved into a new office block, *2-12 Gresham Street*, during 1958.

In 1990, Post Office HQ moved from Grosvenor Place into Old Street, such that RHQ and PHQ were in the same locality.

In 2001 Royal Mail Group became the operating name of what was once the Post Office, as the split of RM and PO would lead to privatisation in 2012. Thus in 2009 Royal Mail (mail handling) moved its HQ from Old Street to 100 Victoria Embankment, EC4.

And in 2015 Post Office Counters Ltd, which became simply Post Office Ltd. in October 2001, moved from Royal Mail House at 148 Old Street to Finsbury Dials, 20 Finsbury Street, EC2.

References

http://britishpostofficearchitects.weebly.com
Post Horn April 2018 (18/127)

Note: *Tomb Raider* (2018) features a pushbike race through Postman's Park.

Outlet 8: GPO Time Services

The GPO in London facilitated the distribution of Greenwich Mean Time (GMT) throughout the UK from about 1870, during an era of communications which pre-dated the telephone. Intricate switching devices relied upon 'clockwork' mechanisms, governed by springs, levers and pendulums, as well as 'galvanic' (electrical) forces that were supplied by battery power. The growing telegraph network centred upon *GPO West* proved an ideal medium over which to transmit time signals.

Later, the adoption of Master Clocks within the GPO telephone exchanges attested to their accurate and regulated time-keeping. The opening of Rugby radio station allowed the broadcasting of the time signal over greater distances, and the *Speaking Clock* gave instant announcements to anyone with a telephone.

Greenwich Time Ball

Time and navigation by the sun and stars historically led to the setting up of the Royal Observatory in Greenwich. Subsequently the Admiralty oversaw the operation and by the early eighteenth century marine chronometers were maintained at Greenwich. In 1833 daily time signals were established by the dropping of a time ball, affixed to a mast, to visibly mark one o'clock.

"For the first time it made Greenwich time regularly available to those ashore who could see it, including much of London."

[Greenwich Time and the Discovery of the Longitude by Derek Howse 1980.]

Time Ball at the Royal Greenwich Observatory (RGO)
© *J. Chenery (2018)*

GPO Time Services

The Need for Uniform Time

The operation of a railway timetable; the timed arrivals and departures of mail coaches, and the accurate timing of a telegraphic message bearing good or bad news, were all concerns of everyday life in the 1840s. The now well-known Bradshaw's railway timetable used local times to record the comings and goings of passenger trains, but the lack of a uniform time across the UK was more than just an inconvenience.

In 1840 it was suggested by Captain Basil Hall of the Royal Navy, that all Post Office clocks throughout the UK be regulated to London time. Similarly, in 1847 Henry Booth of the Liverpool and Manchester railway envisaged that:

"...the ever-varying longitude of a thousand post-towns is made subservient to the metropolitan chime of St. Martin's-le-Grand [GPO HQ]."

[Greenwich Time and the Discovery of the Longitude by Derek Howse 1980*]*

The Electric Telegraph Company

Meanwhile, in 1846, the (private) Electric Telegraph Company (ETC) was established by William Fothergill Cooke and Joseph Lewis Ricardo. At Founders' Court, Lothbury, in 1848, the company set up its Central Telegraph Station (CTS), in the heart of London, opposite the Bank of England. The ETC had agreements with the principal railways and business institutions to provide telegraphic services, and consequently lines radiated out, all over the City. By 1852 its lines reached to distant parts of the UK.

A time ball, not unlike the one at Greenwich, was installed on the

My GPO in London: Trilogy Edition

roof of ETC's premises, opposite Charing Cross Station, at 448 Strand. The time ball was five-foot in diameter, dropped via a 21-foot post. It must have been quite a spectacle to witness it in operation.

Greenwich Observatory Clock System(s)

George Airy (seventh Astronomer Royal) proposed a grand scheme to make galvanic (electrical) time distribution a practical reality. At the request of Airy, Charles Shepherd designed a master clock as part of a time-distribution system for the Observatory, namely:

1. One automatic clock with face and works – Shepherd Master Clock/Mean Solar Standard Clock.

2. One clock with a large dial to be seen by the public - Gate Clock.

3. Three smaller clocks, all to be moved sympathetically with the automatic clock, which were for the Chronometer Room, Computing Room and Flamsteed House (Airy's home).

The Gate Clock was brought into service on Friday 13 August 1852. Additionally, the dropping of the Greenwich time ball at 1 pm was thereafter activated by the system.

Airy further proposed:

"A galvanic connexion between the Royal Observatory Greenwich and the London Bridge Railway Terminus, for the three purposes:

1. Of regulating the principal clocks of London; the Royal Exchange clock and the clock shortly to be constructed for the New Houses of Parliament [Big Ben clock tower].

GPO Time Services

The Gate Clock © J. Chenery (2018)

2. *Of sending every day a time signal to every part of Britain which is reached by a line of galvanic (electric) telegraph.*

3. *Of communicating with the principal foreign observatories."*

Time Network

The master clock at Greenwich sent out one-second pulses to drive additional slave clocks via the South Eastern Railway (SER) telegraph network. Thus, the first electric time signal from Greenwich, at 4pm on 5 August 1852, was received at the London Bridge terminus.

Onward switching arrangements were necessarily complex, because the telegraph lines had to be cleared of normal traffic to accept the *time-current*. By 1859 lines were routed directly to ETC's HQ at Lothbury for switching and transmission to London and Provincial post offices, government buildings and clockmakers.

The Chronopher (aka Time Carrier)

The GMT signals needed a reliable method of being quickly switched to multiple destinations at the appointed hour(s). Mr Varley (consulting electrician with ETC) designed an elaborate, but effective clock and relay system through which the Greenwich time signals could pass. Galvanometers on the main outputs indicated (by a needle moving under glass) the passing signal. And a return current path was incorporated so that an integrity check could be made on the distant clocks too. [See ***Master Clocks*** chapter for more of the Chronopher.]

GPO Time Services

GPO West

The privately owned inland telegraph system was transferred to the State on 28 Jan 1870, following the Telegraph Act of 1868. The Post Office took over 1,058 telegraph offices and 1,874 offices at railway stations. ETC's Central Telegraph Station was transferred, in 1874, into the newly opened *GPO West*.

'The hourly signal at the Post Office is distributed by means of the Chronophers. The old-one originally constructed by Mr. Varley and brought from Telegraph Street on the removal to St. Martin's-le-Grand (GPO West), and a new one, much larger. It is to this that the Greenwich wire is led, and the current transmitted to the different lines.'

Deal Time Ball

A line routed to the old Navy Yard at Deal activated another time-ball from the 1 pm *time current* from Greenwich. A time-gun at Dover Castle was fired at noon. The time ball operated from 1855 until the service officially closed in 1927. Since 2004, as a museum site, the time ball now operates from an MSF signal received from Anthorn.

Time Signal Renters

Private Wire (PW) renters were able to take the hourly time signal from their local head post offices, typically for an annual fee. Details of the *time signal* service were published in the *Post Office Guide* from 1873 up until 1936, when the service was superseded by the *Speaking Clock*.

My GPO in London: Trilogy Edition

BPO Guide April 1873

To transmit from London to the Country:

1. A Ten o'clock Current – including the rental and maintenance of a private wire, from the Local Head Post Office to the renter's house. The charge varied from £12 for a quarter of a mile circuit, to £17 for a one-mile circuit (per annum).

2. A One o'clock Current - £27 and £32 respectively.

The Department undertakes to supply a time signal only where the existing postal telegraph arrangements will permit the work to be properly done.

PO Guide 1920

Where sufficient support is forthcoming special arrangements can be made for the hourly synchronization of clocks. Information as to rates and arrangements can be obtained in London from the Controller, London Telephone Service, 144A, Queen Victoria Street, London, E.C. 4, and in the provinces from the District Managers of the Telephone Service.

By the 1930s it appears that the renters' 10 o'clock signal had again been reverted to 9 o'clock...

[See *Master Clocks* chapter for previous alterations.]

GPO Time Services

Letter from the Secretary to the Engineer-in-Chief

The Secretary,

In papers 122960/29 dealing with the alteration of the Greenwich mean time signal from 10 a.m. to 9 a.m., it was decided that the standard service available for new subscribers should be 9 a.m. and/or 1 p.m. G.M.T.

YR Pervis

for Engineer-in-Chief
27 June 1932

PO Guide Jan 1936

Where telegraph arrangements permit, Greenwich mean time can be supplied by means of a private circuit over which an electric current is transmitted at either 9 a.m. or 1 p.m. (Greenwich time). Information as to rates and arrangements can be obtained in London from the Controller, London Telephone Service, Cornwall House, Waterloo Road, London, S.E.1, (Telephone No. – City 2000) and in the Provinces from the District Managers of the Telephone Service.

Rugby Radio Station

Was opened in 1925 and an international time signal was wirelessly broadcast from 1927.

[See *Rugby Radio* chapter for more]

On the ground floor of the North Dome at Flamsteed House, Greenwich, an elaborate set-up of time-keeping clocks was

My GPO in London: Trilogy Edition

established (in the renamed Rugby Room) specifically to transmit the time signals via landline to Rugby.

'A high-grade mechanism at Greenwich has been supplied by the Synchronome Company, under the personal direction of Mr. F. Hope-Jones, a great authority on electrical clock installations.'

The apparatus consisted of three clocks:

- A free pendulum
- A slave clock
- A signal transmitter

Special circuits were designed to keep all three clocks in exact phase. The physical circuit included an underground line from Greenwich Observatory to the GPO (West) and thence an underground line to Rugby Radio Station.

The time signal was sent twice daily at 09.55 and 17:55 hours.

[Reference: An International Time Signal – POEEJ Vol 21 part 1 1928.]

Notes

Dent & Co. built 'the great clock' at Westminster, with the bell called *Big Ben*. The *Clock Tower* was renamed the *Elizabeth Tower* in 2012 in recognition of the Queen's 60-year reign.

GPO Time Services

Switching panel in GPO West for the International Time Service (1928) showing galvanometers and relays 90A, for both Greenwich and Rugby. © BT Heritage and Archives TCB 417/E05273

A clock no. 24 was associated to control the switching times. The arrangement acted as a sub-Chronopher to switch the Greenwich line through to Rugby at the given hour(s).

My GPO in London: Trilogy Edition

Flamsteed House

The ground floor room of the North Dome of the RGO was initially referred to as the Galvanic Room, but soon became known as the Chronographic Room and then the Chronograph Room. In the late 1920s, it became known as the Rugby Room following the locating of the Rugby time-signal apparatus there.

The Speaking Clock

The GPO established a dial-up time service (TIM) in 1936. [See *Speaking Clock* chapter for more.]

A Timely End

It is plausible that the GPO's hourly Chronopher time-service via switched landlines was then deemed superfluous and was gradually withdrawn. By January 1937 the Post Office Guide no longer had any reference to switched time signals, but instead stated:

TIME SERVICE

'Subscribers or call office users in any part of the country may obtain the correct time by making a call to the speaking clock in London. The only charge payable is the ordinary charge for a call to central London. Full particulars are to be found in the London Telephone Directory.'

References

Greenwich Time and the Discovery of the Longitude by Derek Howse (1980).

Outlet 9: Master Clocks

The regulation of time in the GPO was always essential for the smooth operation of the business. As time-keeping for large factories and business establishments developed, the adoption of electric pulse-driven clocks came to the fore as a method of keeping the accuracy of many clocks, from a single *master* clock, that pulsed-out time to a chain of *slave* clocks, which were distributed throughout the premises.

The Hipp-toggle principle of operation of electric master clocks was devised by Matthaeus Hipp, a Swiss watchmaker, in 1838. And it was this feature particularly which helped keep accurate time and was later specified as the basis for the GPO's master clock systems. Typically, *Gents of Leicester*, established in 1872, was one manufacturer of the Master Clock No. 36 which served the GPO throughout its Strowger telephone exchange era of switching (circa 1912 to 1995).

Time Distribution

From 1855 a method of distributing an indication of the correct hourly time to telegraph offices, railway stations, business and financial institutions was urgently needed. A service had been established between the Royal Greenwich Observatory, the Electric Telegraph Company (ETC) and the South Eastern Railway (SER) for the daily signalling of Greenwich Mean Time (GMT) via the firing of guns, the ringing of bells, and the dropping of a time-ball. Many of these devices were electrically triggered via elaborate clocks and switches sited at the London Bridge terminus of the SER, or the Lothbury HQ of the ETC, upon receipt of the *time-current* from Greenwich. The growing number of telegraph offices, which needed correct time regulation led in 1864 to the ETC's consultant electrician devising a unified switching system for the distribution of the *time-current*. Lines to telegraph offices were solely for telegram traffic; additional lines for the transmission of clock pulses was not considered financially viable.

[*Time-current*: see chapter **GPO Time Services** for more details.]

The Chronopher (Time Carrier)

The Chronopher was a beast of a machine, capable of extending time throughout the UK, and yet with the delicate precision of clockwork it performed its hourly tasks. This long-forgotten device is worthy of recollection, for the implications of its working were widespread and relied-upon during its era.

More accurately, it was a mechanical switch which, at the appointed hour(s), interrupted normal telegraph traffic and transmitted a time signal over the wires to alert telegraph offices, and other important places, of the correct time. Its task completed, the lines were automatically reverted to normal working. The time signal originated from the Royal Observatory, and thus transmitted Greenwich Mean Time (GMT) throughout the land, in an age before the *Speaking Clock*, or radio broadcast *time pips*.

Note: The Electric and International Telegraph Company was the recognised name after the ETC had merged with the International Telegraph Company in 1855.

On the next page is a description of the first *Chronopher* by ETC's electrician, Cromwell Fleetwood Varley:

DESCRIPTION OF THE CHRONOPHER

OR APPARATUS EMPLOYED AT THE CENTRAL STATION OF THE
Electric and International Telegraph Company
IN LONDON,

FOR THE PURPOSE OF SENDING EXACT GREENWICH TIME SIMULTANEOUSLY AND AUTOMATICALLY TO NUMEROUS LOCAL AND PROVINCIAL STATIONS.

INVENTED AND DESIGNED BY

MR. C. F. VARLEY

ELECTRICIAN TO THE COMPANY

The Chronopher (time, I bear) consists of the following apparatus:

I - A *clock* to control the whole of the changes and connections.

II - Various sets of galvanic *batteries* to supply the currents which give the signals to the various stations, and also to put in action the various relays and magnets.

III - A large *commutator* or switch for connecting the lines to the Chronopher when time is to be transmitted.

IV - Two *relays* which give the actual time signal to the different stations.

V - Two electro-magnetic *switches*. [To prevent false signalling.]

VI - Two *galvanometers* to show by the deflection of the needles the passage of the currents.

My GPO in London: Trilogy Edition

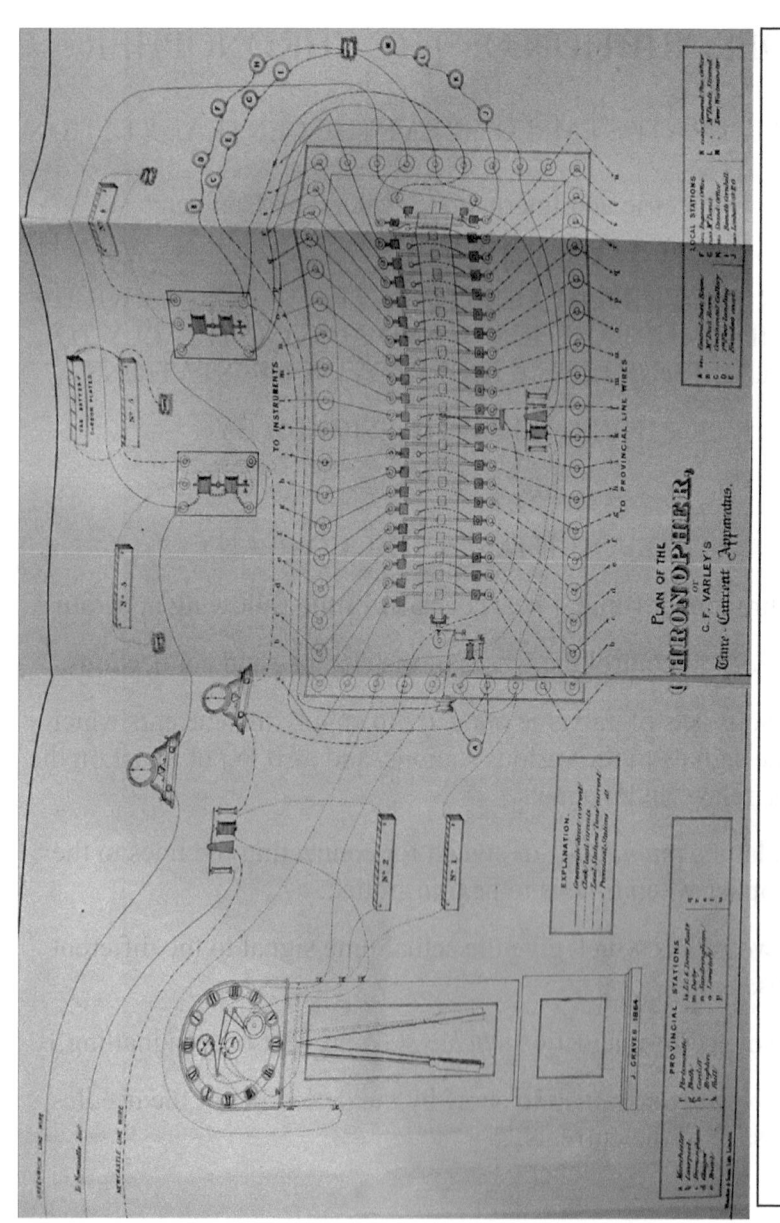

Plan of THE CHRONOPHER 1864

Outgoing Time Feeds

Provincial Stations (*relay*):
- Manchester; Liverpool; Birmingham; Glasgow; Bristol; Portsmouth; Bath; Cardiff; Brighton; Hull; LC and Dover Railway; Derby; Sandringham; Lowestoft.

Local Stations (*relay*):
- Bells: Central instrument room; Mr Dix's room; Continental gallery; 1st floor landing; Founder's court; Engineer's office.
- Time ball: Strand office; Bennett's Cornhill.
- Clocks: Mr Davis's; Lombard Street PO; General Post Office (East); Mr Dent's; Strand; Tower, Westminster.

Newcastle kit: Newcastle castle gun; North Shields gun

Operation

The Chronopher *clock* was timed to operate electrical *switches* at the hours of 10 am and 1 pm. In conjunction with the *commutator* and *relays*, a combination of events could be signalled.

The mechanically-driven *commutator* only activated for the 10 am event to cut-off telegraphic messages and switch the lines through to the time signal circuits, to receive a pulse from Greenwich Observatory.

The *local relay* was to send a current every hour to the local stations, and an arrangement could be made to send time to any single station in connection with the Chronopher at any hour of the day when necessary.

My GPO in London: Trilogy Edition

The *local* and *provincial* relays both operated to send time current at 10 am. The 1pm current fired the time guns at Newcastle. In practice the *commutator* was activated *before* the timed events to allow switching of the lines, and again *after* the events, to restore the lines.

10 am became the countrywide time at which clocks were set and adjusted. The 1 pm relay was historically for mariners to sight the dropping of time balls. The Chronopher had several incarnations and was undoubtedly modified over many decades to perform revised switching patterns.

Postmaster-General's report 1873: *'Greenwich time alone is now kept at all the Post Offices in Great Britain (England, Scotland and Wales).'*

Chronopher Two

Varley's first Chronopher was installed in ETC's premises at Telegraph Street. Following the Post Office's takeover of the telegraph companies, the machine was moved to GPO West, in 1874. Another, larger Chronopher was then built to cater for the popularity of the time signals, and to allow easier distribution over varying length of circuits.

Housed in a piece of furniture (a sideboard with top display cabinet, having two opening doors) that would not have looked too out of place in a dining room, the new Chronopher had six galvanometers, each with a corresponding switching relay. The commutator bar/horizontal cam operated across three sections of electrical circuits to switch the provincial, *short*, *medium* and *long* lines, from telegraphic traffic to the time signal.

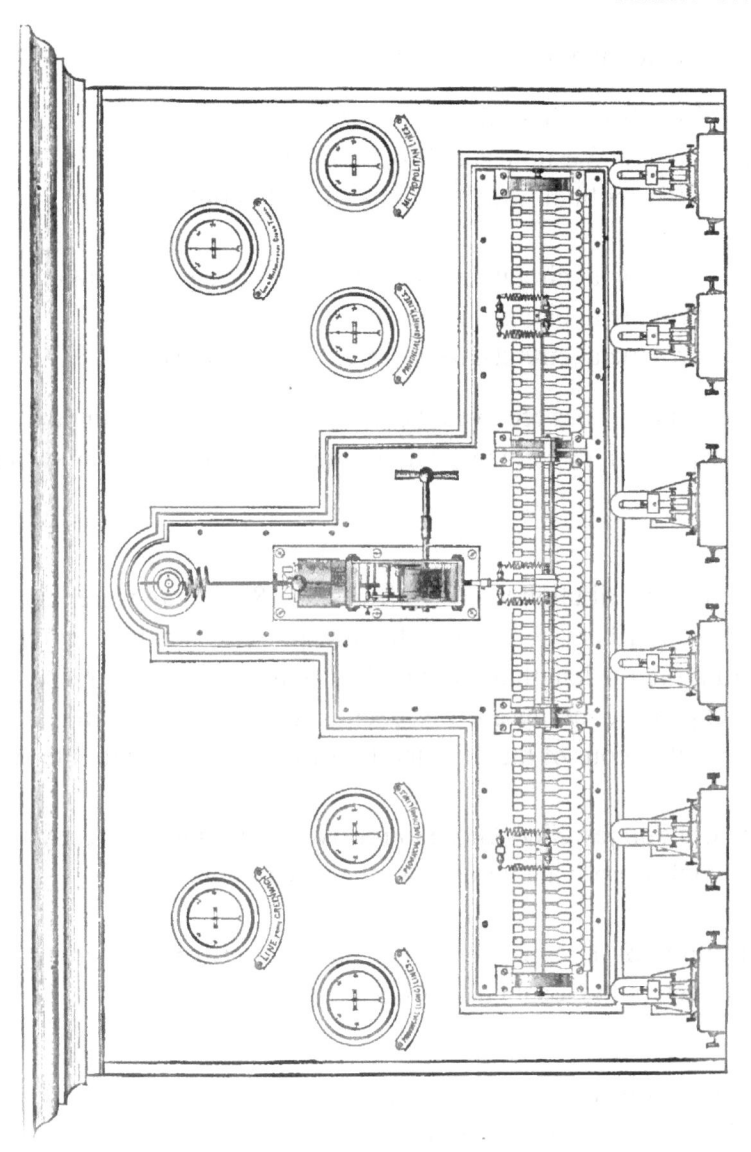

*The newer and larger Chronopher
From 'Time-keeping in London' 1883*

My GPO in London: Trilogy Edition

Galvanometer and relay circuits:

1. Line from Greenwich
2. Line to Westminster (Clock Tower)
3. Metropolitan (local) circuits - London only – hourly time signals
4. Provincial circuits, *short* - 50 miles out e.g. Brighton
5. Provincial circuits, *medium* – e.g. Hull
6. Provincial circuits, *long* – e.g. Edinburgh, Belfast

The provincial lines received the time signal at both 10 am and 1pm, dependent upon the wiring through the horizontal bar switch.

As well as distribution to GPO offices, in 1880, there were 100 private subscribers (renters) of the time pulse(s). Rentals varied according to the length of circuit. Additionally, the 1 pm pulse was more expensive, because it was deemed that telegraph traffic was busier at that hour of the day, and thus more disruptive to interrupt.

Some London jewellers chose to receive a time signal directly from Greenwich via private wires from the observatory.

Distribution of the time signal to certain subscribers was controlled by a switch in the local GPO office, viz.:

"An instruction card, T.E. 224 should be placed in a conspicuous position near the Time apparatus at each local office."

Master Clocks

POST OFFICE ENGINEERING DEPARTMENT.

GREENWICH MEAN TIME DISTRIBUTION.

Instructions for manipulation of Time Switch
at Post Offices, Diag. G.M.T. 12 (B).

(1) At 9.58 a.m. turn Switch to "PREL."
(2) At some time between 9.58 a.m. and 9.59 a.m. the needle of the right hand Galvanometer will deflect to the left. At once, turn the Switch handle to "TIME." (*see note below*.)
(3) At 10.0 a.m. precisely the passage of the momentary TIME CURRENT to the subscriber will be observed on the left hand galvanometer, the needles of both galvanometers being deflected to the right.
(4) Immediately after the passage of the Time Current turn the Switch handle to "INST." The normal circuit arrangements will be restored at 10.2 a.m.

Note: It is important that the switch handle should not be turned from "PREL." to "TIME" while the needle of right hand galvanometer is deflected to the right, or before it shows a steady deflection to the left.

Failures of the signal should be reported promptly to ....to whom also should be forwarded any complaints of failure or inaccuracy made by Subscribers.

Card T.E. 224.

[The card is for the later period of 1927, although illustrates a typical manual switching process.]

My GPO in London: Trilogy Edition

By 1904 the daily interruption of GPO telegraph traffic (at 10 am to switch the time signal) was stated to be particularly disruptive and was causing a backlog of work in suspended requests for telegrams.

Intercommunication Switch

Signal for London Postal Service (LPS) offices to be given at 9.00 instead of 10.00 am.

Letter to the Assistant Controller: 4 March 1904

Whatever the reasons might have been which led to the adoption of the hour of ten for signalling the 'time current', circumstances render it desirable that a change should be made, so far as the Intercommunication Switch is concerned. The stoppage of intercommunication and concentration for even so short a period as two minutes leads to a congestion which terminates that continuity of smooth working which is so necessary for any system worked at high pressure. On giving the warning signal at two minutes to ten, the work of the whole of the staff engaged at the Switch is interrupted, and the connecting cords of those offices intercommunicating have to be withdrawn, and notes taken by the Board Operators of the status quo.

After the signalling of the 'time current', the majority of the 138 stations call, either for intercommunication or for TS; and through the congestion, delay is caused which takes some time to work off, and a considerable number of MQs has to be given.

I am of the opinion that this would be avoided if the working were stopped at nine a.m. in order to signal the daily 'time current' as at that hour there is, as a rule, very little traffic as compared with ten a.m.

Master Clocks

Perhaps you will think the proposal worth submitting to the Controller for the consideration of the L.P.S., seeing that, so far as is known, the 'time current' is only used for the regulation of the office clocks.

James Bailey
Asst Supt.

[TS - Telegraph/telegram Service.]

The change for 10.00 am to 9.00 am appears to have been accepted, for the Intercommunication Switch users, as a later chart reveals.

There was however, some concern of the lack of detailed records of the Chronopher and its capacity for future alterations and expansion.

Chronopher Letters

EXTRACT from Papers Regd. No.66,107/09, File XVI
The Secretary,

Considerable difficulty has been experienced in obtaining particulars in connection with the history of the Time Current and its various arrangements.

The Time Current was originally supplied to the South Eastern Railway Company's Stations at London Bridge, Lewisham, Ashford, and Reigate, and was first transmitted from the Royal Observatory in August 1852. The Time arrangements, so far as the Telegraph service is concerned, appear to have been made by the Electric and International Telegraph Company, the Time Clock, Chronofer, etc., being introduced by C.F. Varley, the Company's Engineer, and the system was no doubt taken over by the Post Office at the time of the transfer in 1870.

My GPO in London: Trilogy Edition

In a communication to Sir G.B. Airy, Astronomer Royal, on the 28th July, 1878, the Department intimated that it would be prepared to distribute the hourly time received from Greenwich from the Chronofer in the Central Telegraph Office. The Admiralty Time apparatus, maintained by the Astronomer Royal, was taken over by the Department in 1887.

The Time apparatus in the Central Telegraph Office has, from time to time, been slightly altered since it was taken over from the Telegraph Company, but not to any great extent.

There is practically no record of the rentals which were fixed by the Department except those at present in vogue.

The drawings for the new apparatus and Clock for the Chronofer Room are not yet completed, and it has therefore not been possible to render a detailed estimate; but it is anticipated that the approximate cost will be £180. This will provide for re-arranging the Time apparatus, providing a new Clock, increasing the capacity of the 10.0 am Chronofer from 60 to 120 lines, and also increasing the capacity of the 1.0 pm Chronofer from 19 to 30 lines. The arrangements will admit of further additions at small cost.

(Sd.) W.A.J. O'Meara
10th April 1908

Notes in pencil: Only one Chronofer now with 23 circuits. Sub Chronofer for other Metropolitan clocks.

[Some memos used the alternative spelling of Chronofer!]

Master Clocks

By about 1910 the design of a third Chronopher was underway.

The already complex arrangements and procedures, for different feeds to various offices and/or renters was still generating correspondence. This related to the Provincial feeds.

The Secretary,

Ten o'clock is considered to be a better time for the signal to be sent.

The staff on duty between 8 and 9 a.m. is of course much less than between 9 and 10 a.m. and would be insufficient to ensure that the signal was transmitted to all points simultaneously when the current was received at 9 a.m. from Greenwich.

The more-lengthy wires are moreover not always in a settled condition at 9 a.m. and it is feared difficulty would ensue in consequence. It is open to question whether business people accustomed to receiving the time signal at 10 a.m. daily would welcome the suggested change.

7th June 1910

Reply 26th July 1910

"The existing arrangement under which the time is sent to Renters at 10.0 a.m. or at 1.0 p.m. need not be disturbed in any way."

The Chronopher was indeed a complex beast!

My GPO in London: Trilogy Edition

The Time Beast aka The Chronopher (2018)

In the far depths of the CTO
Where few folks rarely dare to go.
There lurks a beast of all time
Working with precision very fine.
It ticks away every second
The circuits primed, its springs do beckon!
Just before the appointed hour
Its cams switch-over, oh such power!
Work throughout the land doth pause
In telegraph rooms they hold the calls.

The ten o'clock pulse from Greenwich races
As Big Ben's hands straighten its faces!
Thousands of circuits spring into life
The Chronopher's time-pulse balanced like a knife.
Bells sound, guns fire and time-balls drop
Everyone knows the accuracy of the clock!
Circuits revert as telegrams await
Messages foretelling senders fate.

Its job done the beast goes to sleep
All for Greenwich Mean Time to keep.

George Stow Probationer Telegraphist (1927) stated: *"The only time that we were ever quiet was at two minutes to nine a.m., when everyone was poised to flash a time signal. All sorts of people, not least the bookmakers, relied upon the synchronisation of all the clocks, in all the Post Offices in the UK."*

Master Clocks

Statement shewing the number of offices receiving the Time Signal at 9 am, 10 am, and 1 pm   *[November 1910]*

Time	Signalled by	No.	Remarks
9 am	Hand	21	Tube offices
9 am	Hand	523	Intercommunication Switch offices
10 am	Hand	23	Tube offices
10 am	Chronofer	62	Provincial offices
10 am	Chronofer	8	Metropolitan offices
10 am	Hand	294	Provincial offices
10 am	Hand	29	Metropolitan offices
10 am	Hand	2	Private Wires
1 pm	Chronofer	18	Provincial offices

The Provincial offices change from 10.0 am to 9.0 am was published in the Post Office Circular (POC) during 1911…

Rules for Head Postmasters

GREENWICH TIME

Rule 113. At 9 a.m. daily, Sundays excepted, Greenwich time will be sent to every Telegraph Office in the United Kingdom.

At two minutes to 9 o'clock special attention must be given to the circuit on which the time signal is to be received and to all the circuits on which it will be sent. The word "time" will be signalled at two minutes to nine, and the circuits must then be left free until 9 a.m., and work stopped meanwhile.

My GPO in London: Trilogy Edition

At 9 a.m. the signal "nine" should be received and the first letter "N" should be received precisely at 9 o'clock. Between 8.58 and 9 a.m. the key should not be touched.

On arrival of the "nine" signal, every clock is to be adjusted, except those electrically controlled, which will be synchronised automatically.

On Sub-Office Telephone circuits, the warning signal at 8.58 a.m. should consist of three one-second rings; and at 9 o'clock the signal should be a continuous ring of three seconds, the beginning of the ring marking 9 a.m. The number of rings in the warning signal should be varied if any confusion is likely to arise with the distinctive call of an office.

Some offices receive a time signal directly from Greenwich (by chronopher) at 10.a.m. and 1 p.m.), in addition to the 9 o'clock signal. At these offices a preliminary current should be received at 9.58 a.m. (or 12.58 p.m.), and 10 a.m. (or 1 p.m.) will be indicated by the reversal of the deflection of the indicator needle.

[The change was subsequently reverted to 10.0 am on 23 May 1916.]

Chronopher 3

By 1912 (possibly slightly earlier) the third Chronopher was in service.

"The chronopher, as installed in those early days, is still doing useful service, but has become much overloaded. The temporary disturbance of the telegraph wires has also resulted in such

Master Clocks

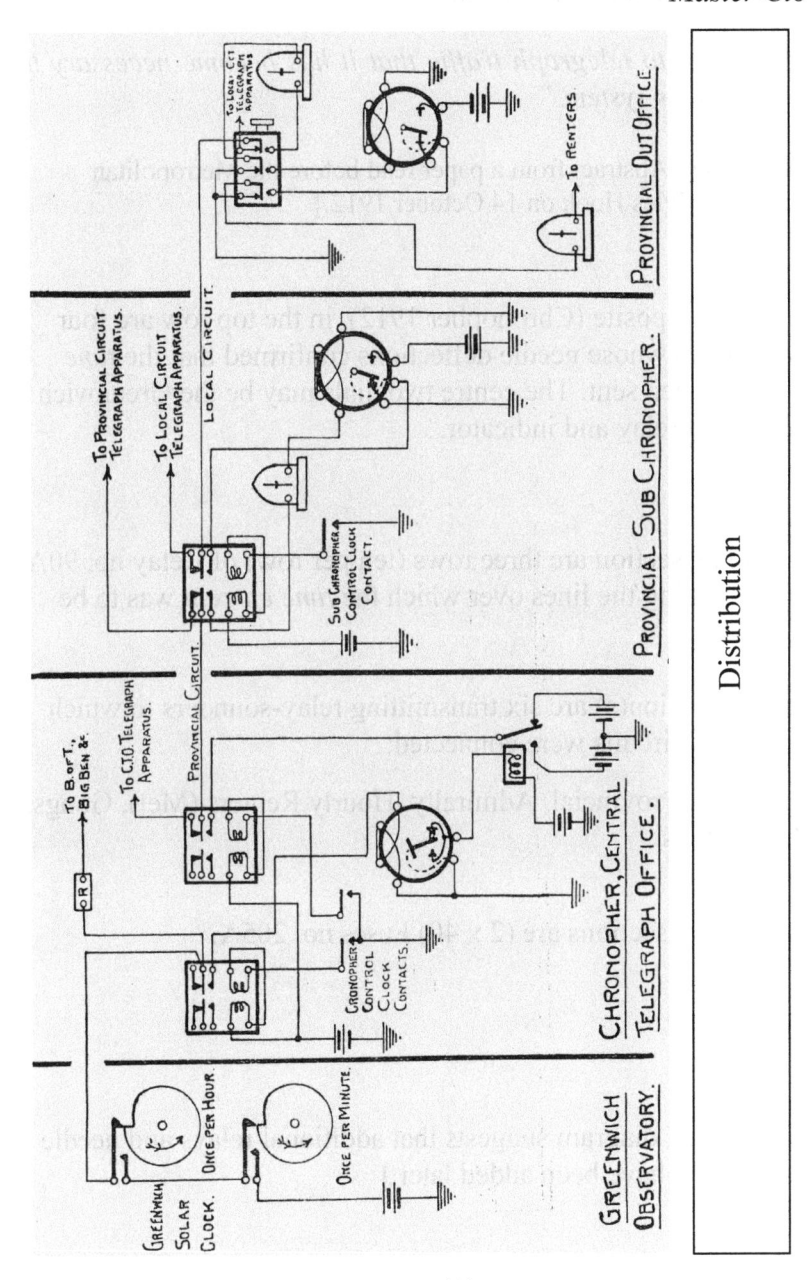

Distribution

My GPO in London: Trilogy Edition

inconvenience to telegraph traffic that it has become necessary to introduce a new system."

[*Correct Time* - Abstract from a paper read before the Metropolitan Centre by R. Myles Hook on 14 October 1912.]

In the photo opposite (Chronopher 1912), in the top row are four galvanometers whose needle deflections confirmed that the *time current* had been sent. The centre two dials may be the Greenwich return current relay and indicator.

In the middle section are three rows (ten per row) of Relay no. 90A for concentrating the lines over which the *time current* was to be sent.

In the next section(s) are six transmitting relay-sounders to which the groups of circuits were connected:

Metropolitan, Provincial, Admiralty, Hourly Renters (Met), Gongs, and Misc. Bells.

The lower two sections are (2 x 40) Fuses no. 205A.

[A 1927 wiring diagram suggests that additional relays and needle indicators may have been added later.]

Master Clocks

The Chronopher (1912)

© *BT Heritage and Archives TCB 475/YB23*

My GPO in London: Trilogy Edition

Sub-Chronophers

The second Chronopher used variable length distribution lines with increasing battery potential to power the longer circuits. The third system was more flexible, because at each main centre the received time signal was passed onto a number of Sub-Chronopher circuits, which in turn distributed the signals ever further.

Pulse Clocks

At the start of the Strowger telephone switching era, accurate clock pulses were needed for call timing purposes, as well as for the clear-down of held equipment.

Master clock systems in the GPO evolved from the early Magneta type, to the Hipp-Toggle type No. 12, which was later superseded by the Clock No. 36, which then became the standard throughout the GPO.

Clock No. 24

From about 1912, an ETS (Electrical Time Switching) Clock No. 24 was specified in Sub-Chronopher circuits.

'A disc controls contacts which form a change-over switch, allowing for connection or disconnection between either the 10 a.m. or the 1 p.m. group relays and contact springs.'

By the mid-1920s, Clock No. 24 was obsolescent and time switching was replaced in future installations by Clock No. 30 (and 32), in conjunction with the new Clock No. 36.

Master Clocks

Clock No. 24 (1922)
© *BT Heritage and Archives TCB 417/E02684*

My GPO in London: Trilogy Edition

Clock No. 30 (1932)
© BT Heritage and Archives TCB 417/E07821
Top row terminals: Time circuit, 9 am, 10 am, 1 pm. Common.

Clock No. 30

In series with the half-minute pulse from a Master Clock No. 36, it controlled the seconds indicating clocks in conjunction with Clock, No. 32 and Relays 90A.

Clock No. 32

Was used for synchronising 1-second clocks, together with Clock No. 30.

Master Clocks

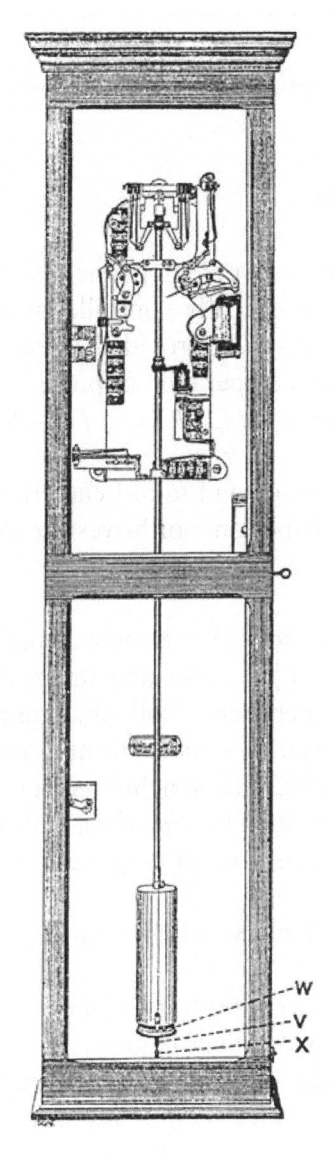

Clock No. 36
EI Misc. Time B 1325 (1959)

My GPO in London: Trilogy Edition

Relay 90A

Was a change-over contacts relay for switching lines into the Chronopher.

Master Clock No. 36

Spanning most of the Strowger telephone era and beyond. Clock No. 36 was an electrically-controlled master clock having a 1-second beating pendulum. It provided 1-second, 6-second, and half-minute pulses for the operation of pulse clocks and telephone apparatus. *[EI Misc. Time B 1325 Issue 3, 12-2-59.]*

Manufacturers were: Magneta Ltd of Leatherhead in Surrey; Synchronome Ltd of Alperton, north-west London; Gillett and Johnson; Gents of Leicester.

The clock was accurate to within 8 seconds per week, hence the desirability for an automatic daily adjustment. The Mk. 1 to Mk. 4 versions included a synchroniser coil which regulated the clock upon receipt of the 10 am time pulse from Greenwich. From the Mk. 5 version (circa 1955) the synchroniser circuit was omitted from the design, but by then the *Speaking Clock* service *TIM* was readily accessible to assist in checking the correct time.

Hourly Signals for Clock Synchronization

'The distribution of these signals to subscribers is effected on a party line basis, each subscriber being provided with a single line spur connected to either wire of the nearest distribution circuit. Each such spur is terminated within the subscriber's premises on a protective device provided by the Post Office.'

Master Clocks

End Notes
An article in the *Post Office Telecommunications Journal* (Feb-April 1954) entitled Post Office Clocks, suggests that *'private wires for time-signals were recovered'* not long after the introduction in 1927 of the *International Time Signal* which was broadcast worldwide, from Rugby. And by 1936, the *Speaking Clock* service had begun. The exact fate of the Chronopher is unknown, but it was most likely destroyed during the WWII bombing of *GPO West*.

Radial Time Recorders
These 'clocking-in' devices were to be found in large industrial premises, which included GPO switchrooms. Inside the box casing was a pen and paper/chart recorder. The recorders 'time-stamped' the instance of an operator's arrival on duty, upon selection with the pointer, of their allocated number on the large dial.

Maintenance of Time Recorders
'All types of radial time-recorders are obsolete. And have been superseded by alternative methods of recording attendances. No new or replacement radial time-recorders will be supplied, but those in service may be maintained while local repair is economical.' EI Misc. Time D 53011 Issue 3 5.1.65

References
Inventions by CF Varley 1864
Time-keeping in London by Edmund A. Engler (1883)
POED Technical Instruction:
XI Clocks and Time Distribution (1927)

GPO Clock Systems by Simon Taylor hosted at
www.lightstraw.co.uk/gpo/clocksystems/

My GPO in London: Trilogy Edition

*GPO Time Recorder in the Science Museum, London collection
British Time Recorder Co. Ltd. 149 Farringdon Road, London. E.C.
© J. Chenery (2010)*

Outlet 10: Rugby Radio

Rugby radio station enhanced the dissemination of London (GMT) time to the rest of the UK and beyond. In later years it underpinned the *Speaking Clock* service and overshadowed Greenwich as a centre for the provision of accurate time-keeping.

Equipment designed for Rugby was a collaboration of ideas and practical application. NPL (National Physics Laboratory) set the standards; the Post Office Research Station, investigated and prototyped feasible designs; the POED (Post Office Engineering Department) and the ETE (External Telecommunications Executive) built and operated the final kit.

Rugby operated a continuously evolving range of kit housed initially in *Battleship Grey* colour enclosures with later racks resplendent in *Light Straw*, through to self-build interfaces of varying shades! Services were a complex mix of time clocks, frequency generators, transmitters and control equipment.

Greenwich Time Signal (GTS)

'The Greenwich Time Signal (GTS), popularly known as the pips, is a series of six short tones broadcast at one-second intervals by many BBC Radio stations.'

The GTS service began on 5 February 1924. The signals were sent from Greenwich Observatory and transmitted by the BBC.

[https://en.wikipedia.org/wiki/Greenwich_Time_Signal]

The signals radiated from Rugby were not the more familiar *pips* that are heard on BBC Radio, but were broadcast for the technical communities. From 1990, the BBC generated its own clock pulses.

My GPO in London: Trilogy Edition

Rugby Radio Station

The Post Office long-wave wireless station, at Rugby, broadcasting worldwide began operating in January 1926. Throughout its life (1926 to 2007) its many transmitters and aerials provided a range of services which included the Greenwich Mean Time (GMT) *time-signals*. Trials started on 8 December 1927 and the official service began from the GBR transmitter on 19 December.

Rugby Aerial Tuning Inductor (ATI) coil at London Science Museum.
© J. Chenery (2016)

Rugby Radio

'The Astronomer Royal is responsible for the measurement of time in this country and the Post Office radio transmitters are employed to broadcast the special time signals provided by the Royal Observatory.'
[PO Research Report 1474 by J L Creighton G Gregory March 1946.]

GBR (16 kHz)

GBR transmitted at Rugby from 1927 until the end of BT's contract in 2003, when the service transferred to VT Communications at Anthorn.

Originally the 16 kHz transmitter broadcast the rhythmic time signal, essentially for navigators, enabling chronometers to be checked to an accuracy of approximately 1/61st of a second. Broadcasts commenced, for five minutes leading up to, the appointed hour of 10 am, and also 6 pm. The time signal service from GBR ended in 1986.

The time signals were generated at Greenwich and sent by landline to Rugby. The delay over the lines made it difficult to keep the required accuracy. The solution was the design of a new type of clock to be installed at Rugby. [See Cold Cathode Clocks.]

POEEJ Oct 1930: *'In the new test room in the basement of the Central Telegraph Office [GPO West] is housed the main chronopher and the sub-chronopher controlling the International Time Signal sent out by radio from the Rugby transmitter.'*

Abinger: About eighteen months before the outbreak of WWII, the time service was moved to the magnetic station at Abinger, Surrey. Two Shortt clocks were transferred from Greenwich and two additional clocks were obtained. The GPO installed the necessary landlines and the installation was all in a blast proof building.

[Abinger and the Royal Greenwich Observatory by Peter Tarplee 1996.]

From about 1960 onwards, GBR was primarily used to relay messages to Royal Navy defences, such as Polaris submarines! The Cold War made Rugby both a key operational site and a major target.

MSF (60 kHz)

The 60 kHz MSF signal was transmitted from Rugby Radio Station between 1st February 1950 and 31st March 2007.

Over the years it was broadcast from several different designs of transmitters and finally evolved into both a time signal and date code that could be received and decoded by a wide range of radio-controlled clocks.

In 2007 MSF was transferred to Anthorn Radio Station, Cumbria, operated by Babcock International Group, under contract to NPL.

Cold Cathode Clocks (1960-1967)

'The daily Greenwich time signals have until recently been generated at the Time Department of the Observatory sited at Herstmonceaux Castle, Sussex. The signals were transmitted about 140 miles over landline to the Post Office radio station at Rugby where they were radiated from the high-power very-low frequency transmitter, GBR, on 16 kc/s and from two additional transmitters in the 10-20 Mc/s band. Equipment has now been installed at

Rugby to generate the time signals and thereby avoid the need for a long line link.'

[POEEJ Vol 53 Part 3 Oct 1960 Automatic Control of the Rugby Radio (GBR) Time Signals by an Electronic Clock.]

The new clocks had a BIS date of 10 am on 1 April 1960.

Speaking Clock (TIM)

When the Post Office *Speaking Clocks* Mk. III were brought into service in 1963, instead of having a time correction from Greenwich, they now referenced the *Cold Cathode Clocks* at Rugby.

'Twice daily or upon request, the landlines were switched through from Rugby to London and Liverpool. The 1kHz audio-tone time pulses sent were 100 ms long for the seconds markers and 500 ms for the minute.'

An Updated GBR

A modernised GBR transmitter came online on 30 November 1966. From 1967 three new Venner digital clocks based on a Varian rubidium-vapour frequency standard were in use. The associated GBR time signal equipment then incorporated the TIM synchronisation facility. The solid state Venner clocks were supplied by NPL and the kit was modified to meet on-site working practices.

A Hewlett-Packard caesium beam frequency standard, atomic clock from NPL (Teddington) was occasionally brought to site for comparative checking.

My GPO in London: Trilogy Edition

Programmable Master Clocks (PMCs)

From 1991 three PMCs supplied by Radiocode Clocks Ltd kept time at Rugby. A rebuild of the monitoring system in March 1992 led to two of the clocks being replaced by an in-house design and these continued in service until station closure in April 2007.

1984 TIM

The Mk. IV version of BT's *Speaking Clock,* then named Chronocal, was equipped with a receiver unit for the 60 kHz MSF correction signal, but continued to use a landline to Rubgy for security of service.

MSF at Anthorn

Rugby's aging aerial infrastructure was ultimately a factor in its losing the bid to continue the MSF contract beyond 2007. Rugby had been a pioneering site in the decades before satellite communication and fibre optic transatlantic cables. No longer a government owned site, market forces determined its fate.

The time at Anthorn is kept by atomic clocks and the MSF signal is transmitted 24 hours a day, excepting downtime during planned maintenance. NPL at Teddington is still the reference for the absolute time standard.

References

The history of RUGBY RADIO STATION by Malcolm Hancock (2017).

National Physics Laboratory: www.npl.co.uk

Outlet 11: Speaking Clock

By the 1930s a variety of hourly time service signals had been developed:

- The hourly *time-current* service to renters of Chronopher private wires (1874)
- The Greenwich Time Signal - BBC time pips (1924)
- GMT signals via Rugby Radio (1927)

For casual enquirers as to the correct time, a phone call to the GPO operator could solicit the time as gleaned from the switchroom clock. In London more than 26,000 requests were received every week!

The GPO's first *Speaking Clock* service used a pendulum clock for timing and glass disks for the voice recordings. The playback on a rotating glass disk was state-of-the-art before the much-later age of the compact disc! Valve amplifiers were the norm, because solid-state devices such as the transistor weren't available until the 1950s.

Mk. I Clock (1936)

'The constituent parts of the announcements are recorded as concentric photographic tracks on four glass disks. The recordings are played by scanning them with six beams of light; the outputs from the photo-electric cells are combined to form a complete sentence.'

The voice was that of telephonist Ethel Jane Cain.

My GPO in London: Trilogy Edition

A main clock and another as standby were installed in the basement of Holborn *Director* exchange and were BIS on 24 July 1936.

[BIS – Brought into service.]

The Speaking Clock installation at Holborn (1950)
© BT Heritage and Archives TCB 473/P04728

Post Office Circular July 22, 1936

'A "speaking clock" for the use of telephone subscribers has been installed in London and will be brought into service at about 4.30 p.m. on Friday the 24th of July 1936. It gives oral announcements of the time at intervals of ten seconds, each announcement being followed by three pip signals (similar to the B.B.C. time signal), the third pip indicating the time with an accuracy within one tenth of a second.'

Speaking Clock

'The charge for a call to the clock from any exchange will be the same as the charge for a call from that exchange to an exchange in central London.'

'Details of the operating procedure at London exchanges are given in London Telephone Service Traffic Instruction No.958 and at Provincial exchanges in Telephone Service Instruction, Traffic Serial No. 19/36.'

Distribution

A dedicated trunk double ring-main distribution circuit linked group (provincial) exchanges so that the *Speaking Clock* service could be made available throughout the UK by simply dialling into an access relay set.

- On Director exchanges, TIM (846) was dialled as the first three letters of TIMe. This changed to 123 (circa 1966) as All-Figure Numbering (AFN) replaced letter codes.

- Non-Director access was via 952 [EI Miscellaneous Time C1100 dated 1954]. In the 1960s Recorded Information Services (RIS) numbers were standardised to use special final selector numbers, so that up to 100 separate services could be accessed. Each RIS was allocated a four-digit code starting 80xx, thus 8081 obtained the Speaking Clock [TI A6 A4301 1972].

- By the mid-1990s, 123 was the UK-wide number.

In 1942 a second pair of clocks was added at Lancaster House, Liverpool.

My GPO in London: Trilogy Edition

Greenwich Correction

'*...the periodical check employs the signal transmitted exactly at each hour from the Observatory.*'

A circuit diagram (GMT 60) from 1948 shows PW (private wire) links to Greenwich and Abinger, for the hourly time correction. Abinger, Surrey was the alternative site for (GMT) time services between the war years and the late 1950s.

After ten years in service, the mark I clock(s) had proved reliable, but technology had improved, so that a new design using modern components was (eventually) preferable to a full overhaul of the original.

Mk. II Clock (1954)

This clock used a quartz-crystal controlled oscillator developed by the PO Research Department to give an improved accuracy suitable for the export market. As part of the Commonwealth it was not surprising that the Australian Postmaster-General ordered clocks for Melbourne and Sydney.

Cold War Calling

Conveniently, by 1962, the new HANDEL nuclear attack warning system (WB 400/600) was configured to use the secure ring-main of the *Speaking Clock* feeds to interrupt the time service and use the network for the sounding of sirens and the transmission of essential voice messages and tones. The Post Office was always seeking ways to fully exploit the use of its circuits!

Mk. III Clock (1963)

BIS dates: London May 1963; Liverpool Oct 1963.

Speaking Clock

An improvement over the mark II clock was the use of magnetic media for the playback of the phrases. Speech was recorded as circular tracks on a thick tyre of magnetically-loaded Neoprene fitted over a rotating metal drum, which was synchronised with the quartz-crystal oscillator. The daily correction signals, now from the *Cold Cathode Clocks*, by landline from Rugby, between 08.55 and 09.00 hrs resulted in an overall error of less than 5 milliseconds. Due to inherent delay on the telephone networks, the published figure was quoted to be *'normally accurate to one twentieth of a second'* (50 milliseconds).

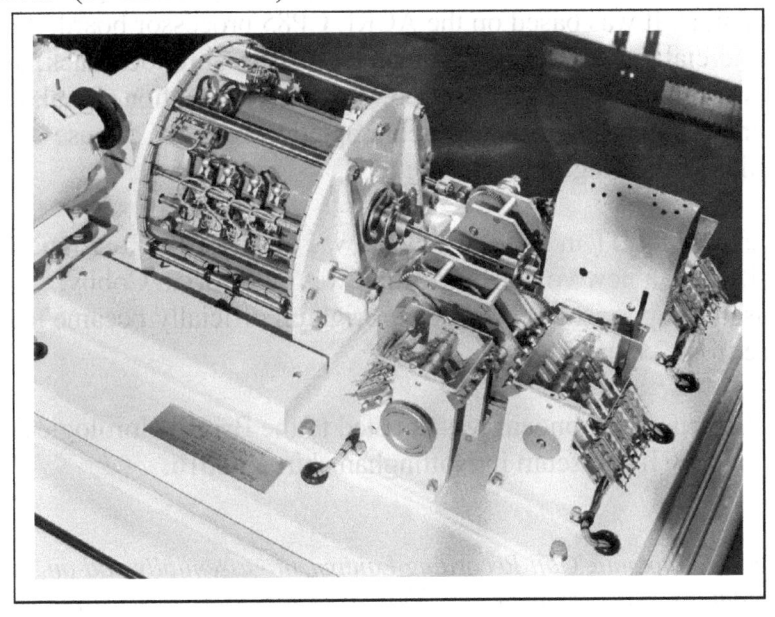

Speaking Clock Mk. III
© *BT Heritage and Archives TCE 361/ARC00844*

Trunk Control North (TCN) was then chosen for the home of the London *Speaking Clock* as a more spacious area that would also look better in publicity photos. Additionally, TCN already had a UPS readily available, which was necessary to maintain continuous service.

The new voice was that of assistant supervisor Miss Pat Simmons, from Avenue exchange.

Mk. IV Chronocal (1985)

A solid-state design, having no moving parts, and using digitised speech was possible for the fourth version of TIM, which was given an evocative name of *Chronocal* (probably meaning time-calculator). It was based on the ACRE CP85 processor board. A commercial radio receiver was included in the Chronocal rack, to allow reception of the standard 60 MHz time-correction signal, but for greater security British Telecom opted to continue the use of landlines from Rugby to take the feed.

Developed by BT in 1983, the clock was quietly BIS circa June 1984, while a new voice competition was held. Brian Cobby, Assistant Supervisor at Withdean, Brighton officially became the voice from 2 April 1985.

The Liverpool Chronocal was donated to the British Horological Institute (BHI) museum in Nottinghamshire in 2016.

[ACRE – Automatic Call Recording Equipment - essentially add-on electronics for auto-manual switchboards before computer-assisted connection of calls was possible.]

RIDE

From 1986 the Recorded Information Distribution Equipment (RIDE) progressively routed calls from the dedicated Recorded

Speaking Clock

Announcement Centres (RACs), with the National Announcement Centre (NAC) overseeing the process at Oswestry. RIDE was developed to handle televoting and high-volume calling patterns while protecting the national network from serious overloading.

In 1992 the early warning system HANDEL was decommissioned, and by 1994 the *Speaking Clock* distribution had migrated onto the RIDE platform.

In 2001 RIDE was replaced and upgraded to new technology and at that point Chronocal was retired.

M211 Master Clock (2001)

"Time & Frequency Solutions have supplied the technology behind the Speaking Clock since 2001. Teligent, the telecoms specialist, supplies the vital switching gear enabling multiple users to access the system at the same time. The time source used is a Time & Frequency Solutions M211 Master Clock Timing System with a redundancy element to ensure continued working even if a fault developed."

Later Voices

Sara Mendes da Costa took on the voice role from 08:00 hrs 2 April 2007. During the 80th anniversary year of the *Speaking Clock*, the service was switched-over live at 19:23 hrs 9 November 2016 on BBC TV's *The One Show*, to the voice of Alan Steadman, a retired Civil Servant from Dundee.

At the time of writing, the *Speaking Clock* currently resides at Oswestry NAC.

My GPO in London: Trilogy Edition

References

POEEJs
Vol 29 Part 4 Jan 1937 *The Speaking Clock*
Vol 48 Part 3 Oct 1955 *The British Post Office Speaking Clock Mark II, Part 1.*
Vol 48 Part 4 Jan 1956 *The British Post Office Speaking Clock Mark II, Part 2.*
Vol 56 Part 1 April 1963 *The New Post Office Speaking Clocks.*

UKWMO History www.ringbell.co.uk/ukwmo
TFS www.timefreq.com
Teligent Telecom www.teligent.se

British Telecommunications Engineering
Vol 2 Part 3 Oct 1983 *The New British Telecom Speaking Clock.*

Post Office Telecommunications Journal Winter 1962 – *New Clocks for TIM.*

RR 20723 *The Post Office Speaking Clock Mark III* (1964)

London Dialling Instruction book (1968)
EI Miscellaneous Time C1100 (1954)
TI A6 A4301 (1972)

Subscribers in London with a dial telephone with letters as well as figures dial 'TIM'. [Evening Standard 1937.]

'PHONE *TIM* FOR THE RIGHT TIME

Outlet 12: King Edward Building

KEB (1910-1996) King Edward Street

Opened 7 November 1910. Grade II listed 6 August 1974.
Architect: Henry Tanner from the *Office of Works*.
This was the first building in London to be constructed from reinforced Portland cement, concrete.

Foundation stone:

> EDWARD THE SEVENTH KING OF GREAT BRITAIN AND IRELAND AND THE BRITISH DOMINIONS BEYOND THE SEAS EMPEROR OF INDIA LAID THIS STONE OF KING EDWARDS BVILDING OF THE GENERAL POST OFFICE ON THE 16TH DAY OF OCTOBER 1905 UPON THE SITE OF CHRIST'S HOSPITAL FOUNDED IN 1552 BY KING EDWARD VI

The GPO's ambitious property acquisition policy secured the bulk of the former land of Christ's Hospital, aka the *Bluecoat School*, for its admin and sorting operations, as it was to relinquish the outmoded *GPO East* site.

It its time, KEB was the home of Royal Mail City & International, the National Postal Museum, and the London Chief Office. Of particular note was the later inclusion of a *Post Office Railway* interchange.

The King Edward Street elevation was faced with Portland stone and granite plinths (photo next page).

My GPO in London: Trilogy Edition

King Edward Building. © J. Chenery (2017)

KEB

For London postal staff, the complex was known as *KEB*, but other names were *The Yard*, because of the large *Sorting Block* and west yard. The sorting office handled foreign and colonial correspondence, as well as mail for London E.C./City District. Other titles were *East Central District Office (ECDO)*, *East Central and Foreign Sections*, and later on, *Royal Mail City & International/London Chief Office*.

The smaller elevation facing King Edward Street contained a new *Public (counters) Office* on the ground floor, and the offices of the Controller of the LPS (London Postal Service) on the four upper floors. The counters building was connected to the *Sorting Block* by a high-level bridge, as was popular with large PO complexes.

Contractors' vans in The Yard at King Edward Building (1931)
© Royal Mail Group Ltd, Courtesy of The Postal Museum, 2018.
[Ref: POST 118/5089 used under licence]

My GPO in London: Trilogy Edition

King Edward Building(s) simplified site diagram.

Royal Mail City & International
London Chief Office

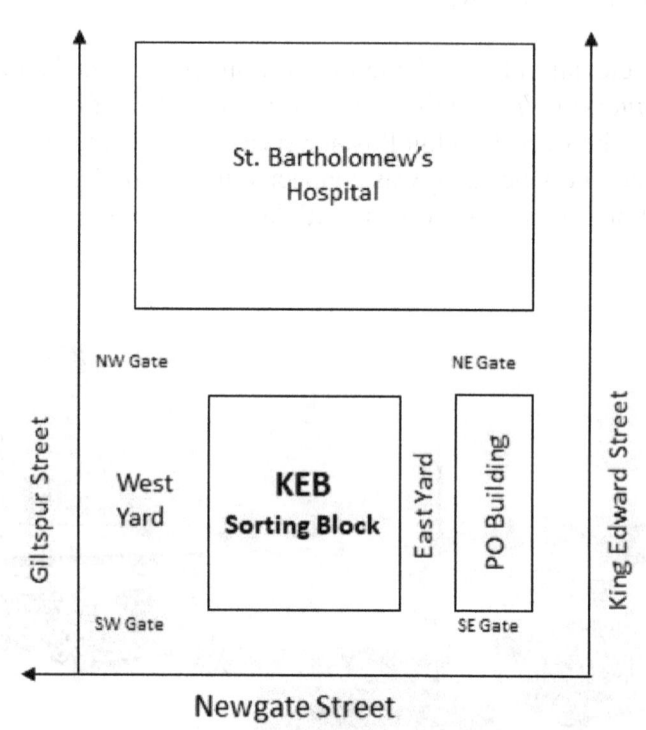

```
                    ┌──────────────────────────┐
                    │                          │
                    │    St. Bartholomew's     │
                    │        Hospital          │
                    │                          │
                    └──────────────────────────┘

         NW Gate                    NE Gate

                ┌──────────────┐   ┌────┐
  Giltspur      │              │   │ PO │   King
  Street  West  │     KEB      │E  │Bldg│  Edward
         Yard   │ Sorting Block│Y  │    │  Street
                │              │   │    │
                └──────────────┘   └────┘

         SW Gate                    SE Gate

                    Newgate Street
```

Entrances: NE and SE gates from King Edward Street
Exits: NW and SW gates to Giltspur Street

© JC April 2018
Not to scale

Rowland Hill Statue

This statue was first erected in front of the Royal Exchange and was moved here in 1923.

Plinth: *Rowland Hill - He founded uniform Penny Postage 1840*

*Rowland Hill statue outside KEB.
Posting slots/boxes: LONDON/COUNTRY/ABROAD
were once let into the sections under each window.
© J. Chenery (2018)*

'Under the public office is the posting room, into which falls the correspondence posted in the big letter-boxes by the public. It is interesting to stand in this room and watch the postal packets pouring down the shoot from the letter-boxes.' [The Post Office and its Story by Edward Bennett 1912.]

My GPO in London: Trilogy Edition

Air Mail

Additionally, from 1937 a blue Air Mail pillar box was also located on the pavement as the Empire Airmail Scheme was introduced to carry first class mail throughout the British Empire at a standard rate. Air Mail bags were loaded onto matching blue-painted Morris vans for transport to Croydon Aerodrome and despatch via Imperial Airways.

Work at KEB was a 24-hour operation on a grand scale.

Sorting Block

London EC (Eastern Central) mail was sorted on the ground floor and work moved from east to west, on band conveyors and in baskets, across the building as sorting progressed. Letters for colonies and abroad were dealt with on the first floor. The third floor housed the kitchen, dining and retiring accommodation, and locker rooms for staff. In 1950 the Engineer-in-Chief's Circuit Laboratory occupied the second floor.

Two miniature rifle ranges were located on the flat roof of the block. Invariably, this was for the territorial unit of *The Post Office Rifles* to practice. In later years the ranges were moved to the basement. Roof access to Post Office buildings generally was once rather liberal.

In the Yard

There was a lot of manual handling of mail bags; York containers (metal trolleys into which bags could be stacked) hadn't yet been devised. Mail to the provinces was taken to Mount Pleasant for sorting and distribution.

The level of activity is difficult to envisage, but in 1912, 1400 postmen were attached to the EC office and a total of 4300 GPO staff were employed at KEB.

Inspection of Messengers/Postmen by Postmaster-General (1917)
© BT Heritage and Archives TCB 417/E01930

The Public Counter

'It is the largest public post office in the country, and measures 152 feet by 52 feet, with a counter running the whole length. '

'The interior of the public office and the entrance halls have been more lavishly treated than usual, as befits the principal post office of the British Empire.'

[The Architect 17 March 1911, p. 17.]

My GPO in London: Trilogy Edition

The public counter at KEB (1962)
© BT Heritage and Archives TCB 473/P07988

As can be visualised in the photo (above), the public counter area was stylishly finished. White-veined Italian marble walls; woodwork of Irish green and matching white-marbled mosaic floors, complimented bronze fittings and plate glass writing-slab tables. Gunmetal windows, and plasterwork finished with Keene's.

Keene's: *A hard-finish gypsum plaster to which alum has been added and which is used chiefly as a gauging plaster in lime mortar for walls (as of hospitals, stores, railroad stations) where an unusually tough and durable plaster is required.*

[*Keene's Cement*. Merriam-Webster.com. Merriam-Webster, n.d. Web. 9 Aug. 2018.]

National Postal Museum (1969-1998)

The Post Office counter in KEB represented the pinnacle of public service, so it was an obvious building in which to showcase a postal history collection.

'This plaque was unveiled by Her Majesty The Queen on the occasion of the opening of the National Postal Museum on the 19th day of February 1969.'

The Phillips' collection at the National Postal Museum in KEB (1969) Note the large slide-out frames, each holding part of the collection © BT Heritage and Archives TCB 473/P10484

My GPO in London: Trilogy Edition

Another information panel read:

'Reginald M. Phillips of Brighton founder of the National Postal Museum. His object was to create a living tribute to the vital contribution that Britain has made to international postal communications through the development of uniform postage and the invention of the adhesive postage stamp. One of the generous benefactions he made to achieve this object was his gift to the Nation on 2nd April 1965 of his unique collection of artists' drawings, proofs and issued stamps of the reign of Queen Victoria now incorporated in the Museum.'

'A selected exhibit from this Collection was awarded the Grand Prix at the London International Stamp Exhibition held at the Royal Festival Hall July 1960.'

The very latest 'interactive displays'! Large slide-out frames held the Phillips' stamp collection of 45 volumes. An HLF (Heritage Lottery Fund) project in 2005-6 digitised the entire collection which can today be viewed online!

The National Postal Museum closed in 1998 as by then the premises had been sold (in 1997) for redevelopment. The former NPM combined with Post Office Archives to form the Heritage Unit of Royal Mail. Items went into storage until the BPMA was formed in 2004, culminating in an exciting new venture, *The Postal Museum* (TPM) which finally opened in 2017.

Post Office Film and Video Library (Sittingbourne)

Between 1988 and 1995 the popularity of VHS (Video Home System) players enabled the Post Office to offer a lending service of educational films to both home and school audiences.

Their booklet in 1991/92 typically stated...

'This catalogue lists all the films and videos currently available for general use. They can be obtained on FREE loan to both individuals and organisations from The Post Office Film and Video Library. No charge is made for this service, though the borrower must pay the cost of return postage.'

I sent off and borrowed *Post Haste* (1988) and *Mail Rail* (1987) which gave a fascinating insight to the workings of *Travelling Post Offices* and the *Post Office Railway*.

On His Majesty's Service (2018)

The King Edward Building, magnificent and grand
Encompassing all, of the former Christ's Church's land.

An impressive public counter for service by division
First time visitors soon find the correct position.

London, country, abroad and overseas
Delivering for the public, forever hard to please!

Van-loads of letters, correspondence and air mail
The Chief Post Office HQ is rarely one to fail.

Messengers and sorters, postmen of all grades
Lined-up outside, inspections to parade.

Rowland Hill's statue, proudly standing tall
Postal reform was the catalyst for it all.

The Post Office Railway, running far below
A once untold secret that everyone does know!

My GPO in London: Trilogy Edition

A public institution for the mail sorting solution
Now electronic communication has prompted its dissolution.

Post Office Railway (*Mail Rail*)

By 1927 the (new) Post Office (underground) railway had a station and platforms connected to the King Edward Building, which was designated the Foreign Section office. A combination of bag elevators, conveyors, and spiral chutes moved the mail between platform level and the building basement. Staircases and lifts provided staff access. [See *Mail Rail* chapter for more.]

The End

Circa 1996 the PO railway station had closed, sorting work was consolidated at Mount Pleasant, and by 1998 the Postal Museum's collections had gone into store. By 2003, Royal Mail's modernisation plans had created a brand new, state-of-the-art international sorting office, near Heathrow, that was open 24-hours daily. With a building area of 430,000 square feet it was equipped to (eventually) handle every letter or parcel to enter or leave* the UK. The HWDC (Heathrow Worldwide Distribution Centre) was comparable to the scale of operations which KEB had been to the 20th century. * Excepting mail between RoI and Northern Ireland.

Roman Wall at KEB

Under the west yard of King Edward Building (KEB) were the remains of London Wall, specifically that of bastion 19 – a build-out in the wall where it turned forming an angle – an *Angle Bastion*. Investigations by Phillip Norman and Francis Reader, circa 1907, during the GPO's redevelopment of the Christ's Hospital site first revealed that part of the Roman wall.

Roman wall at KEB

© JC Aug 2018
Not to scale

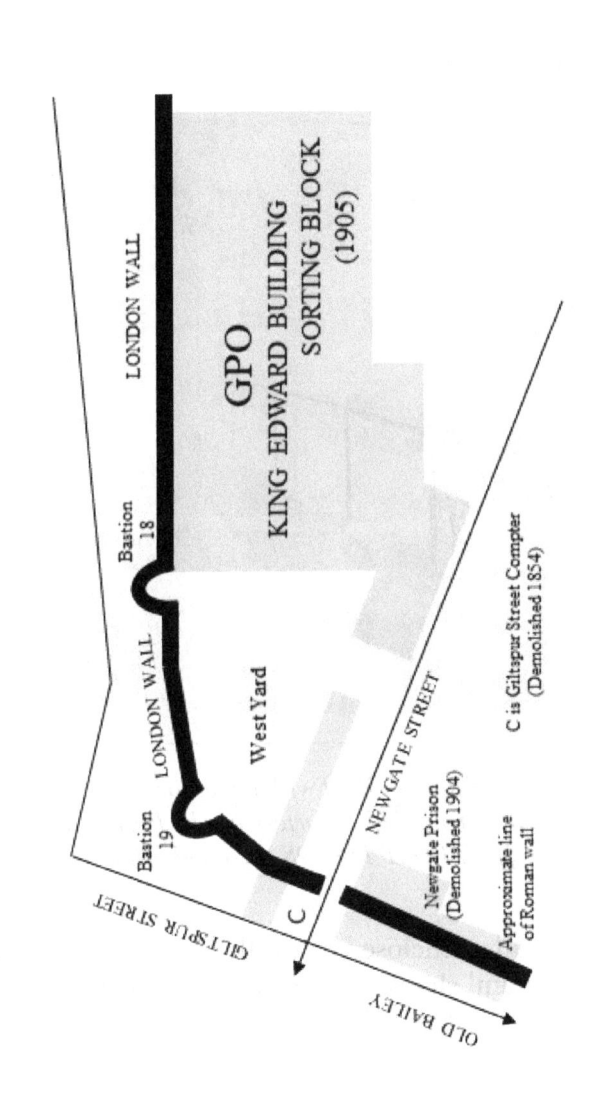

LONDON WALL

GPO
KING EDWARD BUILDING
SORTING BLOCK
(1905)

Bastion 18

LONDON WALL

West Yard

Bastion 19

NEWGATE STREET

C is Giltspur Street Compter
(Demolished 1854)

Newgate Prison
(Demolished 1904)

Approximate line of Roman wall

GILTSPUR STREET

OLD BAILEY

C

My GPO in London: Trilogy Edition

Roman Wall (1936)

*Remains of Roman Wall within the Yard at KEB (1936).
© Royal Mail Group Ltd, Courtesy of The Postal Museum, 2018.
[Ref: POST 118/498 used under licence.]*

The Roman wall as enclosed below the west delivery yard of KEB. Note the 'diagram' showing the plan of KEB in relation to London Wall, Giltspur Street and Newgate.

Roman Wall (2018)

Roman Wall within Merrill Lynch HQ
© J. Chenery (2018)

The Roman wall showcased in the shiny new basement display area which is incorporated into the Merrill Lynch reception of its HQ fronting Giltspur Street.

[A separate (colour) photobook *Roman Wall at Merrill Lynch* by John Chenery is available.]

My GPO in London: Trilogy Edition

Newgate

Bastion 19 was close to Newgate (Street) – one of the gates into the walled City of Londinium. At Newgate by 1225, Franciscan monks seeking sanctuary founded Greyfriars church. Following the dissolution of the monasteries in 1538 the land under bastions 17, 18 and 19 was in disuse, until the founding of Christ's Hospital (*The Bluecoat School*) in 1552. The General Post Office (GPO) purchased the site in 1904 to expand its postal services.
The GPO's King Edward Building and a vast Sorting Block were built over the remains of bastions 17 and 18, but bastion 19 was preserved at basement level. An access stairway, down to the wall, led from a non-descript building in the west yard delivery/parking area close to Giltspur Street.

A redrawn diagram of London Wall in relation to KEB is shown on page 175. Also marked is the site of Newgate prison (demolished 1904) and the Giltspur Street Compter (demolished 1854). The original diagram was prominently displayed in the KEB basement vault which gave access to the wall.

Redevelopment

In 1997 a corporate bank acquired the KEB site for redevelopment into its new London HQ. Although both the KEB and Sorting Block were Grade II listed buildings, an agreement was sought to demolish the rather ordinary Sorting Block, to allow a sympathetic restoration of not only the King Edward Building, but also of a scheme encompassing the ruined Greyfriars church area. Included in the plan was the showcasing of the Roman wall which was carefully incorporated into the Merrill Lynch HQ.

Between 1996 and 2001 Swanke Hayden Connell (Europe) architects, and its partners, transformed KEB and the surrounding area. Limiting factors for the new-build were St. Paul's Heights*, and the close- proximity of the Post Office Railway, in the basement! The former Post Office counters building on King Edward Street was refurbished, and the imposing colonnaded hall at street level was restored as a conference venue.

Notes: Aukett Fitzroy Robinson (AFR) bought up Swanke Hayden Connell Europe (SHCE) in 2013 and now trades as Aukett Swanke.

*St. Paul's Heights (1937): An agreement between the City of London and developers to protect line of sight views of the cathedral.

Merrill Lynch

In 2002, Merrill Lynch received the City Heritage Award for the best conservation and renewal project. At the ceremony, the lord mayor of London said that the development had:

"...transformed a rundown industrial backwater into a vibrant new working area which successfully combines new building with old and is generous with the amount of space provided for public access and enjoyment."

Bastion of the Bank (2018)

From Kentish Ragstone a mighty Roman wall was laid
Now at Giltspur Street it's on parade.

Subtle markers in the courtyard show
Just which way the wall did go.

My GPO in London: Trilogy Edition

Once below the Post Office KEB
Now Merrill Lynch do let you see.

A basement grand footway does curve
With clever lighting to observe.

At Bastion 19 the wall did turn
To Newgate Street the city spurned.

Together with stones from *GPO East*
A history lesson upon which your eyes can feast.

A design award for the layout grand
The whole complex is so well-planned.

References

The Post Office and its Story by Edward Bennett (1912).

The Yard of KEB by F. Heathcote Briant from *Post Office Magazine* 1935.

GPO Headquarters and KEB by Paul Wood in *THG Journal* Issue 33.

Within these walls by Jo Lyon – Museum of London (2007).

(Handout) Merrill Lynch Financial Centre: Background, Facts and Figures.

Special thanks to MLFC for allowing visit to Bastion 19.

.

Outlet 13: On the Grid

The Post Office once had little-known associations with St. Paul's underground station, and the iconic OXO building, which date back to the early 1900s.

St. Paul's (underground) Station (1900)

As a two-storey building, situated on the corner of King Edward and Newgate Street, this *Central Line* underground station was originally named *Post Office*, due to its vicinity to the nearby GPO complex. *Post Office* station opened on 30 July 1900 but owing to the policy of building the tunnels in the footprint of the road structure above, this was a very constricted site. The London Passenger Transport Board (LPTB), formed in 1933, soon had plans to relieve the congestion, as one of many projects to improve transport in the capital. Perhaps with tourism in mind, *Post Office* was renamed *St. Paul's* on 1 February 1937. Ironically, the building of a new station entrance, and below-ground booking hall involved considerable diversion of Post Office lineplant. This included the pneumatic tube system, back-up power supplies for the Central Telegraph Office, Trunk and *Toll A* circuits to Faraday Building, and other utility services. The relocated entrance on the opposite side of Newgate Street opened 1 Jan 1939.

A simplified diagram of the area is shown on the next page:

1 marks the location of *Post Office* underground station in 1900.
2 marks the new location of *St. Paul's* underground in 1937.
LPS in Bath Street was the London Postal School in the 1920s.
KEB was the King Edward Building and Sorting Office and Public Counter from 1910.

My GPO in London: Trilogy Edition

On the Grid

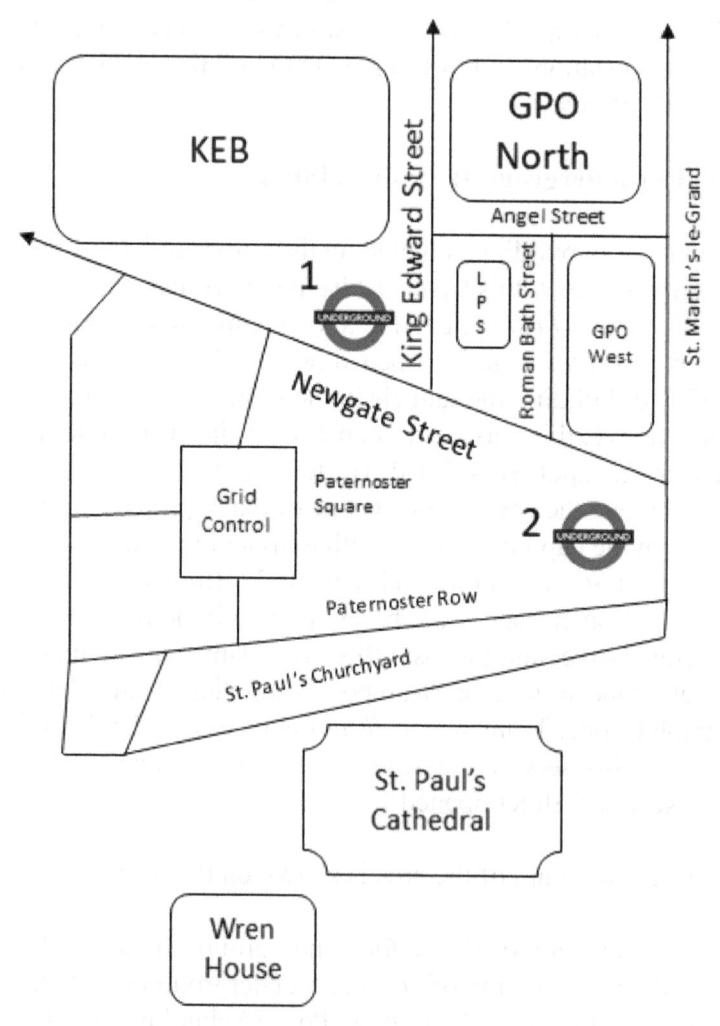

Simplified diagram not to scale   © JC Mar 2018

On the Grid

Roman Bath Street contained the overflow of buildings for departments which could not be housed in the Central Telegraph Office (*GPO West*) due to lack of space.

[See chapter **Roman Bath Street** for more details.]

Wartime December 1940 was particularly devastating for the area as all efforts were concentrated on protecting St. Paul's Cathedral. Regardless, direct bomb hits on *GPO West* (Central Telegraph Office - CTO) and extensive fire-damage left the old station building in ruins. Conveniently, the now disused access shafts (x4) were suitable for conversion into a protected scheme for Grid Control – the London electricity demand, load and generation monitoring centre, which by early 1941 was operational.

During 1943 the CTO was partially rebuilt within its shell, although essential telegraph circuits were switched at alternative protected locations, both within and on the outskirts of the capital. The CTO finally closed in 1962 and was demolished in 1967.

Grid Control moved to a new above-ground facility in Paternoster Square in 1951. The old *Post Office* station building was finally demolished in 1973, and with road junction remodelling, the only obvious remaining part was a new ventilation structure on the traffic island. The area encompassing the CTO and part of the station lift shafts remained unused until final clearance for the new BT Centre (BTC) took place in the late 1970s.

My GPO in London: Trilogy Edition

St. Paul's (tube) Station
© J. Chenery (2018)

MEMORANDUM TO VICE-CHAIRMAN
(FOR SUBMISSION TO ENGINEERING COMMITTEE)

FROM: STATION COMMITTEE. DATE: 27th March 1936.

SUBJECT: NAMING OF POST OFFICE STATION

"St. Paul's would seem to be the most apposite name for the station when the new entrances at the corner of St. Martin's-le-Grand and St. Paul's Churchyard are opened, but this name cannot be recommended for it is already used for the Southern Railway station at Blackfriars on the Holborn Viaduct Line, although that station is about a quarter of a mile from St. Paul's Cathedral.

On the Grid

It is agreed that "Cheapside" is an unsuitable name for Post Office Station, for, even after its reconstruction. The station entrances will be in Newgate Street rather than in Cheapside, and as was pointed out at the Traffic Committee, Cheapside is a long street, part of which will be more conveniently reached from Bank or Mansion House Stations.

The station entrances will still be near the General Post Office buildings, and since the district is known generally as the Post Office District, the existing name would not appear to be inappropriate. But if it is considered desirable that the station should have a more specific name, it is suggested that it be called "G.P.O."

Letter signed off by Secretary of the Station Committee

[Extract from Engineering Minutes via TfL archives]

Subsequently, *Post Office* tube was renamed *St. Paul's* on 1 February 1937. At the same time, the Southern (overground) railway station at Blackfriars was renamed from *St. Paul's* to *Blackfriars*. [Further research would be required to establish if this was a mutual-agreement, or a response to the re-siting of the underground station.]

Power Generation in London (Pre-1900)

In 1829, *GPO East* had relied upon gas lamps for lighting. Electric street lighting was first introduced in 1878 along the Thames Embankment. Telegraph equipment was supplied with direct current (dc) from banks of batteries.

Bankside Power Station, Southwark operated by the *City of London Electric Lighting Company* opened in 1891. It provided ac to power

My GPO in London: Trilogy Edition

street lamps in Queen Victoria Street via cables across Blackfriars' bridge. Wholesale public supply of electricity and a national grid system was yet to be developed.

Note: The later 1947 Bankside Power Station was designed by Sir Giles Gilbert Scott, more famous for the K2, K3 and K6 telephone kiosks.

A Central Power Station for the GPO

In 1899 the Engineer-in-Chief reported that the system which provided the air pressure for working the pneumatic tubes, for the distribution of telegrams at GPO West was obsolescent and inadequate, for the expanding network.

Letter to Treasury November 1900: *"Considerable economy might be effected by establishing a Central Electric Power Station, which would take the place, not only of the plant in General Post Office West, but also that of the Electric Lighting Plant under the yard of the General Post Office East... and similar plant at the General Post Office South and Mount Pleasant."*

GH Murray January 1902: *"...the danger that owing to the engines in the General Post Office being already overworked, and to the fact that the boilers and engines are old, there is a most serious risk of an absolute breakdown of the London Telegraph Service."*

Threadneedle Street BO (Branch Office) was supplied by the *City of London Electric Lighting Company*, but elsewhere the GPO had developed its own coal-fired generating plant in each of its major buildings.

As demand increased, the practicality of producing sufficient power

On the Grid

at each site became more onerous due to lack of space for boilers, coal storage, and manpower. The idea of a local GPO Central Power Station was gaining support.

A site at Hearn Street, Shoreditch E.C. was considered, but the usual process of over-thorough investigation led to the loss of the opportunity. An alternative site was found at Upper Ground Street, on the south bank, close to Blackfriars Bridge. With access to the Thames, coal supplies could be brought in by barge, and cooling water for the proposed turbines could be pumped directly from the river.

The Post Office/Government was sometimes (deliberately) inaccurate in describing the location of its important premises. Thus, the Central Power Station (CPS) near Blackfriars Bridge became known as Blackfriars Power Station, even though it was sited in Southwark.

The map on the next page shows the four wharfs and the public house within the new CPS boundary. The coal wharf was secured in 1902, and the Post Office Sites Act of 1903 assisted purchase of the remaining areas.

PMG Report 1905: *'The building plans for the proposed Power Station at Blackfriars, which is to supply electric current for power and lighting to the General Post Office buildings, have been settled, and building operations will be commenced at an early date.'*

PMG Report 1909: *'The equipment of the Central Power Station at Blackfriars is now approaching completion.'*

Finally, the coal-fired 3.5MW power station opened in August 1910.

My GPO in London: Trilogy Edition

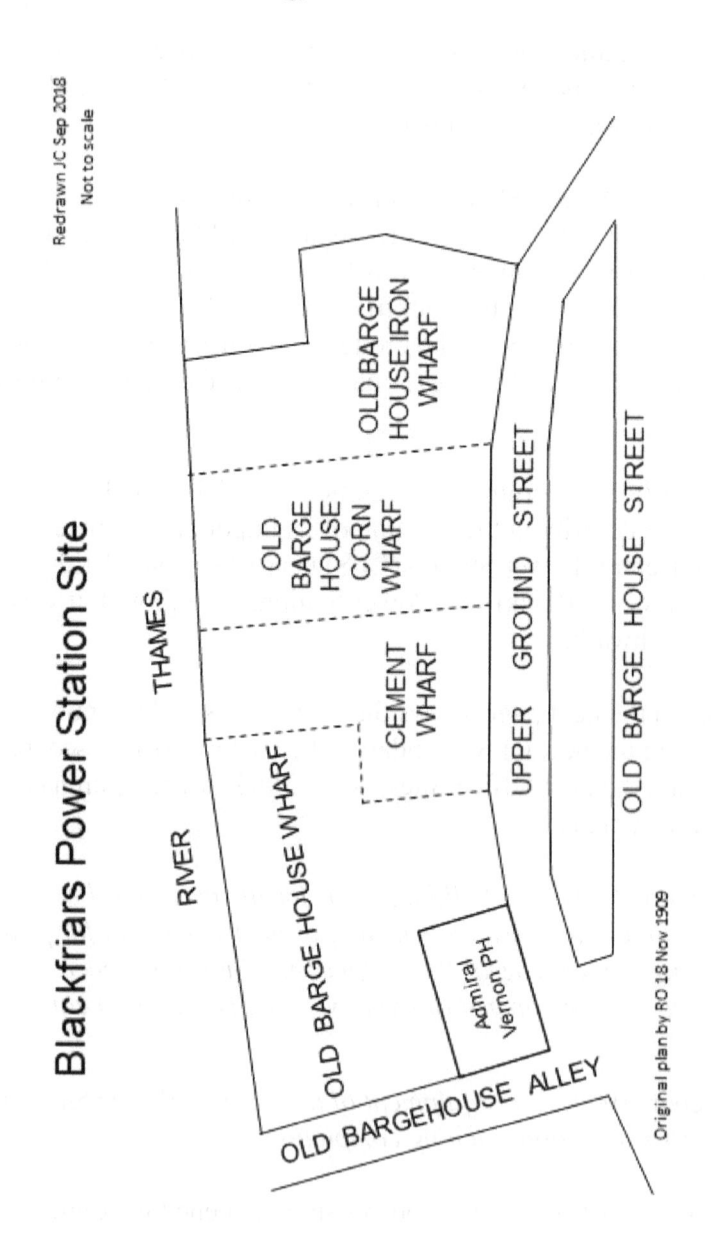

On the Grid

Method of Operation

Three sub-stations were installed:

King Edward Building (KEB) – static transformer giving 110V ac for lighting and 440V ac power.

GPO South - static transformer giving 110V ac for lighting. For cell charging, dc was run from *GPO West*.

GPO West sub-station 220V dc and 3 wire 110V ac, plus a storage battery to improve load factor, and act as back-up.

GPO North was served via *GPO West*.

GPO East closed in 1910, so would not have been included. A sub-station for *Mount Pleasant* was expected to be added at a later date when the CPS added extra generating capacity.

Extract from *The Post Office and its Story* (1912)

'The current by which the whole of the circuits are worked at the Central Telegraph Office [GPO West] *is generated at the Blackfriars Power Station and conveyed by mains to the basement of the building, where the accumulators are charged, and the current distributed from these to the circuits.'*

Post Office (London) Railway Bill – 1913 Debate

The Post Office had intended to extend the CPS to supply the proposed Post Office (underground letters) Railway. The Bill was debated in Parliament where it was suggested that it might be improper for the Postmaster-General to use his 'own' power station, although it was cited that other London railway companies were allowed to generate their own electricity.

Mr Herbert Samuel: *'The electric lighting companies, who appeared to form a common syndicate, asked that this power of supplying from the Blackfriars station should be struck out and that the Post Office should be obliged to go either to the electric lighting companies or to the local authorities for their supply of power. The House of Commons Committee refused this application, but the Committee of the House of Lords has acceded to it.*

Regulation of Electricity Supply (1926)

The *London Power Company* was formed in 1925 with the aim of consolidation by building a small number of very large power stations and to sell the electricity to anyone who wanted it. Their first plant was Battersea Power Station. Operating and technical standards still varied from one company to another and thus the *Central Electricity Board* (CEB) was set up under the Electricity (Supply) Act of 1926 to standardise the nation's electricity supply.

Not surprisingly, this led to the demise of the Post Office's CPS.

The Passing of Blackfriars Power Station

The tender for the Post Office Railway power supply led to a contract covering all HQ buildings. A joint contract was agreed with the London Electric Lighting Co., and the Charing Cross Electric Supply Co. for a term of 25 years. A new sub-station in King Edward Building next to the existing PO scheme transformed the 3-phase 10.6 kV supply down to 6.6 kV. Additional sub-stations at Western District Parcel Office, Liverpool Street, and Mount Pleasant completed the project. Finally, Blackfriars Power Station closed in February 1926.

On the Grid

GPO Power Schemes

Post Office power supplies for the working of telephone/telegraph apparatus and equipment was converted to the required voltages via motor-generators. The supply was fed to an electric motor which turned a generator to produce a different voltage. This practice changed in 1958 as the Engineer-in-Chief's report stated:

'The decision to use rectifiers for very large power plants marks the end of an era during which motor-generators have been employed universally as a means of providing dc at all large telephone exchanges.'

OXO Tower

OXO Tower Wharf © J. Chenery (2018)

My GPO in London: Trilogy Edition

The current OXO Tower Wharf by architect Albert W Moore was a 1928-30 Art Deco reconstruction of Blackfriars Power Station, retaining the waterside elevation. Use as a tinned foods warehouse carried the names *Donald Cook Canned Foods*, and *Dewhurst*. As well as the iconic *OXO* windows in the new tower. The Liebig Extract of Meat Company was the maker of OXO. The overall decline of London's Docklands left the building threatened with demolition until its regeneration in the 1990s as affordable housing and a high-class dining venue! The new reworking of the building by Lifschutz Davidson between 1994-96 was commissioned by Coin Street Community Builders.

References

BT Archives POST 30/4669B Central Power Station, Blackfriars.
City Reborn by Kenneth Powell (2004).
Engineer-in-Chief report 1958.
Hansard [https://hansard.parliament.uk/]
Postmaster-General reports.
London's Secret Tubes by Andrew Emmerson and Tony Beard (2007).

POEEJ 1926 Vol 19 Pt2.

Transport for London (TfL) Archive.
Underground symbol used with permission of TfL/TSBA Group.

Mail Rail

Outlet 14: Mail Rail

The Post Office Railway (POR)

Illustrated within one of the pages of the book *The Post Office* by Nancy Martin (1969), was a strange driverless underground train which ran from London Paddington to Whitechapel.

A 1930s motive unit/car under conservation at Debden (Postal store).
© J. Chenery (2014)

It wasn't until the 1990s when I borrowed a video of *Mail Rail* in action, that I realised just how dynamic and animated the trains whizzing, at speed, through the narrow tunnels would have been!

My GPO in London: Trilogy Edition

During a visit to Amberley Museum in 2008, I discovered a static POR exhibit, but the drive unit was painted POED (Post Office Engineering Department) green, not the bright red colour that I'd seen in videos or that I later saw at Debden in 2014. Both of these sightings seemed somewhat disassociated from the video footage, and because the railway was mothballed in 2003 it was unlikely that I'd experience anything similar...or was it?

History

Opened in 1927, the Post Office (underground) Railway linked mainline train stations and sorting offices to speed the mail across London. The six-and-a-half-mile route connected Paddington Station, Western Parcel Office, Western District Office, Western Central District Office, Mount Pleasant, King Edward Building, Liverpool Street Station, and the Eastern District Office at Whitechapel. Renamed *Mail Rail* (in 1987), the system transported letters, parcels, and *Datapost* using driverless, electric (440V) trains, running on a two-foot gauge track through tunnels which varied from 7 to 25 feet in diameter.

In 1965 a ninth station was added as the new Western District Office (WDO) opened at Rathbone Place. Even then, it was noted:

"Many of the postal-sorting offices in London are due for rebuilding, particularly as they are unsuitable for housing the equipment required for the modernisation of the postal service."

Extensive tunnelling was required to align the railway with the new WDO which could then handle both letters and parcels. Consequently, the old Western DO (at Wimpole Street), and the

Mail Rail

Western parcel office (at Bird Street) stations became disused, although the trains still ran through them. Although it was desirable to relocate other sorting offices to larger premises, the cost of any further tunnelling was prohibitive.

Carrying the Mail

Mailbags descended from the sorting offices above by chutes and conveyor belts to be loaded into carriers which were then wheeled along the platform onto the dropside wagons (also named cars). As the side of the wagon dropped (by a pull on the release lever), its metal plate bridged the gap between the wagon and the platform, thus allowing the mail carrier to be wheeled onto the train.

A disused station mail chute/conveyor © J. Chenery (2017)

My GPO in London: Trilogy Edition

An empty wagon at TPM © J. Chenery (2017)

A car full of mail carriers © J. Chenery (2008)

Mail Rail

Mail train cars/wagons were adapted to accept a variety of mailbag carriers including mini-*Yorks* (a metal roll container/trolley). With a train arriving every few minutes the platform staff were constantly busy pushing and pulling the cars on and off the wagons.

Mail Rail Trains (2016)

Mail Rail trains run with precision
Moving slowly into position.

A car unloading, the trolley rolls
Pushing it firmly a postman strolls.

Turning it from the platform edge
Mailbags in it fully wedged!

Another cart is locked into place
And off into the darkness the train does race.

Datapost priority, for Liverpool Street
An important deadline is one to meet.

Letters and parcels routed through town
Speeding along the underground!

Mail Rail was originally run by a switchman at every station to supervise and control a specific section of track, but by 1993 computer control had superseded the outdated manual lever-control boards and interlocking relays. Nonetheless, the design of the track and gradients already allowed for precise manoeuvring of trains as they stopped and started at designated positions in the stations. Varying track voltages also aided acceleration into and out of the

My GPO in London: Trilogy Edition

running tunnels. It may have been every boy's dream to work there…

Illustration from booklet PA69 (2/73) Post Office Telecommunications.

The Post Office was once responsible for both the postal and telephone services in the UK (excepting Hull). Apprentices joining the organisation had a choice of businesses in which they could work.

 I recall a booklet from *1973 'A Career in Telecommunications Engineering* (PA69 2/73)' which showed '*A Technical Officer on Postal engineering adjusting signalling relays on the Post Office railway in London'.* At the time, it was exciting to think of the variety of jobs in which one might be able to work, as an engineer.

'*You would get practical training on operational equipment under the supervision of skilled engineers in a Telephone or Postal area.*'

Mail Rail

In the event, my career path led me into the clerical side of Post Office Telecommunications, which you can read about in *My GPO Family (2017)*.

Staff employed on *Mail Rail* engineering duties worked on high-voltage power systems, track and signalling, as well as the essential train maintenance. Every task was done 'in-house', unlike modern times when specialist work is usually contracted-out.

Clocks for Post Office Tube Railway (1927)

'The Central Telegraph Office section is installing a system of electric clocks throughout the Post Office Tube Railway System.'
[POEEJ April 1927: London District Notes.]

The efficient running of the railway was to rely upon the Post Office's *Master Clock* system, which it used in large telephone exchanges and telegraph offices, for uniformly distributed time-keeping. [See separate chapter *Master Clocks* for more.]

The POR system comprised of 32 clocks:

- Two *Master Clocks* in the second-floor control room at Mount Pleasant. (2)

- King Edward Street, Western Central District Office and Mount Pleasant: one 12" and four 24" clocks each; the 12" clock is placed in the Control Cabin and two 24" clocks on both Eastbound and Westbound platforms. (15)

My GPO in London: Trilogy Edition

- Eastern District Office and Liverpool Street Station: One 12" clock in each Control Cabin and two 24" clocks on each Westbound platform. (6)
- Western District Office, Western Parcels Office and Paddington Station: one 12" clock in each Control Cabin and two 24" clocks on each Eastbound platform. (9)

Premium Bond

For the 1969 James Bond film *On Her Majesty's Secret Service* (OHMSS), a sequence from KEB (King Edward Building) onto the Post Office Railway was storyboarded, but never filmed.

Synopsis: Across the road from *Faraday Building*, at the College of Arms, Bond chases the Sable Basilisk Pursuivant's assistant, Phidian from the rooftop down to St. Paul's cathedral and along into the King Edward Building. While trying to escape, Phidian slides down a conveyor and onto the platform of the Post Office (underground) Railway. An ensuing fight forces Phidian onto the track into the path of a through-express postal train.

Pursuivants: An officer of the College of Arms ranking below a herald. The four ordinary pursuivants are Rouge Croix, Bluemantle, Rouge Dragon, and Portcullis. Sable Basilisk was used by Ian Fleming in place of Rouge Dragon.

[Reference: *The Making of On Her Majesty's Secret Service* by Charles Helfenstein 2009.]

Mail Rail

Railnet

Royal Mail's continuing evaluation of overground mail-by-rail led in 1996 to the setting up of a major road/rail network hub at Willesden. The PRDC (Princess Royal Distribution Centre) was intended to streamline the interchange of mail from London to major routes on the existing TPO (Travelling Post Office) rail network. Sixteen brand new Class 325 EMUs (purely to carry mail) were commissioned for RM and intended to operate over a 10-year contract to 2006.

The PRDC effectively abolished the running of mail trains out of London passenger termini including Paddington, and Liverpool Street, to which *Mail Rail* specifically connected. Combined with the closure of outdated sorting offices along the *Mail Rail* route, there was no longer justification for keeping an archaic underground system in diminishing use. *Mail Rail* closed in 2003.

Late running due to poor maintenance and administration by Railtrack prompted RM to prematurely end its mainline rail contract and remove postal sorting from the railways permanently. The last TPO service ended on the night of 9/10 January 2004. The fleet of Class 325 EMUs continues to run in a reduced role from PRDC to Warrington, Tyneside and Glasgow.

Sadly, the closure of *Mail Rail* was the impetus to make its history widely known.

[Read further developments in the chapter ***The Postal Museum***.]

My GPO in London: Trilogy Edition

References

An Illustrated History of the Travelling Post Office by Peter Johnson (2009).

Green Paper No.36A: *Post Office Railway.*

Mail by Rail by Peter Johnson (1995).

POEEJ April 1966: *The New Post Office Railway Station at the New Western District Office.*

The Post Office by Nancy Martin (1969).

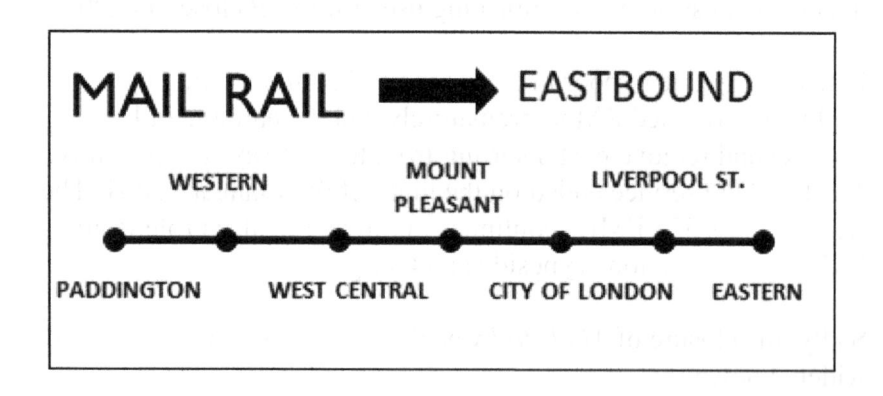

```
MAIL RAIL ➡ EASTBOUND

         WESTERN      MOUNT        LIVERPOOL ST.
                      PLEASANT
    ●———————●————————●————————●————————●————————●————————●
 PADDINGTON    WEST CENTRAL     CITY OF LONDON     EASTERN
```

A typical modern Mail Rail diagram.

Outlet 15: The Postal Museum

When the former *National Postal Museum* (NPM) closed to the public in 1998 it combined with the Post Office Archives to form the Heritage unit of Royal Mail. In 2004, this unified archive and museum service became an independent charitable trust. The trust officially received a donation of the former NPM object collections, and took responsibility for managing the Royal Mail Archive (public records) on behalf of Royal Mail Group, and Post Office Ltd. Thus, the *British Postal Museum & Archive* (BPMA) was the public identity of this trust, preserving a long and fascinating history of postal services.

On 22 March 2012, a press release announced:

"Royal Mail Group will grant a lease of 999 years for Calthorpe House, a property which will provide a secure foundation for the BPMA once redeveloped and extended. Agreements have been signed with Royal Mail and Post Office Ltd (POL) for a £6M long term, low interest loan to fund the conversion of Calthorpe House to meet the basic needs of the organisation. In addition, Royal Mail and POL are providing other support, including a £500,000 grant."

In October 2013, the privatisation of Royal Mail began as 70% of its shares were sold off. By October 2015, the Government had sold its remaining holdings.

A new generic name for the Postal Heritage Trust was devised and thus from 1 February 2016, *The Postal Museum* (TPM) became the new public identity of the trust. The established archive in the Mount Pleasant Mail Centre closed on 11 November 2016 in preparation for transfer to its new home in Calthorpe House, an old Royal Mail property suitable for redevelopment.

Calthorpe House 15-20 Phoenix Place
© J. Chenery (2012)

An Added Attraction

During 2012, with Heritage Lottery funding, the British Postal Museum and Archive (BPMA), in conjunction with RM, developed a bold idea to turn the abandoned Mount Pleasant *Mail Rail* depot and station into a unique visitor attraction/ride and history lesson! One of the fund-raising ideas was to *Sponsor a Sleeper* and have one's nameplate affixed to the running track.

Mail Rail at the TPM (2017)

A special visitor attraction for TPM was to be the re-opening of a section of *Mail Rail* (the former Post Office Railway) with newly built passenger carriages to enable a 'ride-on' experience. In early April 2017 I was excited to receive an e-mail from TPM illustrating the fixing of name-plates to the new sleepers, which included the one that I had sponsored! *A lasting legacy* – well, at least until the wood decayed again. And I looked forward eagerly to the upcoming *Walk the Rails* event to go and photograph my sleeper. Turning the age-old railway into a safe and enjoyable new attraction had required much work behind the scenes, as a news snippet from BT showed.

Recovery of *Cold War* cables (March 2015)

Openreach managed the project to remove redundant cables which its predecessor, the Post Office had laid. It must have been opportune to do this for the scrap value rather than simply cosmetic purposes? Four large, heavy, copper telecommunication cables which had once been a vital link in the *Cold War* communications network, ran the length of the railway tunnels. To aid the removal, a 1.75 tonne Clayton mining locomotive with wagons was hired and duly lowered into *Mail Rail* via the access shaft at Mount Pleasant. The adapted train carried up to 5 tonnes of cable on each run, to recover a total of approximately 180 tonnes of copper.

Delivery of New Trains (Oct 2016)

Two new trains were lowered into the Mount Pleasant depot on 24

My GPO in London: Trilogy Edition

October 2016. Severn Lamb had manufactured the specially designed units in its Alcester factory.

Quotes from TPM: *"There will be two of these trains – one red and one green, the colours of past Mail Rail carriages from different eras. Their design follows that of the original Mail Rail trains from 1987, but with a few tweaks, like a lowered floor to allow passengers to ride comfortably – as the tunnels are just seven feet high! Guests will board the train in the engineering depot at Mount Pleasant and travel through a section of the railway's tunnels and station platforms in a unique, fifteen-minute immersive audio-visual experience."*

A 21st Century Museum

Reading through the background material it was evident that TPM was truly developing a museum attraction that would appeal to all ages. A mix of interactive displays to engage visitors' attentions, merchandising to maximise revenue, and of course, access to the Postal Archive. Within *Mail Rail*, the ability to hire part of the venue for corporate type events would help to popularise the location and strengthen the branding of TPM as more than simply an archive or museum.

7 June 2017 Opening Date Announced

'*We're pleased to confirm that The Postal Museum & Mail Rail – London's most anticipated new heritage attraction – will officially open to the public on Friday 28 July 2017.*'

Mail Rail at Mount Pleasant (2017)

HRH The Princess Royal (Princess Anne) officially opened a new postal museum and *Mail Rail* on 13 June 2017. As a sponsor of one of the many railway sleepers, I was invited to visit *Mail Rail* on 10 July, before it opened to the general public on 28th. With hundreds of visitors expected daily, the people logistics is strictly managed; the staff are generally young and enthusiastic, having been carefully selected for their roles. As £26 million has been invested in the project, the momentum for it to be successful is noticeable, and although still early in its development, its impact as a well-run place to visit is impressive.

The Postal Museum is well-lit and features a diversity of artefacts old, and modern, so as to appeal to visitors of all ages. Many larger items are on display such as, the mail coach and Dodge post bus WNJ 479Y (0750069); K2 and K8 telephone kiosks, as well as a renters' coinbox, and a selection of pillar boxes. Other vehicles include a 1941 BSA motorbike GGY 525 and GPO Morris Minor mailvan BXW 507. Stamps, posters, uniforms and printed media all add to the story of the GPO and the evolution of the postal system. A working pneumatic tube system, sending pods across the room, is a great interactive diversion, encouraging everyone to learn!

The *Mail Rail* attraction utilises the Mount Pleasant maintenance depot of the former Post Office (underground) Railway, which has been turned into a reception and exhibition area, telling the story of mail by rail, including some history of Travelling Post Offices (TPOs).

Mail Rail ride experience and *Walk the Rails*: I'd watched videos of *Mail Rail* operating during its working life, but I'd never been on site, so I wondered exactly what to expect from my visit, ahead of

My GPO in London: Trilogy Edition

the mass public. At least it wouldn't be packed with screaming kids?! At the prescribed time, my friend Kevin Hampton and I descended a new, wide, concrete staircase into a spacious well-lit basement area, which had originally formed the maintenance depot. The floor was naturally divided in two, at the controller's gantry; between the exhibition display, and the running tracks and platform. Standing at the metal barrier afforded a good head-on view straight down the track. My impression of the moment:

"It was new, brand new and technologically slick. It was old, very old; decrepit in parts. The combination of these extremes was somewhat incomprehensible. It was seemingly impractical and yet here it was in operation! I watched almost in disbelief as the low-profile carriages disappeared into the darkness of the tiny sloping tunnel ahead. Some minutes later, as a train returned slowly up the gradient, and the young driver came into view, the realisation dawned. The future was about to take us into the past. We were going on a unique journey of letter to see a worm's eye view of how the Mail Rail trains once negotiated the winding tunnels deep under London."

The top canopies had been raised and the tiny green carriage doors were open, inviting us to see if we could fit inside! Minding our heads, we carefully stepped into the shiny new wagons, unsure of what to expect? The top speaker, only centimetres from my head, started to blare out a safety message and thus the all-encompassing audio-visual adventure began! The lightweight airy carriages were deceptively spacious, and the ride quality was surprisingly smooth. At one point the ride stopped abruptly as a safety feature cut in! These aren't toy trains and do need to be respected by the passengers. The tunnels are well-lit to give as much of a side view as possible, as the trains progress along the very narrow route that a Royal Mail letter wagon once took.

TPM

As the tube opened-up into a station area, projections onto the wall told the unique *Mail Rail* story through the decades. At another section, we were suddenly plunged into total darkness, as the train stopped again; the voice on the speaker informed us that short power outages were common on *Mail Rail*. Wow, that was an effective way of illustrating the story! Our journey continued and without being aware, we had gone around in a loop and were soon back in the depot. It hadn't been a fast fairground ride, but it was every bit as atmospheric and engaging as the designers could make it.

For our special *Walk the Rails* event, we donned helmets and reflective jackets before walking back down the same gradient into the tunnels. For the taller participants, some head-ducking was needed in strategic places. Numbered 'sponsor plaques' had been affixed to the sleepers at the point that the third rail was once located. The director, Adrian Steel's plaque 004 was at the start of our walk; mine 093 was some distance further along! We had to side-step crossovers, points and cables as we made our way towards Mount Pleasant station, in the semi-darkness.

It would not have been surprising to encounter a Yeti or the Tardis, but only carefully-sited redundant engines were to be found as we emerged and stepped up onto the platform to inspect one of the 'cherries' (a button switch) suspended from the ceiling. When in service, the despatcher on the platform would have pressed the 'cherry', or *Train Ready Signal* (TRS) to signal to the control frame that a train had been loaded (or unloaded) and was ready to depart. A corresponding red lamp on the platform indicator would glow, indicating that the train was then not to be touched. Simultaneously, a green lamp in the station switch cabin would advise the switchman to set the route and allow the train to go. [Local switchmen were displaced with central computer control in

My GPO in London: Trilogy Edition

1993.] New lighting and trunking for air-con, as well as CCTV globes were evident against a backdrop of a twilight world from another era. There wasn't any time to explore further; we had to make our way back along the tracks to the depot, so that the next train could safely depart!

Mail Rail is getting lots of media attention. Our driver, Penny was interviewed by BBC News. When asked why people should visit, she replied, *"It's exhilarating, it's in its authentic form...and all the original equipment is still down there."*

Director, Dr. Adrian Steel had a radio slot on the *Robert Elms Show*. Describing the operation of the new ride he said,

"People will turn up in batches like the mail would have done."

The Logistics

Dr. Adrian Steel outlined the challenges of presenting the Royal Mail story of over five centuries of design and communication and operating the new *Mail Rail* ride!

'Signing-off on railway work and physical safety of visitors; no fire exits in tunnels; asbestos removal; no legal right of way to Royal Mail on public land; removing the electric third rail; things they could not afford to change or would not want to; and why would people pay to visit them?'

It must have seemed an improbable aspiration.

[Extracts of this article first published in Post Horn Aug 2017 and THG Journal Spring 2018.]

The Third-Rail

Some eagle-eyed visitors to *Mail Rail* had expressed concern that the track infrastructure had been unnecessarily altered to place the sleeper name-plates. I checked with TPM and they confirmed that the third-rail was removed solely to accommodate the lowered floors of the passenger carriages.

The third-rail showing a raised insulator bolted to the sleeper.
© J. Chenery (2017)

End Note

By Christmas 2017 it was reported that *The Postal Museum* had sold more than 70,000 visitor/ride tickets! It's rare to see the past conserved within a modern visitor attraction; *Mail Rail* blends the two in a mix that is irresistible. Check it for yourself at www.postalmuseum.org and experience it soon.

One of the new train sets parked in Mount Pleasant station.
© *J. Chenery (2017)*

References

The Postal Museum (TPM) at www.postalmuseum.org

BT News via www.bt.com
BPMA Newsletters

See also separate colour photobook: *Mail Rail at Mount Pleasant* by John Chenery (2018).

Telegraphs

Outlet 16: Telegraphs and Telegrams

Overview

In the days before the telephone was invented, the electric telegraph, together with the printed telegram, became the fastest method of communication, second only to the letter post. The system evolved into the telex service – a reliable way to transmit the printed word. In London, the Central Telegraph Office (CTO) was at the heart of these operations until gradually the new telephone service with Subscriber Trunk Dialling (STD) became the most popular means of instant contact. The sending of faxes and e-mails via normal telephone lines eventually displaced the telex service, such that today, broadband internet is about to overtake the use of telephone landlines, as all communications will be sent as data, either over optic fibre to the premises or via mobile cellular links.

The original CTO site operated from 1874 until 1962, and here we trace some of the history of the services centred therein, as the General Post Office strove to cope with the demand. [See also chapters: ***GPO West; Tube Service; Fleet Building.***]

Early Days

In Victorian London, the introduction of the Penny Post (1840) made the sending of letters more affordable, and the volume of mail grew steadily as the essential form of communication. However, this was soon to change as, in 1845, a public telegraph line opened, connecting London and Gosport.

My GPO in London: Trilogy Edition

The emerging Telegraph Service was, very simply, the transmission of characters as coded pulses over a copper line, that could be transcribed at the distant end. The Telegram Service developed as the conveyance of the written (or printed) messages to and from the Telegraph Offices and the public.

For the first time at the State opening of Parliament, Queen Victoria's speech was transmitted by telegraph. The following year (1846), a newspaper report of this now annual event, showed that it was quite a phenomenon.

"...the electric telegraph was brought into active operation on a grand scale, for the purpose of transmitting the Queen's speech to the various large towns and cities throughout England and Scotland. An early copy of the Queen's speech specially granted for the purpose, was expressed from Westminster to the central station. During the two-hours the speech was transmitted over 1,300 miles, to 60 central towns or stations, where one or more manipulators were occupied in deciphering the transmitted symbols. Immediately on its arrival at Liverpool, Birmingham, Rotherham, Wolverhampton, Leeds, Wakefield, Halifax, Hull, Rochdale, Gosport, Southampton, Dorchester, Gloucester, Leicester, Manchester, Nottingham, Derby, Lincoln, Sheffield, York, Newcastle, Norwich, Edinburgh, and Glasgow, the speech was printed and generally distributed, and the local papers published special editions."

The telegraph was quickly becoming the Social Media tool of its time!

Telegraphs

Telegraph Street (TS)

By January 1848 the Electric Telegraph Company (ETC) had opened its *Central Telegraph Station* (CTS) at Founders Court in Lothbury, EC2., opposite the Bank of England. The CTS moved to Little Bell Alley, off Moorgate, in 1860. Little Bell Alley was renamed Telegraph Street and subsequently the telegraphic call-sign became TS. The office handled both inland and foreign telegrams. Such was the extent of the operation that adjacent buildings were connected by pneumatic tubes to pass message papers between the two.

[Note: The ETC is recognised as the origin of British Telecom. See also chapter ***ETC***.]

The privately-owned inland telegraph system was transferred to the State on 28 Jan 1870, following the Telegraph Act of 1868. The Post Office took over 1,058 telegraph offices and 1,874 offices at railway stations.

'...all telegraph circuits emanating from central London were transferred to TS' following the takeover.

Not everyone shared the optimism for the future of the service, and there were many staff changes among those who were used to a faster-paced, more commercial workplace!

"The Post Office by 1868 was a passive, almost inert, amazingly elaborate bureaucracy, with no sense of public service or fiscal responsibility." [http://distantwriting.co.uk/index.htm]

My GPO in London: Trilogy Edition

Despite this, the demand for the service continued to increase, and the Post Office transferred its telegraph plant to a new Central Telegraph Office on St. Martin's-le-Grand, at the corner of Newgate Street, (GPO West) in January 1874.

Remember that the telephone wasn't invented until 1876, so telegrams had become the instant communication media of the day. Urgent news, business news and greetings were all sent by telegram.

The CTO (Central Telegraph Office)

The CTO's role in the history of telecommunications is a significant one. GPO West was a four-storey construction of granite and Portland stone, intended as a new headquarters building on St. Martin's le Grand, bordered by Newgate Street, King Edward Street and Angel Street. [See also chapter **GPO West**.]

'The staff at present employed by the office consists of between seven and eight hundred clerks, of whom about a third are men, and two-thirds women. Of the latter, some come on duty at eight a.m., and leave at four p.m.; others arrive at twelve noon, and leave at eight p.m.'

Walter Thornbury, 'Aldersgate Street and St Martin-le-Grand', in *Old and New London: Volume 2 (London, 1878), pp. 208-228.*

[British History Online http://www.british-history.ac.uk/old-new-london/vol2/pp208-228 accessed 3 November 2018.]

Telegraphs

The Engineer-in-Chief's office was situated in a single south wing on the ground floor. All manner of telegraphic devices filled the instrument galleries. The popularity of the telegram was such that accommodation originally intended for postal business was surrendered, and as early as 1884, a fourth floor was added to the building.

Telephones

The first London-Paris telephone service (via submarine cable) was inaugurated on 1 April 1891 and was operated from the CTO until 1904 when it transferred to the Central exchange in GPO South, where telephone services continued to develop.

Telegram Messenger Boys

Messenger boys were always an important link in the operation of the service. The GPO Film Unit produced the film *Job in a Million*, which depicted new recruits serving a two-year probationary period upon leaving school. In smart uniforms, they represented the public face of the GPO, not only delivering the telegrams, but also being expected to take back a reply, at the appropriate cost, when requested.

'Whether you are to be a postman or sorter or the Director General himself, you must always remember that part of the responsibility for the organisation will fall on your shoulders. On your faithful performance of a public service will depend the future greatness of the Post Office. It's a vast organisation and you as a small part of that will be called upon to put public service before anything else.' [Quote from 1936 GPO film Job in a Million]

My GPO in London: Trilogy Edition

Until the first world war, telegrams were delivered on foot or by pedal cycle messenger. The motor cycle was introduced from 1933.

'The abolition of the Boy Messenger grade has now been virtually completed. Telegrams are delivered mainly by young postmen who also perform some postal work wherever composite duties can be arranged. It is probable that the 125c.c. motor cycle will be adopted as standard for telegraph delivery work.' [POTJ Nov 1949.]

Telegram Terms

The principles here evolved into various combinations of working as the technology improved.

- **Telegram**: A (written) message accepted at a counter and delivered locally by hand or sent over a distance by telegraph, transcribed and delivered by hand.
- **Telegraph**: Electrical apparatus for transmitting messages by code over a distance.
- **Teleprinter**: A telegraph instrument providing a direct printed record of messages between any two machines. Early teleprinters did not produce a copy of the message being sent.
- **Phonogram**: Verbal dictation of a telegram between a telephone subscriber and an accepting Post Office or *CTO*.
- **Telephone-Telegram**: Verbal dictation of a telegram from one Post Office to another.

Telegraphs

Tube Working [See also chapter *Tube Service*.]

Within London, telegram messages between the *Central Telegraph Office (CTO)* and delivery/acceptance offices, and many important buildings were transmitted by pneumatic tubes under the streets.

Pneumatic Tube Systems

In 1870, as the Post Office took over the operation of the Telegraph Service, its first street tubes were run from the *CTS in Telegraph Street* * to Temple Bar and Charing Cross.

Over the years, a vast network of pipes under the streets of London connected telegram branches with the *CTO*. Worked by pneumatic air, the paper telegrams were inserted in a plastic carrier, which in turn was placed into the tube system for conveyance to a distant office.

"The down carriers are forced along the tubes by air pressure, and those in the up direction are drawn through the tubes by the application of a partial vacuum."

Street tubes were made of lead, in iron pipes, and were buried at shallow pavement level. A standard tube was two and a quarter inches, internal diameter, but three-inch tubes were provided on busy or longer routes. The plastic carriers were five or eight inches long. Up to 20 telegrams could be placed in a single carrier. The network extended to a total of 75 route miles.

*Until the Post Office's own *CTO* at Newgate Street opened in 1874.

My GPO in London: Trilogy Edition

Instructions for Operating Pneumatic Tubes

- The message should be placed firmly inside the carrier and should not project outside.

- The carrier should be inserted in the tube so that the felt buffer is foremost in the direction of travel.

- The carrier should not be inserted until the operator is satisfied that the previous carrier has reached its destination.

- Only one carrier should be in the tube at any time.

- If a blockage occurs the matter should be reported immediately to the office in charge of the telegraph instrument room and no more carriers should be inserted.

The Coming of Telex

Methods of working continued to change…
[In the *CTO*] *"The number of teleprinters continues to increase. These are chiefly the No.3A type. …the old metal-framed tables are being superseded by wooden ones of solid construction. It is hoped that by this means, vibration will be practically eliminated."*
[POEEJ Vol 21 1929.]

By the late 1920s, the spread of loaded trunk cables, primarily for telephone use, were not well-suited for the transmission of the dc telegraph signals. Multi-Channel Voice Frequency (MCVF) working was established, using convertors at each end, to enable telegraph and telephone traffic to be effectively carried within the

Telegraphs

same cables (on separate pairs) without excessive interference or degradation.

The sending of a telegraph over a wire, was an exchange of teleprinter messages, hence the term:

TELeprinter EXchange (* shortened to TELEX).

[* Concise Oxford English Dictionary - Telex: Teleprinter + Exchange]

However, by the mid-1950s, Telex was more specifically a business dial-up teleprinter service network, which had evolved separately from the already established public telegram service.

Maintenance engineers working on customer lines could distinguish telex circuits by the greater shock they received, 80 volts dc as compared to 50 volts dc for telephone working!

Printergram Service (1932)

The *Telex Printergram* service was introduced on 15 August 1932. With the necessary additional signalling equipment (voice frequency convertors), this enabled a telephone subscriber to use a teleprinter no. 7A on his telephone line. This could be used for intercommunication with another telephone subscriber with a teleprinter, or primarily for sending messages (Printergrams) to the *Central Telegraph Office*. Essentially, this was one of the first 'dial-up' services, long before the concept of home computing was conceived.

On (London) *Director* exchanges, telephone subscribers dialled TLX to be routed to the operator for a high-grade trunk connection.

On *Non-Director* exchanges, level 98 was utilised. The Teleprinter 7A was quickly superseded by the 7B to conform with CCIT (Comite Consultatif Internationale Telegraphiques) standards.

...And over PWs (Private Wires)

Additionally, the continuing growth of trunk telephone cables enabled the GPO to offer some of the first Renters' Private Wires (routed partly) over the derived phantoms of existing circuits.

Tariff A - Simplex service for teleprinters 7A between renters' premises with all kit maintained by the Department.

Tariff B – Duplex telegraph circuit for renters' own kit, or that provided and maintained by the Department.

Note that the Department provided steel tables as part of the new teleprinter 7 installations.

Although the interchange of cables for either telegraphy or telephony was possible, by 1941 it was decided that a dedicated *Telegraph Network*, separate from the *Telephone Service*, was needed for the growing use of teleprinters. An automatic switching system based upon existing *Zone Centres* was desirable, but events delayed this scheme...

Wartime

Throughout wartime, important communication centres were obvious targets, and the *CTO* suffered during both world wars. The damage in 1917 during the First World War was relatively minor, but the Second World War (1 September 1939 to 2 September 1945) saw much more substantial damage. After a raid on 29

Telegraphs

December 1940 the *CTO* was set alight by burning debris from adjacent buildings and the interior was totally destroyed.

A pre-planned contingency allowed *CTO* working to be switched to the reserve offices:

- CTO R which was in King Edward Building
- CTO X which was at a remote underground location
- CTO Y for phonogram circuits
- CTO Z for overseas circuits

The shell of the building was refurbished to the first and second floors, and the unsafe upper floors dismantled. The *CTO* reopened in June 1943, although by this time plans were well-advanced for relief switching centres.

Devolved Trunks

The wartime bombing of the *CTO* had demonstrated the vulnerability of concentrating all the telegraph trunk lines in one location. Of course, the nature of telecoms is generally that lines converge to a central switch. Multiple sites are more desirable for diversity and safeguarding the service in the event of disruption at a single site, but this tends to be costly to implement.

Up to that time, the main telegraph network had point to point circuits which converged on major sites (*Zone Centres*), which mostly coincided with the growing telephone trunk network. A policy of decentralisation of the telegraph work at Provincial Zone Centres by transfer to *Area Centres* was adopted in 1941. In the interim, *Ring Centres* to safeguard the *CTO* circuits were established in Acton, Addiscombe, Hendon and Stratford.

Two distinct networks, the DTN and the TMS were developed

DTN: Defence Teleprinter Network (1939)

A separate Defence Teleprinter Network (DTN) was planned and implemented, for government and military communication. As DTN work took priority, the Public Telegraph Service also adopted a new resilient manual switching system based upon triangle clusters of nodes to ensure security of service.

TMS: Teleprinter Manual System (1944-47)

Configuration of the TMS with *Area* switching was phased over the six *Zone Centres* in 15 stages, from January 1944 up to completion in late 1947. Use of additional *Area Centres* increased the number of telegram re-transmissions, but development of an automatic switching system was not practical during wartime. The TMS used 1547 switching circuits with 134 switchboard positions and carried approximately 75% of all public telegraph traffic.

Sending a Telegram (1946)

From South Kensington to Scotland. *"The telegram is handed over the Post Office counter, stamped and despatched to the CTO. It can arrive via pneumatic tube, by teleprinter, or be telephoned, according to the sending office. After being sorted and stamped it is carried by a fast-moving conveyor belt, winding round desks and between tables to the Gallery which deals with the despatch of*

Telegraphs

telegrams to Scotland. From there it is teleprintered to its destination for delivery."

[Abridged from *The Post Office went to War* by Ian Hay 1946.]

History of Teleprinter Automatic Switching System (TASS)

In 1935, the Intersectional Telegraph Switching Committee had carried out a detailed study into the feasibility of providing a national automatic switching system for the Inland Public Telegraph Service. This was prompted by the Retransmissions Committee. At this time, circuits connected together intermediate telegram offices, but often several re-transmissions were needed to reach the final destination. By 1937 the decision was taken to convert the Inland Telegraph Network (also known as TMS - Telegraph Manual Switching) to automatic working. This was delayed by World War II, but by the summer of 1945 a revised conversion plan was issued.

TASS

Teleprinter Automatic Switching (TAS) System (TASS) was built in stages between 30 October 1950 and 1954. TAS removed the need to physically transmit telegrams, and cut down on re-transmissions too. The TAS System was based upon the provision of 24 Strowger switching centres. TAS (Strowger) selectors were similar to those developed for telephone use but used different switching and signalling functions.

Transmission of a Telegram by TASS

The Transmission of Telegrams

Minor	Printergrams Phonograms Public Counter	Teleprinter Automatic Switching System	Printergrams Phonograms Public Counter	Minor
Acceptance Office	Appointed Office	Main Teleprinter Network	Appointed Office	Delivery Office

Notes:
Minor Offices are those that only handle their own traffic.
Appointed Offices also handle traffic on behalf of other offices.

© JC Nov 2018

Telegraphs

The 24 TAS centres were divided into:

- Zone Centres {6}
- Area Centres Class I (12)
- Area Centres Class II (6)

The London TAS Centres

By 1952 the London Telegraph Auto Switching Centres were listed as:

- London Centre JTS (Judd Street) Area Centre
- London North JXN (Brent Building) Zone Centre
- London West JXW (Chiswick ATE) Zone Centre

[See *London's Trunks, Tolls and Telex* book for more.]

Instrument room equipment for TASS comprised:

- A Teleprinter No.11B
- A separate dialling unit

    The dialling unit included, a dial, dial lamp, and four keys:
    Dial and clear
    Incoming reset
    Paper-failure alarm cut-off
    Out-of-service facilities
    A green connection lamp, and a red paper-failure alarm lamp.

My GPO in London: Trilogy Edition

Telegraph Service

Telegram volumes rose from 45,000 in 1880 to a staggering 82 million per year by 1913. By the end of WWII 1945/6 the number peaked at just 64.9 million, as the telephone service expanded and became the more convenient method of timely communication.

At the CTO

In its heyday the Central Telegraph Office had direct communication with every large town in the UK and was the largest telegraph office in the world.

'It houses both Inland and Foreign Operating Galleries. The Inland Telegraph Gallery is equipped with nearly 500 teleprinters and they sometimes have to deal with 200,000 telegrams per day.'

Galleries: a reminder of the time when the telegraph instruments were operated in galleries running around the public office.

[GPO booklet: Central Telegraph Office.]

By 1957 the *CTO* street tube system served 40 London District and Branch offices, two postal sorting offices, two railway station offices, three service departments, and a branch of the Accountant General's Dept.

By now, traffic was on the decline:

'At present some 10,000 telegrams are conveyed each day to and from the CTO.' [Approx. 3.65M per year – POTJ Spring 1957.]

Telegraphs

In 1958 the wartime *Ring Centres* closed and returned to the *CTO*, as a move to the new *Fleet Building* was to handle future traffic. Continental telegrams transferred from the *CTO* to *Electra House*.

The original *CTO* at *GPO West* had served the public well, but its complicated network of pneumatic tubes belonged to another era. The war-torn building had reached the end of its life and closed in 1962. By then, annual telegraph/telegraph traffic was down to 13.3 million, falling to 6.7 million by 1972.

As more messages were sent over the expanding Telex Network, the last TASS centre in London JTS (Judd Street) closed in 1977. In later years, Telex switching was to undergo a digital transformation, but that too is another story.

A Greetings Telegram (1967) Artwork: Edward Ardizzone.
© BT Heritage and Archives TCB 480/67a

My GPO in London: Trilogy Edition

Telemessages

Telemessages were introduced in early 1982 as a printed overnight message (dictated by phone or telex) sent by first class post, guaranteed to arrive the following day. Essentially the same as a telegram but delivered by normal post rather than by special messenger. Telemessages superseded the inland telegram service on 30th September 1982. [Note: 1981 was the year that British Telecom split from the Post Office.]

'TELEMESSAGE is British Telecom's new electronic mail service, which offers you ease of sending, and next working day delivery, in a distinctive high impact envelope.'

References

POTJ:
Nov 1950 *Automatic Switching for Telegraphs*.

POEEJs:
Vol 60 Part 2 July 1967 *Ninety-Seven Years of Engineer-in-Chief*.
Vol 54 Part 3 Oct 1961 *The Closing of the CTO*.
Vol 38 Part 4 Jan 1946 *Safeguarding Telecommunications in Wartime*.

IPOEEJ Printed Papers:
No. 189 *Development of Telegraph Switching in Great Britain Telex Service* (1944).
No. 195 *The Introduction of Automatic Switching to the Inland Teleprinter Network* (1949).
No. 215 *The Automatic Telex Service* (1959).

Outlet 17: Electra House

Overseas telecommunications were established by companies other than the Post Office, providing networks of telegraph (submarine) cables, and radio links, across the world.

Eastern Telegraph Company (1872-1929)

Of particular note the Eastern Telegraph Company was established in 1872 from the joining of several smaller firms. Merging with other international companies it finally became Cable & Wireless Ltd in 1934.

Electra House, 84 Moorgate. Architect: John Belcher

Opened in 1902, Electra House was the first home of the Eastern Telegraph Company.

Electra House, Victoria Embankment

Company admin was transferred to a new building on 11 May 1933. Bomb damage to Moorgate in 1941 prompted a full move to Victoria Embankment.

Transfer to the Post Office

The *Cable and Wireless Act 1946* enabled the UK government to purchase all of the remaining shares of Cable and Wireless Ltd effectively nationalising the company with effect from 1 Jan 1947. The *Commonwealth Telegraphs Act 1949* sought to regularise the running of the services and thus allowed integration of staff into the Post Office from 1 April 1950.

My GPO in London: Trilogy Edition

Electra House at Victoria Embankment (1950)
© BT Heritage and Archives TCB 473/P04705

ETE (External Telecommunications Executive)

The Post Office's ETE was established in 1952 to control the activities of the newly enlarged overseas services. Continental telegram work was progressively transferred from the *CTO* to *Electra House*. ETE became the International Division in 1979 changing to British Telecom International (BTI) in 1981 as it split from the Post Office. BTI continued until 1991 as the 'BT Piper' identity signalled a reorganisation of the company.

Electra House

The ETE at Electra House spanned an era from when worldwide communications were primarily by telegraph, and few households had their own telephone, through to the period of rapid growth in the provision of high-capacity overseas submarine cables, satellite links and international direct dialling of telephone calls.

'The main operating gallery at Electra House covers about one-third of an acre, for 64 radio and 17 cable circuits.' [POTJ Autumn 1955.]

As the technology developed, OTOs (Overseas Telegraph Officers) used a wide variety of systems to keep the messages flowing:

ARQ (Automatic error correction), MSU (Manual Switching Unit), Gentex, tape-torn OTRU (Overseas Telegrams Relay Unit), MRCs (Message Relay Centres) and TRCs (Telegram Retransmission Centres).

The later MRC and TRCs were located in Cardinal House.

'The overseas telegraph system comprises the public telegraph service, the Telex service, and a rental service for commercial organisations.' [POTJ Summer 1962.]

'The Overseas Telegraph Service at Electra House has 93 point-to-point routes using 115 two-way channels. 15 outgoing and 17 incoming teleprinters are connected to the International Telex Exchange to dispose of Gentex traffic. Nearly two-thirds of the point-to-point circuits are provided by high-frequency radio links, supplemented by the old Commonwealth network of single-core telegraph cables... and a steadily increasing number of trans-oceanic submarine cables.' [POTJ Spring 1964.]

My GPO in London: Trilogy Edition

Gentex (General Telex)

Allowed operators to transmit telegrams direct to the appropriate delivery office.

'Gentex is an international standard (ITU F.20) for the transmission of telegrams over the Telex network.'

Signing Off

The opening of the TRC in Cardinal House greatly reduced the staffing need in Electra House. The final transfer of the TRC to Coventry in 1991 ultimately led to the closure of operations in Electra and the building was subsequently demolished.

References

POTJ Autumn 1955: *The Central Station of the Post Office Cable and Wireless Services.*
POTJ Summer 1962: *The Nerve Centre on the Embankment.*
POTJ Spring 1964: *Speeding the Overseas Telegraph Service.*
POTJ Summer 1966: *A New Relay Unit.*

International Telegraphs:
www.spencerweb.net/telegraphs/index.html

One World by Ian Elliott and Andrew Bailey (1991).

BT Archives: *Events in Telecommunications History.*

Outlet 18: Fleet Building

Fleet Building (1959) was one of the Post Office's biggest office blocks to be devised in the years after the war; the forthcoming decades were to be a boom in telex growth and development.

Fleet Building on the corner of Shoe Lane and Stonecutter Street.
© J. Chenery (2012)

My GPO in London: Trilogy Edition

Of all the office-type telecommunication buildings in London, Fleet was perhaps the only one to display (on the outside) graphic clues of the industry worked within. Commissioned in 1960, the tiled murals by Miss Dorothy Annan gave a public identity to an otherwise non-descript building. Even so, the massive telecommunications complex had been designed (like many others) to fit the available plot and maximise usable space; it wasn't an architectural masterpiece!

By the time I got to view the murals (in 2006) they had become weathered and faded and the building looked derelict.

Fleet Building murals on Farringdon Street © J. Chenery (2006)

Fleet Building

Fleet Building was designed by W.S. Frost under guidance from chief architect Eric Bedford, of the *Ministry of Works*. The 15-storey building was completed in 1960 and occupied a large site between 40 Shoe Lane and 70 Farringdon Street.

Dorothy Annan Murals

Public service buildings of the era represented a showcase of the industry thus Dorothy Annan's multi-tiled, colourful murals were especially themed to depict aspects of telecommunications. The nine panels inlaid into the Farringdon Street elevation were:

1. Radio communications and television
2. Cables and communications in buildings
3. Test frame for linking circuits
4. Cable chamber with cables entering from the street
5. Cross connection frame
6. Power and generators
7. Impressions derived from the patterns produced in cathode ray oscilligraphs used in testing
8. Lines over the countryside
9. Overseas communication showing cable buoys

Note: A 27-page full-colour A5 photo-booklet *Dorothy Annan Murals for Fleet Building* by John Chenery (2018) illustrates the wonderfully restored artwork.

See www.mygpofamily.com for details.

My GPO in London: Trilogy Edition

'Radio communications and television' mural.
© J. Chenery (2016)

Miss Annan thoroughly researched the topic for the murals by visiting other GPO premises and gathering photos of the proposed themes. The ceramic tiles, manufactured by Hathernware Ltd, were hand-scored to give the textures for the mural. The final rich, deep-coloured, glazed decorations were applied and then fired in Annan's own studio.

At the opening ceremony of Fleet Building on 10 April 1961, the murals were inspected by London Mayor Sir Bernard N Waley-Cohen, together with the Postmaster-General the Right Honourable Reginald Bevins, and Miss Dorothy Annan.

Reference: English Heritage Advice Report, Case no. 463962 (2011)

Fleet Building

Floor Allocation

The main entrance was in Farringdon Street, but due to the slope of the land, the staff entrance in Shoe Lane was designated the first floor. Six lifts served the massive complex

The lower six floors (including sub-basements) were designed for heavy equipment, while the upper nine floors were allocated for office space.

The Refreshment Club occupied the ground floor level facing Stonecutter Street. An assembly hall and stage, as well as conference rooms catered for all types of meetings.

The fourth floor was specially designed for a Sales Bureau and apparatus demonstration area. A recruitment centre for telephonists applying to LTR (London Telecommunications Region) was situated on the sixth floor.

The top floor was used for staff training. Other floors housed two *TMOs* (Telephone Manager's Office), LTR's City and Long-Distance Areas, one of which included Waterloo's *Traffic Office*.

Additional training areas temporarily utilised the ground floor spaces which were allocated to Inland Telegraphs, due to occupy them upon full closure of the Central Telegraph Office (*GPO West*) which was scheduled for late 1962. The large open-plan areas were ideal for exhibitions. Notably, the *Commonwealth Technical Training Week* (29 May to 3 June '61) and *A House Style for Post Offices* (Oct '62).

House Style was the work of Eric Bedford. House Style: *"Traces the development of Post Office design and points the way to the future."*

Permanent Exhibitions (1961)

Long before the days of the *BT Museum*, Fleet held displays of telecommunications equipment and techniques. A double-needle telegraph instrument, circa 1851 from Buckingham Palace was just one of the exhibits. Exchange demo sets included a display of Subscriber Trunk Dialling equipment, which at the time was a new system for the UK. By 1969 Fleet was listed as one of the recommended Post Office buildings in London to which the public could visit.

Auto Telex (1960)

In August 1958 Shoreditch (London), and Leeds automatic telex exchanges became the first to transfer from a manually switched service. The rest of the UK followed, culminating in the completion of the project in December 1960 with the opening of Fleet auto-telex.

The 874 subscribers on Shoreditch all transferred to Fleet. Installation had begun in May 1959 when the building was partially completed, such was the urgent demand for equipment space! Fleet was now a *Zone Centre* handling telex calls not only for London, but also (as hypothetical units) for all of Home Counties, excepting Cambridge.

Auto-telex was a new network for telex subscribers to dial their

Fleet Building

own calls. Spread over two floors, Fleet's telex capacity was for 20,000 subscribers and it was hailed as the largest *automatic* telex exchange in the world! By 1963 the forecast demand had increased to 60,000 stations, such that two additional telex exchanges (and buildings) for London were envisaged.

During 1961 additional units allowed for the direct dialling of international telex calls to many European countries.

[Telex was a dial-up public-switched teleprinter network for the transmission and delivery of printed messages between subscribers.]

Central Telegraph Office (*CTO*)

The original *CTO* had occupied the majority of accommodation in *GPO West*, on Newgate Street, since 1874. Over many years it had developed into the hub for sending and receiving inland (and later) international telegrams. An extensive network of pneumatic tubes, buried under the roads, carried paper messages between key offices within London. More than 5,000 staff worked in the building, which was filled to capacity, as it struggled to keep pace with the complexities of newer signalling methods, and instruments, and the popularity of its services.

During the war it had been extensively damaged such that essential switching of telegraph/telegram traffic had been relocated to protected adjacent and distance centres, i.e. the *King Edward Building*, and newly built *Ring Centres* outside of London.

My GPO in London: Trilogy Edition

Post-war, in a much-depleted state, the *CTO* continued to operate the public telegram service amidst the mechanisation of its switching (TASS) and the emerging telex and telephone services, which both added complexity to the variations of equipment needed and the additional staff to operate them. The established network of pneumatic tubes had been re-instated from war damage but digging the road up to repair blocked tubes was becoming an expensive business.

From about 1958 the outstationed offices were consolidated back to the *CTO* and a new plan of inter-working inland/international telegrams, and telex, suitable for implementation in a modern building was being devised. Thus from 1960 began the run-down and closure of *GPO West*, and its tube systems.

The New *CTO* (1962)

The *CTO* re-opened in *Fleet Building* on 21 October 1962. On 12 November, Lord Geddes of Epsom sent a teleprinter message to officially inaugurate the centre.

The new telegraph instrument room was installed on the third floor of Fleet – a space originally reserved for an additional telephone switchroom but reviewed as the Post Office's plans for London had changed since the first concept of the building. Specialisms included: Telex EQ and DQ, Phonograms, Circulation, *Combined Positions*, Printergrams, *TAS* Forwarding, Multelex, Abbreviated Addresses, Tracing and Delivery.

Fleet Building

Terms

Telegrams were handed over the counter (in person) at an Acceptance Office i.e. a Head Post Office, Post Office or Sub-Post Office.

Phonograms were telegrams which were rung over the telephone i.e. dictated to the Acceptance Office.

Printergrams were telegrams which were accepted by teleprinter (i.e. Telex).

CTO: Streamlined Printergram positions (1962)
© BT Heritage and Archives TCB 417/E27625

My GPO in London: Trilogy Edition

Combined Positions/Working

The telegraphist accepted a *Phonogram* on the telegraph typewriter and then transmitted it on the associated teleprinter signalling/dialling unit to its destination office. All at a single workstation.

CTO: Phonogram Combined Working (1962)
© BT Heritage and Archives TCB 417/E27626

Staffing of the *CTO* was to be 750 compared with the 5,000 who were once required at *GPO West* in its heyday. A reduction of operating positions from 249 to 178 was also possible, due to new

Fleet Building

work processes. Fleet was the telegram DO (Delivery Office) for EC1 and EC4, plus all of London during the night.

FLEet Street ATE

The FLE Strowger Director unit had opened in *Faraday Building* and was transferred into *Fleet Building* circa 1962. With all-figure numbering, this served 01-353 subscribers, and later with a TXE4 unit for 01-583 numbers. Both converted to System X which closed and was absorbed back into *Faraday Building* circa 2001.

Fleet Street AMC

Assistance calls were via a Cordless Auto-Manual Centre on the fourth floor. This was listed as 40 Shoe Lane.

Subscriber Trunk Dialling

STD for London was being rolled out progressively from July 1961. An inauguration ceremony took place in the assembly hall in Fleet Building on 10 October 1961. As part of the telephone trunk network, *Varley* Non-Director I/C exchange opened on the first floor of *Fleet Building* in 1968. *Varley* used ferrite core RTs (Register Translators).

London to Paris ISD (1963)

The first ISD (International Subscriber Dialling) call was made by the Lord Mayor of London (Sir Ralph Perring) at 11am on 8 March 1963. Calling from Fleet Building, he dialled 13 digits and was connected to Monsieur Jacques Marette, the French Minister of Posts, Telegraphs and Telephones, in Paris.

A transcript of leaflet *PH 1015* (February 1963) explains the system and charges. This was before the UK adopted decimal money. 1s (shilling) was 5p. 1d was less than one new penny (1p). Telephone charges were timed for 2d (twopenny) unit-pricing.

INTERNATIONAL SUBSCRIBER DIALLING

Dial **Paris** on the **twopenny telephone**

1. **Dialling to Paris**
   You can now dial your own calls to Paris. The procedure is very similar to dialling an inland trunk call. First you dial a code to get Paris, then the Paris number.

2. **Tones from Paris**
   For a few seconds after you have finished dialling you will hear a short burst of tone indicating that the automatic equipment in Paris is putting your call through.

   When the call is connected you may hear the Paris ringing or engaged tone.

   The **Ringing tone** is a three-second medium-pitch tone, alternating with three seconds of silence: pee-ee-eep; silence; pee-ee-eep; etc.

   The Engaged tone is a medium-pitch tone, half-second on half-second off: peep-peep-peep-peep, etc.

   If you would like to hear these tones free of charge dial **MINcing Lane 8711.**

Fleet Building

There is no Number Unobtainable tone. Instead you would hear a recorded announcement in French.

3. **Charges in 2d. units**
Dialled-calls to Paris will be charged in 2d. units of 4.28 seconds with no three-minute minimum. Thus, a call lasting 1 ½ minutes would cost 3s. 6d., a two-minute call 4s. 8d. and so on. You pay only for the time you are connected. The units will be registered on the meter at your exchange and will be charged in your account with your inland dialled-calls.

4. **Save on Personal Calls**
The minimum charge for a three-minute Personal Call, connected by the operator, is 9s. 4d. (including the Personal fee of 2s. 4d.) With I.S.D. it costs 1s.2d. to speak for half a minute on a call you dial yourself. This may be long enough to find whether the person you want is available, or to make an appointment if he is not.

5. **Calls connected by the Operator**
Should you want the operator to get your Paris call, dial **104**. Also dial **104** for all calls to the rest of France. The three-minute minimum charge (now 7s. to *all* parts of France) will continue on calls made through the operator.

Please keep this dialling code list in your STD Dialling Codes booklet. If you would like more copies please ask your exchange supervisor (dial **INF**).

M. & M. LTD LONDON   PH 1015 2/63

My GPO in London: Trilogy Edition

Telex International Cordless Switchboards (1963)

Many international routes could not yet be dialled direct, so up to 12,000 calls per week had to be handled manually. New telex boards equipped with the Teleprinter No.12 allowed for modern working. Two suites of cordless of 36 cable and 36 radio positions were BIS during 1963.

CTO: Cordless Telex Switchboards (1961)
© BT Heritage and Archives TCB 417/E28071

The switchboards used specially modified teleprinters no.12 supplied by Creed & Co, Ltd. The positions were constructed of French Cameroon Iroko timber and the sloping desktop was covered with light-green vinyl plastic. New 'fully-adjustable' chairs were also a feature of the switchroom.

Fleet Demolition (2015)

The twenty-first century saw both a contraction and amalgamation of BT's activities in London. Office working was becoming call-centre based outside of town(s). Telephone exchange premises needed only a small footprint, and the UK telex service had been superseded by other electronic communications, e.g. e-mail and web-based solutions.

Typically, bankers Goldman Sachs acquired the *Fleet Building* site to build a new corporate HQ. [Bankers had a proven habit of buying BT premises in prime sites!]

Dorothy Annan's murals, which had once captured the optimism and excitement of the so-called *White Heat of Technology* of the 1960s, were faded and reminiscent of public services before the digital age. Fortunately, English Heritage had listed the murals as Grade II protected in 2011 and ownership was transferred to the Corporation of London.

Time Capsule

Buried beneath the foundation stone of *Fleet Building* was a 'time capsule' - a brass cylinder, which contained the latest technological developments of the services provided by the Post Office. The capsule was unearthed during the excavations for Goldman Sachs' new HQ on the Farringdon Street site and was finally passed to BT Archives in October 2016. BT's Head of Heritage, David Hay remarked, *"The contents look as pristine as when they were put in it, probably because it was filled with nitrogen gas before being sealed."*

My GPO in London: Trilogy Edition

A transcript of the notes which were enclosed with the artefacts is reproduced here:

"This container was placed beneath the foundation stone of the new Fleet Building on Monday October 20th, 1958 by the Lord Mayor of London, Sir Denis Truscott, T.D."

Fleet time capsule and contents on display at BT Archives.
© J. Chenery (2018)

"In the life-time of many present at the ceremony, man has learned to fly and now pauses tensely on the very fringes of space. He has harnessed the power of the sun, first for destruction and then for more peaceful purposes. By science he has ensured longevity even if he has not made it universally tolerable by his social wisdom.

Fleet Building

In the hope that world understanding will come from free intercourse and peace from understanding, these examples of present development in Telecommunications are placed here for the interest of posterity."

3000-TYPE STANDARD RELAY

Developed jointly by the Post Office and Equipment Contractors, this relay is widely used in all types of telecommunications because of its reliability. Different contact combinations, thinner contact springs or special armatures may be used depending on circuit requirements. About 80,000 relays are used in each large telephone exchange where 2-motion selectors are employed.

700-TYPE TELEPHONE HANDSET

A rocking armature receiver is used in the 700-type hand-set which will shortly be supplied to all new Post Office telephone subscribers. Apart from its modern design, the receiver can be used on subscriber's lines of up to 1000-ohms resistance with potential saving in cable costs.

POLYTHENE SUBSCRIBERS CABLE

The compound, polythene, which has recently been developed is being used for insulation in subscriber's underground distribution systems. In this 50-pair telephone cable each conductor is insulated with an extruded covering which is coloured to a specified code for identification purposes. The laid-up core is also sheathed with an extrusion of polythene.

At first used as an alternative to small lead-covered, paper core cables for subscribers' networks, this type of cable with far larger pair capacity is undergoing field trials. The toughness of the polythene makes physical damage less likely than in lead-covered cables and the compound is impervious to acids which might cause corrosion and lead to breakdowns in older types.

TELEX ANSWER BACK UNIT

The automatic connection of subscribers over the TELEX network makes it necessary to ensure that the connection is made to the correct address. The 'Answer Back' unit carries the code of each subscriber and when connection is made sends this recognition signal automatically to the transmitting end. The code is repeated again at the end of transmission. In this way misrouting is avoided.

Handbook: A LONDON TELECOMMUNICATIONS REGION (internal) directory, displaying the 'GPO crown' logo on its cover, was also included in the capsule.

My Postscript

It may not have been envisaged for the capsule to be discovered again so soon, but it is surprising how much the technology has changed in less than a lifetime, though our needs to communicate remain just as important, while our social graces are still far from perfect.

Of Fleet

As to the exact functioning of the departments, and the detailed provisioning of switching equipment, together with the daily procedures, this was best-known by those who worked there, but they have probably long forgotten the designations of systems, and how they interconnected!

The Telex Fleet (2018)

In the Sixties age so bold,
A new *CTO* was foretold.

A *Ministry of Works* design
This architecture wasn't fine.

Fifteen storeys rising above
Not the sort of thing you'd love.

But a telegraph office spacious and new
With cordless switchboards running through.

Fleet Street numbers connected too
A telephone exchange also new.

Outside displayed for civic pride
Dorothy's murals weren't hidden aside.

Themed telecom panels forged in the *White Heat*
With a technology hall for folks to meet.

A telex centre at the very heart
Several floors below the Annan art.

Now swept away for another bank
Corporate HQs in London rank.

The murals? Well, they've been restored
So they can still be well-adored!

My GPO in London: Trilogy Edition

References

Leaflet PH 1015 2/63 *Dial Paris on the Twopenny Telephone.*
Engineer-In-Chief's Report Year Ending March 1963.

POTJs:
Summer 1961 *Fleet Building Opened* and *Combined Working in Telegraph Instrument Rooms.*
Winter 1961 *Fleet Permanent Exhibition.*
Summer 1963 *The New CTO at Fleet.*
Autumn 1963 *New Switchboards Speed Overseas Telex Calls.*

POEEJs:
October 1958 *Automatic Switching for the Telex Network.*
April 1961 *Fleet (London) Automatic Telex Exchange.*
October 1961 *The Closing of the Central Telegraph Office.*
July 1964 *A Cordless Telex Switchboard.*

Booklet PG239 10/62 The New Central Telegraph Office:

THE NEW CENTRAL TELEGRAPH OFFICE

Outlet 19: At Doctors' Commons

Within sight of St. Paul's Cathedral in the area known as Doctors' Commons, the Post Office Savings Bank, and later the International Telephone Exchange were established. Some history of the area sets the scene...

The *Doctors' Commons* was a familiar name given to the College of Advocates and Doctors of Law which was founded in 1511. It was a requirement for admission as a fellow to have attained the degree of *Doctor of Civil Law* from either Oxford or Cambridge University. The Commons had shared facilities, such as a common dining/meeting hall, a group of clerks and scribes, and probably a common waiting room.

Doctors' Commons
© *BT Heritage and Archives TCB 473/P03672*

My GPO in London: Trilogy Edition

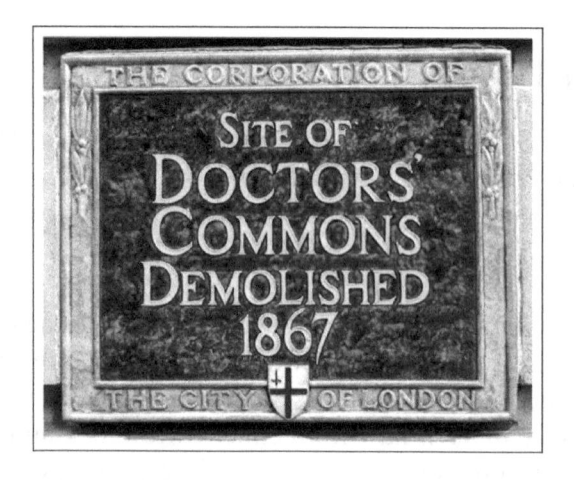

Site of Doctors' Commons plaque on BT's Faraday Building
© J. Chenery (2005)

Doctors' Commons: A society of ecclesiastical lawyers within premises on or close to the present Knightrider Street, described in *David Copperfield* and referred to by Sherlock Holmes.

Holmes: *"And now, Watson, we shall order breakfast, and afterwards I shall walk down to Doctors' Commons, where I hope to get some data which may help us in this matter."*

[*The Adventure of the Speckled Band*, Arthur Conan Doyle.]

There were five courts within the Commons:

1. The Courts of Arches
2. The Prerogative Court
3. The Court of Faculties and Dispensations
4. The Consistory Court of the Bishop of London
5. The High Court of The Admiralty

[From *Hand-Book of London*, 1850 Peter Cunningham.]

Doctors' Commons

The *Commons* held records of marriage licenses, divorces and wills. The society was dissolved in 1857, and the building was finally demolished in 1867.

Thomas Linacre

Thomas Linacre practiced medicine in London and was the appointed physician of King Henry VIII. This was an important and influential position, with notable patients being Cardinal Wolsey, Archbishop Warham and Bishop Fox. In those early days, there were many imposters who were not qualified to practice medicine, and it was through this need to raise standards that the Royal College of Physicians was founded. From his home on this site, Thomas Linacre established the College and became its first president.

Thomas Linacre plaque on Knightrider Street
© J. Chenery (2001)

My GPO in London: Trilogy Edition

In 1518 The Royal College of Physicians was founded by King Henry VIII.

'The Royal College of Physicians is a registered charity that aims to ensure high quality care for patients by promoting the highest standards of medical practice. It provides and sets standards in clinical practice and education and training, conducts assessments and examinations, quality assures external audit programmes, supports doctors in their practice of medicine, and advises the Government, public and the profession on health care issues.'

Queen Victoria Street

A new road, Queen Victoria Street opened from Mansion House to Cannon Street in October 1869 and was finally completed 4 November 1871.

'Queen Victoria Street was constructed by the late Metropolitan Board of Works as a continuation of the Victoria Embankment, with the object of providing London with a new main artery from the Mansion House to Charing Cross. It was the greatest improvement carried out in the City of London during the nineteenth century. Not only did it provide invaluable relief to the enormous traffic of Cheapside, but it completely altered the appearance of the City centre.'

[Extract from The Face of London by Harold P. Clunn.]

Conveniently, a new Post Office Savings Bank HQ was built, circa 1880, at 144 Queen Victoria Street. This appears to be the first occupation of the site by the Post Office.

[See **POSB** chapter for more history.]

Doctors' Commons

Bakehouse Court

Although the *Doctors' Commons* was demolished in 1867, the site was still referred to by that name as its history had become a part of the area. Towards the end of the nineteenth century, Bakehouse Court (at 6 Godliman Street) had been built on the site of St. Paul's Bakehouse. The original 'bake house' had supplied bread for the Church.

The new bakehouse wasn't a law court although some solicitors were based therein: 'Arthur S Joseph and Co., 3-4, Paul's Bakehouse Court, Godliman Street, E.C.4, Solicitors.'

By the late 1930s, Bakehouse Court was an empty derelict building on the corner of Carter Lane and Godliman Street. And so, in 1938, as the Telephone Service was rapidly expanding, the GPO applied to compulsory purchase the site, primarily because it was situated adjacent to *GPO South*.

Spectacularly, on 4 August 1939 a 48-inch gas main ruptured causing an explosion which demolished the empty Bakehouse Court and caused damage in the surrounding area of St. Paul's. In the telephone exchange, telephonists at work reported

"The whole building shook and the [switchboard] plugs were jerked out of our hands." The Chief Supervisor stood up and in a clear voice said, *"It's quite all right girls, go on with your work, and I will find out what has happened."*

[References: *Telecommunications Heritage Journal* Nos.90/91 and 92 (2015) *A Narrow Escape for Faraday* Parts 1 & 2 by Richard Truscott.]

My GPO in London: Trilogy Edition

In the photo below, the high-level bridges between Faraday South and Faraday North can be seen. The part of Bakehouse Court still standing is propped up onto Faraday South-East, which is under construction.

Bakehouse Court (September 1939)
© BT Heritage and Archives TCB 417/E11308

Doctors' Commons

Faraday South East Block

Viewed from Godliman Street, the debris of Bakehouse Court is shown on the right. On the left is the steelwork for the *South East Block* of Faraday Building to house new automatic exchanges.

Faraday SE Block and Bakehouse Court
Godliman Street (September 1939)
© BT Heritage and Archives TCB 417/E11306

My GPO in London: Trilogy Edition

Subsequently Toll A O/G (outgoing) Auto exchange opened in Faraday *South East Block* in 1942. With the advent of World War Two, the area was to be subjected to more devastation and with this in mind, by 1945, the GPO had built its own 'telephone fortress', *The Citadel*, on the site of Bakehouse Court.

Bell Yard

Bell Yard off Carter Lane, showing the original position of the Shakespeare tablet © J. Chenery (1999)

Bell Yard linked Carter Lane to Knightrider Street, but in bygone years this was a private right of way, save for deliveries and access. Bell Yard is steeped in history as it was named after the Bell Tavern which once stood upon this site.

Doctors' Commons

> UPON THIS SITE FORMERLY STOOD
> "THE BELL" CARTER LANE
> FROM WHENCE RICHARD QUINEY
> WROTE THE LETTER TO WILLIAM
> SHAKESPEARE DATED THE 25TH
> OCTOBER 1598. THIS IS THE ONLY
> LETTER EXTANT ADDRESSED TO
> SHAKESPEARE AND THE ORIGINAL IS
> PRESERVED IN THE MUSEUM AT HIS
> BIRTHPLACE, STRATFORD UPON AVON.
>
> THIS TABLET WAS PLACED UPON
> THE PRESENT BUILDING BY LEAVE OF
> THE POSTMASTER GENERAL 1899.

A stone tablet, once affixed to the wall of GPO South

Reigning Monarchs

- Queen Victoria 1837 to 1901
- King Edward VII 1901 to 1910
- King George V 1910 to 1936
- King Edward VIII 1936
- King George VI 1936 to 1952
- Queen Elizabeth II 1952 to date

Queen Victoria died in 1901 and thus the Victorian era of the GPO, which had established the modern postal system, came to an end. However, Queen Victoria Street was to become the centre of savings and later that of telephonic communications.

My GPO in London: Trilogy Edition

The photo below shows the Knightrider Street elevation of *GPO South* and the ironwork which supported one of the link bridges between Faraday *North* and *South* Blocks.

One of the ornate VR (Victoria's Reign) portico entrances to GPO South © J. Chenery (1999)

[See chapter **GPO South** for the continuing story of the area.]

Doctors' Commons

The Bell Tavern at 6 Addle Hill

The Bell, 6 Addle Hill (1982)
© *London Metropolitan Archives, City of London.*

My GPO in London: Trilogy Edition

References to *The Bell* tavern date as far back as 1598. The final premises were demolished in 1998. Not surprisingly, *The Bell* was popular with telephone employees, more so because of its location opposite *Faraday Buildings*. In the photo (page 265) the netted railings of Knightrider Street are propped against *North Block*.

Refreshment Clubs
These were an enhanced form of 'tea club' which many Post Office employees joined. Run by a committee and selected members, the clubs enjoyed access to affordable food and drink, and in some premises a licensed bar too! In 1903 the aim of the *GPO North Refreshment Club* was: *'To provide the members with good and substantial refreshments at moderate prices.'*

During the Civil Service era of the Post Office, clubs were regulated by the Treasury. Hansard 26 November 1952 Volume 508: *'Post Office refreshment clubs exist for the purpose of providing food and drink for the staff during the period of their duties and extensions of this function are discouraged.'*

Post-privatisation, telecom catering functions were outsourced to Compass/Eurest, and overseen by Monteray/Facility Services. The Post Office's own catering division, Quadrant Catering Ltd became a JV with Compass and continued to be contracted by RM.

Godliman House
At 21 Godliman Street, Godliman House was on the corner of Knightrider Street. During the 1960s, Godliman House was home to *Fault Control* – an engineering test desk (office) conveniently located opposite Faraday Building.

POSB

Outlet 20: Post Office Savings Bank

As a child during the 1960s, I had a Post Office Savings Bank account, which my parents had opened for me. On the special occasions that my aunt came to visit us, she sometimes left me with a crisp 10/- (ten-shilling*) note. I was usually encouraged to 'spend half and save half', thus a trip to the local Post Office and sweet shop was a necessity. Entries into the passbook were written in biro, initialled and then date stamped by the clerk. The handstamp was inked on a special pad and then pressed onto the book. The familiar, 'thump-thump' noise of the stamping process was all part of the atmosphere of the Post Office during that era!

* Ten shillings is 50p in decimal money.

History

In 1861 the Palmerston government set up the *Post Office Savings Bank* - a simple savings scheme aiming to encourage ordinary wage earners *'to provide for themselves against adversity and ill health'*.

The 1861 Post Office Savings Bank Act enabled the General Post Office (GPO) to provide this service and thus the Post Office Savings Bank (POSB) opened for business on Monday 16 September in two small rooms within the Post Office headquarters, (*GPO East*) St. Martins-le-Grand, London. By 1863 the bank occupied a warehouse at 27 St. Paul's Churchyard.

A new road, Queen Victoria Street opened from Mansion House to Cannon Street in October 1869 and was finally completed 4 November 1871. Conveniently, a new POSB HQ was built, circa 1880, at 144 Queen Victoria Street. This appears to be the first occupation of the site by the Post Office.

My GPO in London: Trilogy Edition

PO Savings Bank HQ:
Queen Victoria Street elevation (1880)

The five-storey Post Office Savings Bank building was subsequently completed and occupied from 1880.

Post Office Savings Bank HQ at 144 Queen Victoria Street (c.1880) This building was demolished circa 1929. The current-day Bible Society building can be seen on the far left. On the right is a 'Pirelli' tyres business. © BT Heritage and Archives TCB 475/ZE18

POSB

The GPO Estate

The Postmaster-General's report from 1874 highlighted the accommodation difficulties:

'The new Post Office [GPO West] in St. Martin's-le-Grand has been completed and brought into full occupation; but I regret to state that owing to the transfer of the Telegraphs to the Post Office, the building is not sufficient for the purposes originally contemplated; the consequence being that the Money Order and Savings Bank duties have still to be carried on for the present in detached offices.'

GPO East was fully utilised for postal services:

'The average number of bags despatched daily from the Chief Office is 5,872 and the number of bags received 5,573.'

In 1877 the Postmaster-General's report stated:

'A new building is about to be erected in Queen Victoria Street to accommodate temporarily the Central Savings Bank, until permanent provision can be made for that and other Departments, for which there is present no accommodation in the General Post Office buildings, St. Martin's-le-Grand.'

By 1878, GPO West was taking the expansion of the telegraph service:

'The estimated number of telegrams delivered in the London Postal District during 1878 was 4,816,000, or about one fifth of the total number delivered in the United Kingdom; viz. 22,792,000.'

My GPO in London: Trilogy Edition

Post Office (Sites) Act 1885

48 & 49 Vict c.45 (Source www.gbps.org.uk)

'An Act to enable Her Majesty's Postmaster-General to acquire lands in London, Birmingham, Bristol, and Newcastle-upon-Tyne for the public service.'

The GPO was still actively seeking additional sites as the Postmaster-General's report of 1885 shows:

'The Report of the Committee appointed by your Lordships in 1883 to examine the subject of obtaining improved accommodation for the Central Departments of the Post Office in London has been presented to Parliament, and a Bill has been introduced to give effect to the recommendations of the Committee, and to acquire by compulsory powers the site of the Queen's Hotel, and other properties adjoining it, for the purpose of erecting on these sites a building in connection with the General Post Office and for the accommodation of the administrative staff.'

The new admin building was to be *GPO North*, but the 1885 Act was essential in order to secure further sites.

Continuing growth in the Savings Bank business required additional accommodation, which was located across the other side of the street at no. 147. Hansard reports of the poor state of the overflow premises:

POST OFFICE SAVINGS BANK DEPARTMENT, QUEEN VICTORIA STREET— INSANITARY CONDITION.
HC Deb 28 February 1887 Vol 311 cc692-3

DR. CAMERON *Glasgow, College)* asked the Postmaster-General, Whether his attention has been called to the insanitary and inadequate nature of the accommodation provided for the staff of the Post Office Savings Bank Department at 147, Queen Victoria Street; whether the gross cubic space of one room, in which 40 employees have to work, allows less than 360 cubic feet of air per head, and the rooms are dark, ill-ventilated, and disturbed by the noise and vibration of adjacent machinery; and, whether, in view of the fact that these conditions are unquestionably detrimental to health, and that several years must necessarily elapse before a new building can be erected on the site which has been purchased under the sanction of Parliament, he will at once take steps to provide suitable accommodation in some other building or buildings?

THE POSTMASTER-GENERAL (MR. RAIKES) *(Cambridge University)* I have personally inspected the premises, No. 147, Queen Victoria Street. They have been taken for a temporary purpose only, and were the best that could be obtained, it being necessary to have the accommodation as near as possible to the main Savings Bank Office. The premises are not all that could be desired; but I do not think they can be considered as very objectionable for a mere temporary purpose. I will, however, make inquiry whether improvement can be effected in the ventilation. Attention is also being given to the question of obtaining additional temporary accommodation to meet increase of business, and of thus relieving any inconvenience which may exist at present.

[No. 147 QVS was across the street where *Baynard House* is now located.]

My GPO in London: Trilogy Edition

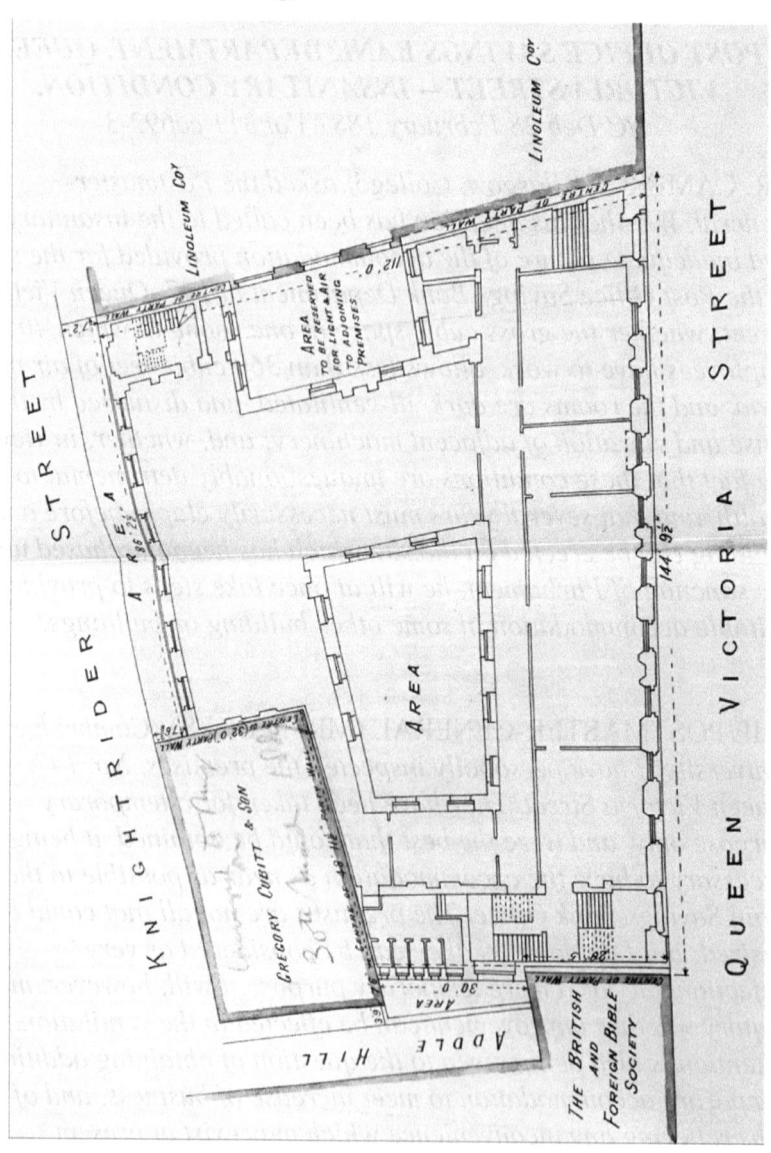

*Plan of Post Office Savings Bank HQ
at 144 Queen Victoria Street, circa 1880.*

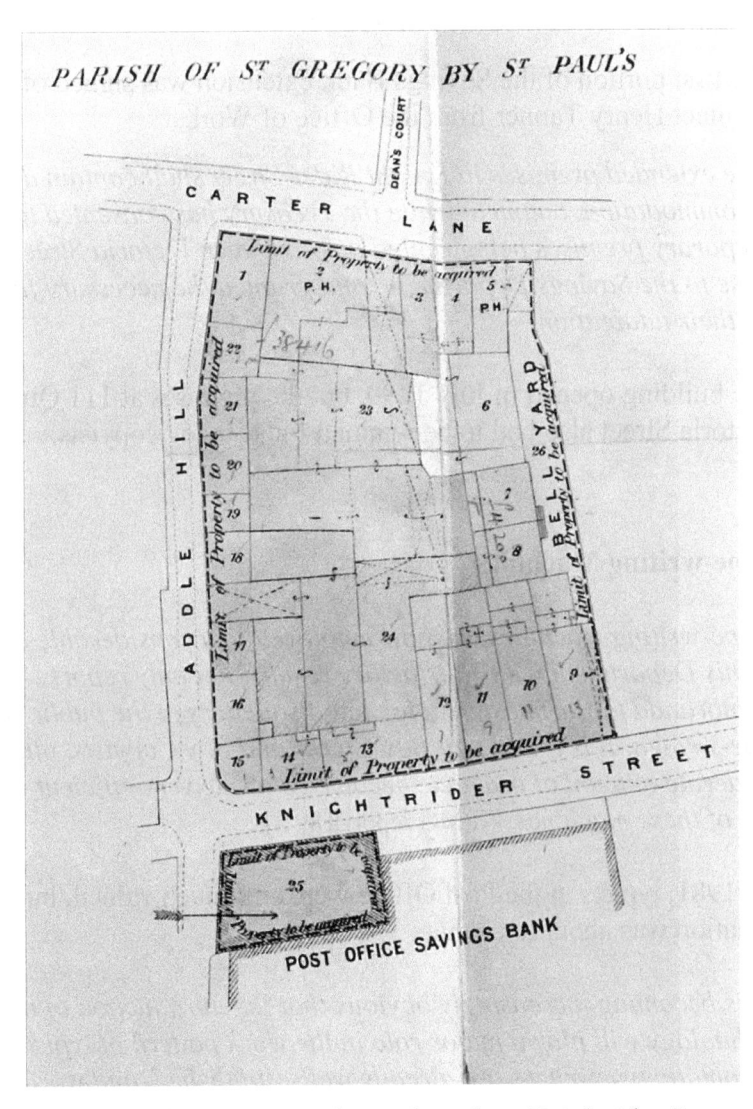

Plan of properties to be acquired stretching from Knightrider Street to Carter Lane. Note the many separate plots to be purchased.

My GPO in London: Trilogy Edition

Knightrider Street/Addle Hill (1890)

The first portion of the Savings Bank extension was signed off by architect Henry Tanner from the Office of Works.

'The extended premises in Knight Rider Street shall contain dining accommodation, but meanwhile the Treasury has consented to temporary premises being rented at 140 Queen Victoria Street, close to the Savings Department, and granted the necessary funds for their adaptation.'

The building opened in July 1890, but the premises at 111 Queen Victoria Street also had to be retained for 150 boy copyists.

Type-writing Machines

'Type-writing machines are now employed to a considerable extent in this Department with satisfactory results, not only reports, memoranda to Postmasters, etc., but also letters to the public being type-written. It is found that Boy Clerks and Boy Copyists, after a moderate amount of practice, become as a rule very efficient in the use of these machines.' [PMG report 1891.]

By 1981, typists in the Post Office were still much valued, but the situation was about to change:

'It is becoming increasingly obvious that the introduction of new technology will play a major role in the work pattern of typists. Automatic typewriters are already well-established, and word processors are under trial.' [CPSA Annual Report.]

Working Practices

'The introduction in last year [1893] of machinery for folding purposes was an alteration of great importance. Until then the acknowledgements, warrants, and advices were folded and sealed by women sorters and boy messengers, and the task of arranging daily for the disposal, in time for the mails, of a mass of documents averaging about 60,000, and sometimes reaching as high a number as 120,000, was no easy one.' [PMG report 1894.]

Progress in Building

'Active steps are being taken to extend the Central Savings Bank Building, which when completed will stretch from the frontage in Queen Victoria Street as far back as Carter Lane.' [PMG report 1895.]

Carter Lane/Addle Hill (1894)

The rest of the site has now been cleared of its old buildings, and the walls of the new building are rapidly rising. The additional accommodation is needed not only to meet the constant growth of the Department, but also in order to dispense with the outlying premises in which portions of the Staff have now to be located, with obvious disadvantages.' [PMG report 1895.]

The second portion of the new buildings of the Post Office Savings Bank has been completed and occupied during the year, and the whole staff is now housed in spacious blocks, which though divided by Knightrider Street, are practically one building, as they are connected by bridge and tunnel. [PMG Report 1897.]

My GPO in London: Trilogy Edition

The towering floors of Faraday North Block as it was then known when photographed in 2002 © J. Chenery

POSB

Carter Lane…

*'Savings Bank Extension' on Carter Lane which became the entrance to
Faraday telephone switchrooms © J. Chenery (2002)
Note the VR (Victoria's Reign) portico entrance on the left.*

My GPO in London: Trilogy Edition

...and Addle Hill

Savings Bank Extension on Addle Hill © J. Chenery (2002)
The wire netting was to prevent debris falling into the basement area.
This was predominantly a wartime precaution, although just as effective
in modern times.

Telephone Exchanges

The Queen Victoria Street/Carter Lane premises had always been intended as simply a temporary site for the ever-growing Savings Bank. By the turn of the century a much larger site had been acquired in West Kensington.

The popularity of the telephone in London required the progressive opening of new manual exchanges to connect more subscribers and to handle the calls.

'Considerable progress has been made with the central exchange for the London Telephone System, which will ultimately occupy a large part of the present Savings Bank Buildings in Queen Victoria Street; and outside premises have been hired in order to provide temporarily for the Savings Bank Staff displaced.' [PMG report 1901.]

'The Chief Money Order Office was removed in November from Fore Street to the premises in Queen Victoria Street, vacated by the Savings Bank and now known as the General Post Office South.' [PMG report 1904.]

[See **GPO South** chapter for more.]

Many decades later, a telephone engineer working in *Faraday Buildings (circa 1970/80s)* remarked:

"The room which housed the safe for the PO Savings Bank was in the North Block basement. And it still had the original safe door fitted when I was there on the International Exchange construction group; we used it as a store room. No combination lock system, just a very robust key operated lock."

My GPO in London: Trilogy Edition

Blythe House (1899) Completed 1901

At 23 Blythe Road, West Kensington. The architect was Henry Tanner from the *Office of Works*. Listed Grade II status in 2004.

The new Savings Bank occupies a site of about five acres lying between Brook Green and Addison Road Station. The building already erected covers some two acres, consists of six floors, and will accommodate 4,000 people. It is capable of considerable extension. In constructing and fitting up the building every effort has been made to secure the maximum of efficiency, convenience, and comfort for the staff. [PMG report 1903.]

>   THIS STONE WAS LAID BY
>   HIS ROYAL HIGHNESS THE PRINCE OF WALES K.C.
>   ON BEHALF OF
>   HER MAJESTY THE QUEEN
>   ON THE 24TH DAY OF JUNE 1899.

Foundation stone at Post Office Savings Bank HQ Blythe House
© J. Chenery (2010)

Knight of the Garter (KG). The Most Noble Order of the Garter, founded by Edward III in 1348, is the senior British Order of Chivalry.

Transfer of Business (1903)

Post Office Savings Bank HQ Blythe House
© J. Chenery (2010)

The Blythe Road Savings Bank was a most grand, capacious building in which it was anticipated to finally house all the departments of the business. The move from Queen Victoria Street was phased between January and April 1903 so as not to interrupt the daily workings of the bank.

My GPO in London: Trilogy Edition

Business as Usual

Post Office Savings Bank HQ Blythe House (1946)
© BT Heritage and Archives TCB 417/E14042

Blythe House more details

On 25 October 1961 the centenary celebrations of the Post Office Savings Department and Department for National Savings included a special visit by Her Majesty Queen Elizabeth the Queen Mother, to the Headquarters in Blythe Road, West Kensington. The Queen Mother opened the new Chetwynd Exhibition Hall, the modern inquiry office, and the centenary gates, and she unveiled a plaque in

POSB

the main entrance hall to commemorate the event.

The centenary gates at Blythe House show a crown on each post, with the date(s) 1861 and 1961 shown underneath.

[Reference: POEEJ Vol. 54 Part 4 January 1962.]

Post Office Savings Bank HQ Blythe House (1946)
© BT Heritage and Archives TCB 417/E14039

My GPO in London: Trilogy Edition

West Kensington DO (Grade II listed 2004)

West Kensington DO was built to service the adjacent POSB building which, in its heyday, was said to have generated approximately 100,000 letters daily.

West Kensington DO. © J. Chenery (2010)

National Savings move to Glasgow
at 150 Boydstone Road, Cowglen.

Blythe House continued as the main operational centre of the bank until about 1963 when the Government agreed a gradual dispersal of jobs to Glasgow. Blythe House was vacated circa 1977/78.

The Savings Bank office in Glasgow was established with 11 staff in April 1966. By 9 May 1977 this totalled 4,768½.

[Hansard: HC Deb 23 May 1977 vol 932 cc342-5W]

The Cowglen site continued the *GPO Family* ethos that several generations of staff all worked for the Post Office over a period of many decades. The architecture of Boydstone Road was typically that of modern three or four storey, square and rectangular 1960s-style office blocks, built in clusters as the requirement for staff and facilities increased.

Charles House (1948-2010) – London HQ

Most likely this was an additional building for the POSB, which then became their London HQ when the main operations moved to Glasgow.

*Charles House, West Kensington © Ruth Sharville (2010)
See www.geograph.org.uk/photo/1700695 copyright terms*

My GPO in London: Trilogy Edition

Charles House at 375 Kensington High Street, West Kensington, London, W14 was built as offices between 1948 and 1950 to the designs of Arthur S Ash. To many people, this was just another anonymous government building, but a question in Parliament explains it...

HC Deb 23 October 1950 vol 478 cc290-1

'Sir Waldron Smithers asked the Minister of Works for what purpose Charles House, opposite Olympia, has been leased by the Government; what is the floor space and rent; which Department will use it; and how many persons will work there.'

Mr Richard Stokes (replied): *The Ministry of Works have leased Charles House in order to provide accommodation for staff of the Post Office and other Departments previously working in scattered requisitioned premises. The building contains about 309,000 sq. ft. of office space and 41,000 sq. ft. of storage space. It will be occupied by about 3,200 staff of the Post Office, Inland Revenue Department, Ministry of National Insurance, National Assistance Board, Ordnance Survey Department, Ministry of Supply and Ministry of Works. It is not the practice to disclose the rents paid by the Ministry.*

Kensington Computer Centre

British Telecom's Kensington Computer Centre was based in Charles House. In 1981, computers listed in operation were an ICL LEO 326 which had been the mainstay of Telephone Billing, and the updated New Billing system which ran on the ICL 2970.

Drummond Gate, Pimlico

NS & I moved to 1 Drummond Gate, Pimlico, London SW1V circa 2010 due to Charles House being demolished.

'One of the significant changes for our staff during the year was the move to our new offices in Pimlico, London, as our old building in west London was being demolished. We found an alternative tenancy in a vacant, government owned building. The project was delivered on time and under budget, and within an hour of arriving in our new offices staff were working as normal.'

[NS & I report 2010/11.]

Money Order Office

The Money Order Office which had operated from *GPO East* was displaced to Fore Street in 1898, due to accommodation pressures. In 1904, space was found in the new Central Savings Bank in Queen Victoria Street until 1912 when a dedicated building in Manor Gardens was constructed.

10-12 Manor Gardens, Holloway (1912)

Architect Jasper Wager (*Ministry of Works*) with John Rutherford.

The first Savings Certificates went on sale on 21 February 1916. This work expanded, thus the building was extended between 1929 and 1932, and became the known as the Savings Certificate Office. By 1938 about 3000 staff were on site.

The work dispersed to Durham in 1963. A new (Brutalist) building, Milburngate House at Framwelgate Waterside was commissioned between 1965-1969 and designed by TF Winterburn. The architects were Gollins, Melvin, Ward and Partners.

My GPO in London: Trilogy Edition

Manor Gardens (2014) © Julian Osley
See www.geograph.org.uk/photo/3959536 for copyright terms

In 1981 PO/BT correspondence courses were still being administered from 10-12 Manor Gardens e.g., from THQ/TPD the Operational Telecommunications Systems (OTS1) programme. The Post Office/BT vacated the site during the 80s.

ERNIE

To finish the Post Office story about the Savings Department a reminder that the Electronic Random Number Indicating Equipment (ERNIE), the Premium Bond computer, was born in London at Dollis Hill research station, conceived of Sidney Broadhurst and his team. It was then installed at Lytham St. Annes by Preston Telephone Area staff.

The generation of random numbers (in the GPO) was first devised circa 1947 for the Artificial Traffic Machine, and this technique was then used for ERNIE.

Bonds and Stocks Office

On the established government site at Moorland Road, Lytham St. Annes, the Bonds and Stocks Office was opened in 1956 to accommodate the drawing of the first Premium Bond prize on 2 June 1957. The transfer of Government Stocks from Harrogate in 1963 ultimately required a move to larger premises, thus in 1978 ERNIE (mark 2) moved to Mythop Road, Marton, Blackpool.

Disposal of Key Sites

As with the bulk of the Post Office and BT estates, by early 2000, staff numbers and the need for large rambling premises had declined with the pace of technology, automation, self-service, and outsourcing of work.

NS & I statement: *'In April 1999 NS & I signed a pioneering Public Private Partnership with Siemens Business Services, which was subsequently purchased by Atos in 2011. Over 4,000 staff were transferred from National Savings to Siemens IT Solutions and Services (now Atos), who now manage the operational components*

My GPO in London: Trilogy Edition

of our business, including the service delivery of our products, operation of our customer call centres, IT and systems upgrade and support for our services.'

By 2012 the disposal of NS & I outdated sites had been agreed and were out for tender. This was to release 23 acres at Blackpool, 32 acres at Glasgow and 5 acres at Durham.

Glasgow: Operational work moved to the Atos Capella building in May 2015. Mail processing and scanning went to Atos, Orbital House, East Kilbride by October 2015. The Cowglen site was sold in 2016.

Durham: NS & I moved to Freemans Reach, Riverside Place, Durham in mid-2015. Demolition of Milburngate House began in November 2016.

Blackpool: The Moorland Building (probably named after the original home of ERNIE) was extended in a £2.6M contract design by architects Hulme Upright. Demolition of the remainder of the site (Mython Road) included the detonation of the 1970s styled eight-storey ERNIE building on 26 February 2017. Blackpool is still the home of Premium Bonds!

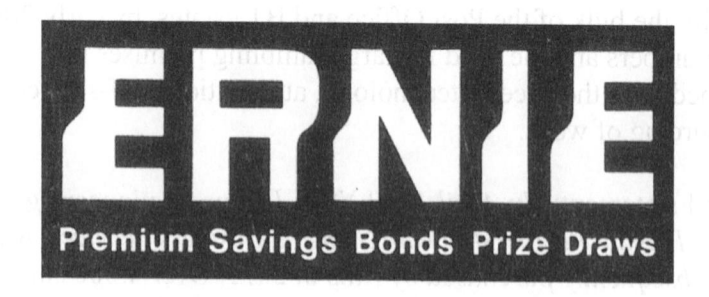

ERNIE
Premium Savings Bonds Prize Draws

Outlet 21: GPO South

GPO South

The Post Office site between Queen Victoria Street and Carter Lane was one that had been gradually extended over the 20 years from 1880 when the Central Savings Bank HQ had first been built. By 1903 the Post Office Savings Bank had moved into much larger, purpose-built premises at *Blythe House* in West Kensington. Regardless, accommodation was still problematic as various departments of the GPO were transferred and restructured as the need arose.

'The Chief Money Order Office was removed in November 1903 from Fore Street to the premises in Queen Victoria Street, vacated by the Savings Bank and now known as the General Post Office South.' [PMG report 1904.]

Marconi

In those early days, any telephonic or wireless communications were operated from *GPO West* – the Central Telegraph Office (CTO). Thus, when Marconi came to the UK to demonstrate a wireless link, it was set up from *GPO West*. A plaque at *BT Centre* (site of the CTO) records this event.

On 27 July 1896 Marconi, assisted by George Kemp, made the first public transmission of a wireless telegraphy system, over a distance of 300 metres. The transmitter was situated on the roof of the *CTO*, and the receiver on the roof of the *Savings Bank* annex in Carter Lane, at the top of Addle Hill.

My GPO in London: Trilogy Edition

London Telephone Service at GPO South

The growing popularity of the Telephone Service had the Post Office planning where to site its new *manual* telephone exchanges.

'The provision of the Post Office Metropolitan Exchange System is progressing satisfactorily. In connection with the works now proceeding, there are to be exchanges at Queen Victoria Street, E.C. (Savings Bank Buildings), Westminster, Kensington, Chiswick, Putney, Richmond, Twickenham, Kingston, Wimbledon, and Croydon. Ultimately there will be about 40 exchanges in the London area.' [PMG report 1901.]

Underground pipes were being laid, cables drawn in. and buildings were being adapted for use as exchanges. By March 1902 the *Central* exchange had been opened, with a capacity for 5,400 lines, on the fourth floor of *GPO South*. The switchboard was extended to approximately 14,380 lines, but demand was so great that *City* exchange was BIS by November 1907 with a capacity for 18,000 subscribers.

Trunk Service

GPO West had become the telegraph centre for London and now *GPO South* was to be developed for the expanding telephone service. The trunk wire (telephone line) terminations into London had previously been routed through *GPO West*, but in 1904 a dedicated new switchboard was installed into Carter Lane as the *Long Distance Exchange* was opened. Later known as *Faraday Buildings, North Block*, the Trunk Service radiated out to eventually provide connections to the whole of the South-East of England.

Although the original Savings Bank site had been extended and annexed many times, ever more space was required...

'A fifth storey has been added to the General Post Office South (Carter Lane Block), to provide additional accommodation for the London Telephone Service. Further space for telephone purposes will shortly be gained in that building by means of the removal of the Central Metropolitan Engineer and his staff to quarters in the disused London Bridge Parcel Office.' [PMG report 1908.]

Trunks and Tolls

Historically, telephone traffic evolved from centres of population and radiated out from capital cities. In the 1920s it was envisaged to interconnect the UK with just 12 Zone Centres for all of the trunk traffic. In those early days of the telephone service, calls over 15 miles were handled as trunks and had to be connected via an operator. Subscriber Trunk Dialling (STD) of long-distant calls was not possible before 1958. Consequently, the London Zone, controlled by operators in *GPO South*, covered a 70-mile radius around the capital!

The Long Distance exchange had cable routes to many, if not all, *Group Centres* in the catchment area. Trunk calls were expensive and were not routinely made, although people wanted to keep in touch, and businesses needed to trade, so the service experienced rapid growth.

To relieve the growing demand on the Trunk Service, 350 shorter-distance trunk lines were diverted from *GPO South* to the first (manual) Toll exchange which was opened on 17 September 1921 at 3-5 Norwich Street, Fetter Lane. Subscribers within the new Toll Area could ring their local operator, ask for the Toll operator and be quickly connected to other exchanges within the Area.

Toll Service

Toll A Manual opened on the 5th floor of *GPO South* on 3 December 1927, handling traffic from the Toll Area to *outside* of London.

Toll B Manual (still at Fetter Lane) handled traffic from the Toll Area *into* London.

[See chapter ***Trunks and Tolls*** for further details.]

Demolition of Savings Bank

[London Trunk & Toll 'A' Committee Memorandum]

Thus far, all the telephone services had been accommodated in the Savings Bank annexes, i.e. the block of buildings between Carter Lane and Knightrider Street. Areas were designated as:

(A) Addle Hill - Carter Lane wing
(B) Bell Yard wing
(K) Knightrider Street wing.

Such was the demand for additional equipment, it was quickly realised that the four-storey Savings Bank building would be unsuitable for the needs of a fully automatic telephone system, and support staff, in London. A revised floor allocation for the complete site was proposed thus:

GPO South

*Faraday Buildings: North Block viewed from Knightrider Street (1931)
In the foreground is the cleared site of the original Savings Bank
elevation onto Queen Victoria Street. Addle Hill is on the left.
© BT Heritage and Archives TCB 417/E07232*

My GPO in London: Trilogy Edition

Carter Lane

- Basement: Batteries and Power (A) Engineering staff (K)

- Ground floor: Main frame and testing (A) Operators quarters (B), Wireless (K)

- First floor: 100 trunk positions and records (A) Trunk apparatus (B), Wireless (K)

- Second floor: Trunk apparatus (A) and (B) 90 trunk positions or eng. plant (K)

- Third floor: 260 trunk positions (A) and (K) Cord circuit repeaters (B)

- Fourth floor: 238 trunk positions (A) and (K) Trunk or Toll manual apparatus room (B)

- Fifth floor: 204 Toll or Trunk positions (A) and (K) Writing staff (B)

Proposed floor allocations in a new QVS building:

- Basement: Batteries and Power. Heating

- Ground floor: City and Central MDF and Test Desks Engineering Staff

- First floor: Central automatic exchange

- Second floor: City automatic exchange

- Third floor: Trunk and Toll repeaters

- Fourth floor: Toll Auto.

- Fifth floor: Toll Auto, VF Telegraphs, City and Central Keysender apparatus
- Sixth floor: City and Central manual boards
- Seventh floor: Operators quarters
- Eighth floor: Operators quarters

[Source: *London Trunk & Toll 'A'* Committee meeting 27 July 1928.]

After much planning, the demolition (circa 1929) of the Savings Bank on Queen Victoria Street had proceeded. The new building was predominantly to accommodate the conversion from *manual* to *automatic* switching of the *Central* and *City* exchanges, long distance signalling, and the automatic switching for *Toll* calls, as well as additional operator switchboards.

Faraday Building (1933)

'Faraday Building, named after the great scientist Michael Faraday, whose discoveries have done much to make modern telephony.'

By 1931 the Savings Bank building on Queen Victoria Street had been demolished. Its replacement was the massive *Faraday Building* designed by A.R. Myers (*Office of Works*). (See photo on page iii.)

The new premises formed the *South Block* of the complex that was then collectively known as *Faraday Buildings*.

My GPO in London: Trilogy Edition

Postmaster-General, Sir Kingsley Wood MP, welcomes the Lord Mayor of London to the Faraday Building. Author's collection (1933).

The Postmaster-General made a speech greeting the Lord Mayor to the Faraday Building, the home of the new International Exchange. He explained the wonders of the new exchange:

"The opening of Faraday Building marks an important stage in British Post Office development and is a considerable event in telephone history. My Lord Mayor, I think I can say, that we are indeed, living in an age of miracles. Today by lifting the receiver of a telephone in London, a British subscriber can speak to Canada, the United States, South America, Australia, South Africa and nearly every other country, except China and Japan."

GPO South

The international switchboards were actually situated in the older *North Block*, but the inauguration for whole building signified the expansion of worldwide telephony. The new *South Block* a building of 11 storeys, linked to the existing *North Block* by bridges and subways.

Walkway/bridge connecting Faraday South Block to North Block. © J. Chenery (2001)

Continental and International Services

Continental telephone services began in 1891 with the laying of a submarine cable between England and France making possible communications from London to Paris. This was controlled from *GPO West*, the Central Telegraph Office, until the transfer to *GPO*

My GPO in London: Trilogy Edition

South in 1904. Cables routes to many other countries followed. International telephone services were established by the opening of a radio link between London and New York on 7th January 1927.

As planned, *Faraday ICC* (International Control Centre) opened on the 1st floor of the *North Block* (Carter Lane) on 4th May 1933 as a sleeve-control board of 121 positions; 93 Continental and 28 Radio working. The Radio Telephony Terminal (RTT) was situated on the same floor.

Local Auto Exchanges

In 1934, installation of automatic switching equipment began in the new *South Block*, with expected BIS dates of April 1935 for *Central,* and July 1935 for *City* exchange.

Switchrooms

As the growth in telephone calls dictated, equipment and switchroom designations were reallocated and moved between floors. The second floor, *North Block* had housed the *manual* board for *Central* exchange, but after the automatic exchange had opened in the *South Block*, the vacated space was to be used for additional trunk switchboards. Thus, the annexe switchroom (2A) was equipped with 42 new trunk positions.

The *North Block* boasted 435 positions, the switchrooms being named, Inland, Trunk, Trunk Provincial, Trunk Country, Toll Manual, as well as International.

Telephonists who worked in Faraday will recall the endless rows of positions in *Main* and *Annex* switchrooms over many floors, many of which looked identical!

GPO South

South East Block

In 1939 a new steel-framed building was being erected next to Faraday *South Block*. Subsequently Toll A O/G (outgoing) auto exchange opened in Faraday *South East Block* in 1942.

North East Block

To the north east of Faraday on the derelict Bakehouse Court site the *Citadel* was built during 1941. A 'fortress type' structure, it was constructed to withstand the consequences of World War II. Of reinforced concrete, and without windows, the walls were between 6 ft. and 3 ft. thick, topped with a roof 7 ft. 6 inches in thickness.

[See chapter *At Doctors' Commons*, for more about Bakehouse Court.]

The scheme for the *Citadel* trunk exchange was planned to meet the following two principal conditions:

1. To provide a limited trunk service if both the Faraday *North Block* and *South Block*, which accommodated the existing trunk equipment, were destroyed.

2. To operate in conjunction with the trunk switchroom in Faraday *South Block* if the switchrooms in the *North Block* were lost.

The Citadel manual trunk exchange was fitted with 204 standard sleeve - control positions (each 6 feet, 8.5 inches high):

- 136 of these were demand or delay positions
- 41 as incoming positions
- 27 as dual-purpose positions

My GPO in London: Trilogy Edition

It was a very large switchroom requiring the staff to work long hours, in far from ideal conditions. Faraday telephonist Barbara Ball recalls...

"*North East Block - I remember that in the winter, we did not see daylight. There were no windows and it was dark when we arrived and dark again when we went home.*"

Additionally, the *Citadel* included:

- Dormitories
- Artesian well
- Fuel storage tanks
- Air conditioning & gas filtration plants
- Standby electricity provided by diesel engine powered alternators

Post-War Years

Faraday Buildings survived the central London bombings of WWII, although they suffered some minor damage in October 1940. Telephone services continued to be automated after the war, culminating in the introduction of STD (Subscriber Trunk Dialling) AFN (All-Figure Numbers) and ISD (International Subscriber Dialling). The sprawling switches and wiring of the predominantly Strowger system(s) filled the building to overflowing, until the steady build-up of digital switching reversed the trend in the mid-1990s.

The End

The hideous bulk of concrete that had been the *Citadel*, and the much-extended *North Block* were prime candidates in BT's 21st century property rationalisation. In 2005 the entire *North East* and *North Blocks* were demolished. *The Grange St. Paul's Hotel* was constructed between 2006 and 2010.

A new entrance into Faraday Building was established along the re-formed Knightrider Street.

Faraday Building 1 Knightrider Street, London, EC4V 5BT
© J. Chenery (2010)

My GPO in London: Trilogy Edition

The Grange St. Paul's Hotel

The Grange St. Paul's Hotel:
Carter Lane entrance using Faraday North Block portico.
© J. Chenery (2010)

References

Postmaster-General Reports (various years).
Post Office Engineers' Electrical Journals (various years).

[POEEJ Vol XXVII Oct 1934 Part 3 – *The London Trunk Centre.*]

Outlet 22: Trunks and Tolls

Before 1958, all trunk calls had to be connected by a switchboard operator who manually selected the route, either by plugging the call through to another exchange operator, and/or by dialling additional digits to set-up the call. The roll-out of Subscriber Trunk Dialling (STD), throughout the UK, required the provision of many new cable routes and dedicated switching equipment and thus was not fully completed until 1979!

A plug-cord switchboard © J. Chenery (2012)

Manual Exchanges

In the long-ago days of manual telephone exchanges, a subscriber would lift his or her telephone receiver (no dial) thus causing a signal lamp to light on the operator's switchboard. Upon plugging into the associated socket, the operator would answer with the expression '*Number Please?*' soliciting the subscriber to advise the number to which he or she wished to be connected. If the required number was on the same local exchange, the operator would simply plug another cord into the correct socket for the other subscriber. Numbers on adjacent exchanges would require an operator-to-operator call, to set up a connection between the two. Calls requiring intermediate or longer routings were usually concentrated on a *Trunk Centre* which specifically dealt with onward traffic.

Local operators had direct cable routes to some intermediate exchanges if the traffic was sufficiently justified, but otherwise dialled specific routing digits to reach the trunk operator. A variety of signalling systems and switchboard operating procedures were established, viz:

- Straight order wire working
- Split order wire working
- Ringing junction working
- Lending junction working

Auto Exchanges

Subscribers on automatic exchanges, had dial telephones, and were able to set up *own exchange* calls, and those to adjacent local numbers, depending upon the cable routes provided. Long distance calls still had to be requested via a trunk operator.

Auto Exchange Types

Most of the UK developed *Non-Director* exchanges, which used a logical sequence of number steps during the call set-up process. In the big cities, including London, the *Director* system of exchanges, translated the dialled number to affect a route connection.

Trunks, Tolls, and Tandems

Dedicated exchanges to route longer-distance calls through London developed over the years, from simple intermediate switches, *Tandems*, as well as longer-distance *Trunks*, and shorter-distance *Tolls*. Much later, *Sector Switching Centres* (SSCs), decentralised through-London traffic to more manageable portions. These systems evolved as the volume of calls grew, and traffic management became smarter!

Central and City Exchanges

The first of the Post Office's (manual) telephone exchanges in London, was *Central* which opened on the fourth floor of *GPO South* on 1 March 1902. To cope with the very heavy demand for service, a second exchange, *City*, opened in November 1907. The *Central* and *City* switchboards connected calls between local London subscribers who could afford the luxury of a telephone.

Early Days of Trunk Calls

"The Post Office trunk telephone system had opened to the public on 16 July 1895 when trunk lines linked London to Glasgow, Belfast and Dublin for the first time."

The service first terminated in a cable room of *GPO West*, otherwise known as the *Central Telegraph Office* (CTO). However, after the Savings Bank had moved out of Carter Lane, telephone operations were then centred onto *GPO South*. Thus in 1904, 144 trunk, and 274 junction circuits were transferred to establish the *Trunk Exchange* in what was later known as *Faraday North Block*. As is commonplace with any technology, the descriptions and names evolved as the service offerings grew.

My GPO in London: Trilogy Edition

From 1912 the Post Office had officially taken over the National Telephone Company's (NTC) network, thus the number of trunk lines was considerable.

Routing Concepts

Historically, telephone traffic evolved from centres of population and radiated out from capital cities. London particularly, routed a disproportionate volume of through-traffic, which was to prove most challenging to accommodate physically, and to devise practical methods of switching.

Recap: {In the 1920s it was envisaged to interconnect the UK with just 12 *Zone Centres* for all of the trunk traffic. In those early days of the telephone service, calls over 15 miles were handled as trunks and had to be connected via an operator. Subscriber Trunk Dialling (STD) of long-distant calls was not possible before 1958. Consequently, the London Zone, controlled by operators in *GPO South*, covered a 70-mile radius around the capital!}

The *Long Distance/Trunk exchange* had cable routes to many, if not all of the *Group Centres* in the catchment area. Trunk calls were expensive and were not routinely made, although people wanted to keep in touch, and businesses needed to trade, so the service experienced rapid and continual growth.

Toll Exchange

To relieve the growing demand on the *Trunk Exchange*, 350 shorter-distance trunk lines were diverted from *GPO South* to the first (manual) *Toll Exchange* which was opened on 17 September 1921 at 3-5 Norwich Street, Fetter Lane. Now subscribers within the new *Toll Area* could ring their local operator, ask for the *Toll*

Trunks and Tolls

operator and be connected without delay (no delay working) to other exchanges within the Area. *Toll Area* working was extended in 1923 and again in 1928, so that eventually Southampton, Portsmouth, Reading, Bedford, Colchester and the whole of Kent and Sussex were within the *Toll Area* Boundary!

Demand and Delay Working

Because of the limited service, trunk calls were connected, with delay working. The subscriber rang the operator, asked for *Trunks* and was called back when a free trunk line was available, at which time the call would mature (be completed). However, by the early Thirties, the Post Office introduced the Trunk service on demand - no more waiting to be called back!

Connecting Trunk Calls

There were three methods used to effectively deal with the volume of trunk calls connected by the operators:

- No Delay Working
- Delay Working
- Demand Working

No Delay Working was possible on the shorter trunk routes, but for the longer routes it was not practicable to provide sufficient circuits from all main exchanges to give full service during the busiest periods.

This led to the practice of **Delay Working** whereby trunk (long-distance) calls were booked in advance with the operator who would then call back when a circuit was available to complete the call. This tended to even out peaks in traffic levels but had the disadvantage that all subscribers had to wait, even if circuits were free.

A compromise was **Demand Working** with calls connected within a predetermined search period of one minute. If lines were busy and the call could not be connected, then Delay Working applied.

Trunk Service on Demand

In 1932, a combined No Delay and Demand Working procedure was introduced, attempting to connect calls within a 50-mile radius of a switching centre without any delay. This was a more flexible scheme that could be adjusted to meet local conditions. The area within these boundaries became known as the *Toll Area*.

This improvement was possible as a result of a new transmission and routing plan which divided large *Zone Centres* into *Groups*. The principal (or main) exchange in each *Group* had control of all originating (outgoing) traffic for all the dependent exchanges in the *Group*. Later with STD, these *Group Centres* became *Group Switching Centres* (GSCs).

Routing and Charging Plans

The switching of calls in the UK was determined by a *Routing Plan* which designated the *main* exchanges and the number of links between them, as well as the type of switching equipment.

It's difficult to precisely define the exact state of the switching protocols at a given year, as *Routing Plans* were necessarily flexible, changing to meet growth in traffic and the availability of equipment and operating staff.

Trunks and Tolls

London routings followed a more complex plan which will be discussed shortly, but regardless these had to interface with switching outside of the big cities. The state of progress from about 1920 up to the late 1950s just before the introduction of STD is a good period to explain the evolution of charging.

Manual Trunk System: Local (dialled) Calls

Before STD was introduced, local call charges were based upon the radial distances between exchanges and a measuring point was determined for every exchange in the country.

In 1921, two-step charging allowed calls up to 7.5 miles to be untimed. By 1935, a four-tier charge structure was in place.

Calls up to 15 miles, point to point, could be dialled direct, were untimed, and the following unit charges were automatically recorded on the subscriber's meter:

- 1 unit for calls 0-5 miles
- 2 units for calls 5-7.5 miles
- 3 units for calls 7.5-12.5 miles
- 4 units for calls 12.5-15 miles

The meter pulses were calculated from the code digits used to route the call.

The London Director Area was a single charge group, so local calls within and to adjacent areas were charged at 1 unit.

My GPO in London: Trilogy Edition

Manual Trunk System: Long Distance Calls

All calls over 15 miles were classed as trunk calls, had to be connected via the operator (by dialling O) and were charged by both distance and duration. Charges for operator calls were raised by means of a ticket prepared by the operator.

Simplified Charges

Up until 1 Jan 1958, manually connected calls were billed in one of 11 charge steps, associated with a complex charge letter system.

1. Local (up to 5 miles) 1 unit
2. Fee (up to 7.5 miles) 2 units
3. A/B (up to 12.5 miles) 3 units
4. C (up to 15 miles) 4 units

All the above were untimed. The following were timed and charged according to whether it was Day/Night, or Full/Cheap rate:

5. D (15-20 miles)
6. E (20-25 miles)
7. F (25-35 miles)
8. G (35-50 miles)
9. H (50-75 miles)
10. I, K (75-125 miles)
11. L-Y (over 125 miles)

Trunks and Tolls

With more than 6000 exchanges in the UK, the point to point distances/charges were different for each one. RRQ- *Route and Rate Quoting* duties were held at every *Group Centre*.

With a new scheme, 639 *Charge Groups* were created to simplify the process, together with just 6 charge steps, preparing the way for cheaper calls, and Subscriber Trunk Dialling (STD).

Dial O for Operator

As automatic (*Director*) exchanges were introduced in London, the letter/number O was allocated to call the operator.

'*Dial 100 for the operator*' was introduced in April 1959 as a precursor to STD, because the letter O was then reserved to dial trunk calls, giving access to GRACE (Group Routing And Charging Equipment).

The Basic Network for Operator Controlled Calls

Calls were connected from the *Dependent* originating exchange through to the nearest *Zone Centre*. And then to the distant *Zone Centre* and thence to the *Dependent* terminating exchange.

Dep-Minor-Group-Zone-Zone-Group-Minor-Dep

Seven links (maximum) end to end

This scheme formed the *Basic Network* in the *Manual Trunk System*. Further auxiliary routes were provided as the traffic between exchanges justified.

My GPO in London: Trilogy Edition

Zones
[18 by 1947]

The UK was divided into a number of *Zones*, each one having a *Zone Centre* to handle all the long-distance traffic into and out of the area. All *Zones*, except Belfast and Tunbridge Wells were fully interconnected.

Groups
[175 by 1947]

Larger exchanges acting as a *Group Centre* for an area of minor exchanges. Thus. the *Zone Centres* and *Group Centres* were fitted with all the control, timing and supervision equipment necessary for the manual connection of trunk calls. Later, the *Group Centres* were renamed *Trunk Group Centres*.

Minors

An exchange having direct connections to the *Trunk Group Centre*.

Dependents

An exchange dependent upon a *Minor* exchange for its long-distance communication.

Subscribers on manual exchanges made calls by asking the operator for the exchange *name* and *number,* e.g. Whitehall 1212. Upon conversion to automatic working, subscribers' telephones were fitted with lettered and numbered dials. Thus, in *Director* areas they might have dialled WHI 1212 – the code was (usually) the first three letters of the exchange *name*.

Pre-War Trunk and Toll

© JC Sep 2018

		TRUNK Area handled by **Trunk Director & Trunk Manual**			
Beyond Toll Area	TOLL Area	12.5 to 20 Mile belt	London Director AREA	12.5 to 20 Mile belt	TOLL Area	Beyond Toll Area
Incoming			**TOLL Area** handled by Toll A (manual) Toll A (auto) Toll B (manual) Semi-mechanical Tandem			Outgoing

My GPO in London: Trilogy Edition

Trunking Plan (Pre-War)

The diagram on page 315 shows the relationship between Trunk and Toll call handling in London.

Toll A and Toll B (Manual)

Toll calls were increasing and with the start of *Director* working it was more practical to divide the traffic into incoming and outgoing groups, thus:

•*Toll A Manual* opened on the 5th floor of *GPO South* (*North Block, Faraday*) on 3rd December 1927 handling traffic from the *Toll Area* to *outside* of London.

•*Toll B Manual* (still at Fetter Lane) handled traffic from the *Toll Area, into* London.

- The *Toll Area* was approximately a 70-mile circle around London.

- Toll A (manual) handled all incoming and outgoing traffic for the *Toll Area*.

- Toll A (auto) later switched all outgoing traffic from both the *Director Area* and the 20-mile belt around London to the *Toll Area*.

- Toll B (manual) provided for incoming calls to the *Director Area* from the *Toll Area*.

- The *Semi-mechanical Tandem* gave access to the *Director Area* from the *Toll Area* via order-wire routes.

Trunks and Tolls

Trunk Manual handled all other trunk calls and some toll calls as well.

Trunk Director (1937) switched traffic to the London Director Area (LDA) from distant *Zone Centres*.

Designations

Switching areas were measured as irregular circles, or belts centred on Oxford Circus. Thus, the London *Director* (exchange) Area was between 0 to 12.5 miles. The *Non-Director* area was 12.5 to 20 miles. The *Toll* area covered 70 miles. Beyond the Toll area was Long Distance, switched by the *Trunk Director* (exchange).

Director Exchanges

The first London *Director* exchange opened on 12 November 1927, at 270 High Holborn, so before very long it was possible for subscribers to call (with their lettered dial):

- TRU for TRUNKS Operator
- TOL for the TOLL Operator

Holborn customers could dial their own calls!

Holborn Tandem

Throughout the modernisation of the UK telephone service, tandem or main switching unit(s) capability was invariably established in advance of local subscriber units.

My GPO in London: Trilogy Edition

Accordingly, the first *automatic* exchange in London, the *Holborn Tandem* had opened at 10.00 a.m. on Thursday 18 August 1927. Tandems switched calls between exchanges, thus this was the beginning of mechanising the London telephone service.

The introduction of the *Holborn Tandem* exchange had been a major undertaking which had required the re-arrangement of all the junction routes between existing London exchanges, as well as a new method of connecting calls between manual and automatic exchanges.

The 70-mile *Toll Area* around London made the planning of switching capacity more urgent as the volume of calls handled continued to grow. *Devolved Trunks* and wartime contingencies, such as the *Citadel,* all added to the mix in the short term.

Devolved Trunks

By the early Thirties, the control of London's Toll traffic was devolved to local automanual switchboards. In 1932, sleeve-control boards were introduced, allowing any kind of circuit termination, leading to greater flexibility in connecting toll calls and any other types of traffic.

Wartime

In the event, (29 December 1940) the whole area around St. Paul's Cathedral was ablaze with incendiary bombs, but *Faraday* fared far better than the Central Telegraph Office (*GPO West*), which had to be partially demolished and rebuilt.

Trunks and Tolls

St. Paul's at War (2018)

In the shadow of St. Paul's
Operators plug in calls.

As the wartime bombs fall
It could be the end of it all.

But *Faraday* holds alone
Straight through for those who need to telephone.

While the Central Telegraph Office shakes
And incendiary fires spread and outbreak.

The electricity Grid Control is holding steady
As the currents fade and sometimes eddy.

The Post Office communications last
Engineered to outsmart many a blast.

Devastation is all around
But the (new) St. Paul's station can still be found!

The Cathedral stands (almost) magnificent throughout
While fire crews attend numerous shouts.

The heart of London remains forever strong
War at any time, is so wrong.

In the aftermath of the Central Telegraph Office devastation – the CTO didn't reopen until June 1943 – contingencies were put in place to safeguard the telegraph and telephone services. A policy of decentralisation of telegraph work at Provincial *Zone Centres* by

My GPO in London: Trilogy Edition

transfer to *Area Centres* was adopted in 1941. At *Faraday Buildings*, more extensive preparations were necessary.

Faraday Citadel (1941)

A massive reinforced-concrete (windowless) building began construction on the north east corner site of Faraday Buildings in May 1941 to safeguard trunk switchboards in the event of further wartime bombings. The fortress-like structure was completed in just seven months.

Faraday Citadel switchroom (1945)
© BT Heritage & Archives TCB 417/E13765

Trunks and Tolls

The *Citadel* manual trunk exchange was fitted with 204 standard sleeve - control positions (each 6 feet, 8.5 inches high):

- 136 of these were demand or delay positions
- 41 as incoming positions
- 27 as dual-purpose positions

Faraday Citadel with post-war cladding - looking down Carter Lane. Two rows of windows denote the 1960s upper extension.
© J. Chenery (2002)

My GPO in London: Trilogy Edition

G.R. Yeats from the *Office of Works* designed the modern extension over the *Citadel* in June 1962.

Toll A (1942)

On 14 November 1942, *Toll A (Auto)*, exchange opened in Faraday South East Block to switch outgoing traffic from the *Director Area* to the 12.5 to 20-mile belt. A new *Toll A (Manual)* was also opened.

Trunk traffic still had to be routed via Faraday Building and it wasn't until after WWII that further progress in decentralising switching was possible.

References

Events in Telecommunications History (BT Archives).
POEEJ Vol XVIII Jan 1926
POEEJ Vol 20 Part 3 Oct 1927 *Mechanical Tandem Exchange.*
POEEJ Vol 27 Part 2 July 1935 *Telephone Transmission – VI.*

POTJ Autumn 1957 *Full Automation of the Telephone System.*
POTJ Winter 1958 *Simplified Charges.*
POTJ Autumn 1963 *London's Trunk Switching Units.*

Charge steps info – Thanks to Simon Chappell.

Outlet 23: Trunk Mechanisation

"Until the conversion of London to automatic working is fully completed, which may occupy a period of from 15 to 20 years, manual working will exist side by side with automatic working and arrangements are necessary to ensure smooth operation between the two systems during the interim period."

Trunk Mechanisation

The connecting of telephone calls via manual switchboards would not have kept pace with the popularity and growth in the service, therefore when the technology to automate became available it was gradually introduced alongside existing methods.

Director Working

Seven digits (3 exchange code, plus 4 number) were required to connect a call between *Director* exchanges. The *Director* (equipment) received the 3-digit exchange code(s) and generated routing digits to connect the call over the available junctions to the distant *Director* exchange.

Holborn Tandem

Also referred to as the semi-mechanical tandem, because many calls were still connected with the assistance of an operator. This was an interim solution, well before the concept of STD (Subscriber Trunk Dialling) was devised.

The first *Director* and the first *Tandem* switch had both opened in Holborn exchange in late 1927. Until other *Director* exchanges were BIS, these switches had to work predominantly to other

My GPO in London: Trilogy Edition

manual exchanges. Holborn *Tandem* was well-planned with trial positions installed at *City Exchange* and the *Automatic Training School*, before full implementation began.

"It will be appreciated that before the first equipped automatic exchange can be brought into use, the whole of the existing manual exchanges in London must be equipped for call indicator working."

Call Indicator equipment was installed at 74 manual exchanges.

"In order to cater for traffic from manual exchanges, each automatic exchange will therefore be equipped at the outset with a suite of cordless 'B' positions equipped with keysenders."

'A' positions were the originating operator(s), and 'B' positions were the distant operator(s). Thus, incoming calls to the *Tandem* were answered on 'B' positions, of which there were 108 at Holborn.

"The mechanical tandem exchange is now being installed in the same building as the Holborn automatic exchange. In it will be concentrated the outgoing and incoming junctions from the smaller exchanges as well as a number of junctions to practically all the other London exchanges."

The *Tandem* acted like another *Director* exchange because it generated the digits necessary to route calls.

Improvement in speech transmission; new *loaded* cables were provided between the *Tandem* and the various exchanges on the London area.

Loaded – with added inductance coils to affect a compensated profile on the transmission characteristic of the line.

Trunk Mech

Holborn Tandem B Cordless Position (1927)

Cordless 'B' Position switchboard of Holborn Tandem (1927)
© BT Heritage and Archives TCB 417/E05131

Each Tandem position was equipped with digit-key strips 0-9 (keysenders).

My GPO in London: Trilogy Edition

1 2 ABC 3DEF 4GHI 5JKL 6MN 7PRS 8TUV 9WXY 0O
Example of a keyboard sending strip (keysender).
© J. Chenery (2012)

At the 74 manual exchanges in the scheme, Call Code Indicator (CCI) lamps were provide on each B position.

*Representation of Code Call Indicator (CCI) display.
Lamps light to show 4-digits of Sub's number.*

0	0	0	0
123	123	123	123
456	456	456	456
789	789	789	789

Trunk Mech

Tandem Call Types

The *Tandem* had to discriminate between automatic and manually routed calls. In London, seven digits (3 exchange code, plus 4 number) were required to connect a call. The exchange code was usually the first three letters of the exchange name. Thus WHItehall 1234 was shown and dialled as WHI 1234. It wasn't until 1966 that All-Figure Numbers (AFN) began to replace letter codes.

Auto to Auto

The originating exchange selects whether local, direct trunk, or tandem call. The *Tandem* routes to 1st, 2nd or 3rd selectors. The final 4-digits operate the selectors in terminating exchange.

Auto to Manual

The dialled exchange code through the *Tandem* seizes a CCI Code Call Indicator and free Coder. When the distant manual exchange operator answers, the CCI lamp field displays the required number from the Coder. The operator plugs into the appropriate sub's jack to complete the call.

"Each call indicator position is equipped with 36 cord circuits and it is expected that each operator will handle 450 calls during the busy hour."

Manual to Auto

Order wire to *Tandem*; B operator at Holborn answers and allocates a free junction back to the A operator. *Tandem* operator loads the keysender with the 7-digit telephone number. Three digits operate the Coder to route the call, and the 4 final digits then operate the

My GPO in London: Trilogy Edition

Sender to automatically dial the final selector number on the distant auto exchange.

Manual to Manual

Same as above, but the Sender translates the 4 subscriber digits to operate the CCI lamps in the terminating exchange. The B position distant operator then completes the call by plugging into the required sub's jack.

Post-War Relief

World War 2 had severely disrupted the development of new switching units, but additional auto-manual centres were soon to reduce the concentration of circuits and traffic through Faraday.

Trunk Control Centres 1949-1951

By 1945, 40% of trunk traffic was controlled by local auto-manual centres. To give further relief, three Trunk Control Centres were planned:

1. TCC City opened in Monarch TE in 1949 [Wood Street]

2. TCC Bloomsbury opened in the old Museum TE in Chenies Street 16 October 1950

3. TCC North opened in Kelvin House, Judd Street in 1951

In 1951 the first generator signalling circuits were introduced on routes to Canterbury, Portsmouth, Southampton and Winchester. These allowed the setting up of calls by a distant operator via *Toll A* exchange without the assistance of a *Toll A* operator.

Trunk Mech

Post-War (1946)
Trunk and Toll
© JC Sep 2018

TRUNK Non-Director

	Incoming						Outgoing	
Beyond London Zone	London Area	TOLL Area	12.5 to 20 Mile belt	London Director AREA	12.5 to 20 Mile belt	TOLL Area	London Area	Beyond London Zone

Toll A (Auto)

Toll B (Faraday)

Toll B (Holborn)

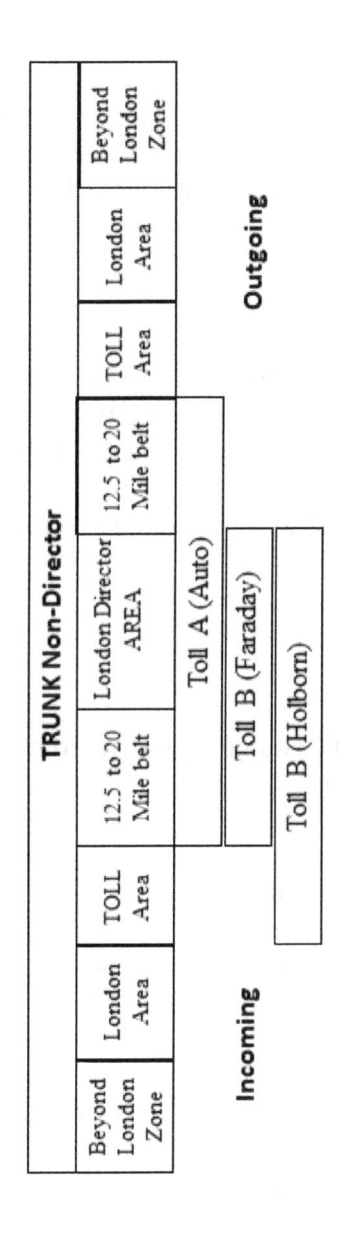

329

My GPO in London: Trilogy Edition

Post War Mechanisation

A major development in Trunk Mechanisation was the opening of *Faraday Trunk Non-Director* exchange on 27th February 1954 on the first floor of the South East Block. The unit was split into two parts due to a policy decision to limit the trunk terminations to 5000.

Trunks

Faraday Trunk Non-Director (1954)
Incoming traffic to Director Area 1955
Outgoing traffic from Director Area 27 Feb 1954

Kingsway Trunk (Tandem) Non-Director (1954)
Through traffic
20% terminal traffic

Toll

Toll A (Faraday) For outgoing traffic from the Director Area to the 12.5 to 20-mile belt.

Toll B Director (Faraday) For incoming traffic to the Director Area from the 12.5 to 20-mile belt.

Temporary Toll B Non-Director (Holborn) took over the function of switching traffic to the London Director Area from within the Toll Area, but outside of the 20-mile belt.

In reality, temporary Toll B ND (Holborn) opened in 1946 followed by Toll B Director (Faraday) in 27 June 1949 at which time the Semi-Mechanical (Holborn) Tandem was closed.

Trunk Mech

Kingsway

In 1941, a deep tube shelter consisting of two parallel tunnels was constructed beneath Chancery Lane tube station. This was one of eight war-time shelters or Citadels as they were more correctly known. Each tunnel was approximately a quarter of a mile long and sixteen feet in diameter with provision for 2 floors in each section. The shelters were built underneath the existing Northern and Central Line stations as part of a possible extension to the railway networks in later years.

In 1949, the Kingsway site became part of the Post Office's 'deep level tunnel scheme' and the original workings were extended to the south of High Holborn to house the new trunk exchange. Work started in 1951 and the exchange was brought into service on 30 October 1954 with a permanent staff of 150, connecting 13,000 long distance lines, with a capacity for switching 5000 trunk circuits.

The unit further enabled single-operator control of operator dialled trunk calls.

Kingsway was a *Zone Centre Non-Director* unit. Two other underground *Zone Centres* were:

- *Anchor* below Colmore Lodge in Birmingham which opened 9 November 1957
- *Guardian* below Piccadilly in Manchester which opened 7 December 1958

At the opening of *Kingsway,* the boundary of the *London Group* was reduced from 20 to 12.5 miles, i.e. that of the London Director

My GPO in London: Trilogy Edition

Area. The Toll A area still stretched beyond the 20-mile belt and the Trunk Director was still in use.

TAT 1

International telephone services were established by the opening of a radio link between London and New York on 7th January 1927.

A Trans-Atlantic Telephone (TAT1) cable system became operational on 25 September 1956, primarily linking London to New York and Montreal. The main switching equipment was located within *Kingsway*, with controlling circuits extending to *Wood Street* TE, and *Faraday Building*.

D-Notices

All 3 *Zone Centres* were protected by *D-Notices (Defence Notices)* until 1967 when they were de-classified.

Defence Notices were instructions issued to the Press not to publish or disclose specified subjects which might otherwise harm national security, particularly in wartime.

Although WWII was over, the *Cold War* was simmering in the background right until 1991 and the dissolution of the Soviet Union.

New Dialling Codes in London

From *Post Office Telecommunications Journal* Summer 1959

The new dialling codes, preliminary to the start of Subscriber Trunk Dialling in London, were introduced in the London Director Area on April 6. [1959]

Trunk Mech

"O for Operator" – which was introduced in London in 1928 when the first automatic director exchange was opened in London – TRU for Trunks and TOL for Toll, are replaced by 100. DIR replaced TKD for Trunk Directory Enquiries. INF was introduced for customers seeking general information about the service, or to call the Supervisor.

ENG (Engineers), CON (Continental), INT (International) and TEL (Telegrams) with 999 for emergencies, remain.

Subscriber Trunk Dialling (STD)

The system allowing every subscriber to dial every other subscriber in the UK was begun in *Bristol Central* TE on 5 December 1958 when the Queen dialled 031 CAL 3636 to call the Lord Provost of Edinburgh. It wasn't until 1979 that the 'dial everywhere' network was completed!

031 was the code for Edinburgh
CAL was the CALedonian telephone exchange.
3636 was the local subscriber's number

GRACE

Group Routing And Charging Equipment (GRACE), essential for STD calls, was accessed by dialling 'O' to seize a *Register Translator* (RT), which routed and calculated the charges for each trunk call.

Citadel Outgoing RT (1961)

Citadel Exchange, was the first centralised STD unit for the *London Director Area* and was brought into service on 1 July 1961, in Faraday North East Block. Initially it allowed STD access from

My GPO in London: Trilogy Edition

the *Metropolitan, Moorgate* and *London Wall* exchanges. Thus, the inaugural call from City Area was made on 3 July 1961 by the Lord Mayor, Sir Bernard Waley-Cohen, to the Lord Mayor of Bristol.

Read more about STD, numbering and charging in the next book of the *My GPO* series: *London's Trunks, Tolls, and Telex*.

References

Edinburgh Director Area *Code Card* Nov 1955 from THG.
Events in Telecommunications History (BT Archives)
POEEJ Vol 18 Part 4 Jan 1926 *The Post Office and Automatic Telephones.*
POEEJ Vol. 42 Part 2 July 1955 *London Trunk Kingsway Exchange.*
POTJ Autumn 1963 *London's Trunk Switching Units.*

STD
IS CHEAPER
YOU PAY ONLY
FOR WHAT YOU USE

You pay only what you use. It costs even less if you make your social calls in the Cheap Rate Period. 6 p.m. to 6 a.m. every day, and all day Sunday.

BT Heritage and Archives: TCB 473/P09581 (1967)

Outlet 24: Bloomsbury and Fitzrovia

Post Office Tower

Elaine Harwood of *English Heritage* once remarked of the *Post Office Tower*:

"The slimness of it and the way that nothing was demolished to create it. It sneaked up right in the middle of Georgian London's townscape. It doesn't disturb historic London, it just adds to it."

The BT Tower sneaking up behind Trunk Control Bloomsbury (L/TCB) Chenies Street © J. Chenery (2006)

My GPO in London: Trilogy Edition

[In the photo (page335) the outline of the Eisenhower Centre can be seen on the left. In wartime this once formed an entrance to the Goodge Street Deep Level Shelter. A serious fire on the night of 21 May 1956 closed the shelter.]

At Bloomsbury

Serving the locality of the British Museum, a manual telephone exchange opened in Chenies Street on 20 April 1914. *Museum* CB1 (Central Battery) exchange was equipped with 113 A-positions and 43 B-positions to cater for 9720 subscribers. ['A-position' sections were for subscribers' lines. 'B-position' sections were for incoming junctions.]

At Fitzrovia

In reality, acquisition of the existing plots and buildings in Howland Street for the use of the General Post Office (and ultimately the PO Tower) was already underway with the passing of the Post Office (sites) Act 1936. As already discussed in previous chapters, the GPO often had a multitude of new sites under consideration, in order to (eventually) meet the increasing demand for its services. The detailed planning for telephone and postal services in London were well-advanced before the wars (WWI & II), although many contingencies were developed as a consequence of them.

The Howland Street site was to have been a mix of postal and telecom use, but the popularity of television, and the growth of the telephone after the war seems to have dictated how the development was to proceed.

Bloomsbury

Museum TE (Howland Street)

In Parliament: *"Mr. Bartlett asked the Postmaster-General when the Museum Exchange will be transferred from manual to automatic operation; and what steps he proposes to take in the meantime to render it less inefficient."*
[Hansard - HC Deb 26 April 1944 vol 399 c759.]

Museum auto exchange opened in a new building in Howland Street on 29 July 1944. The older building on Chenies Street became L/TCB (Trunk Control Bloomsbury) on 16 Oct 1950.

Museum TE in Howland Street © J. Chenery (2008)

My GPO in London: Trilogy Edition

London to Birmingham Links

As BBC TV resumed after WWII it was agreed that the GPO should manage the transmission of sound and vision between the transmitters and the studio locations/outside broadcasts. *Museum* exchange was conveniently located along the coaxial cable route between Alexander Palace and Broadcasting House and thus by 1947 had developed into a focal point for programme transmissions. A coaxial cable to carry 405-line TV between London and Birmingham was in the planning process.

"...*The main cable will form part of the Post Office trunk network and terminate at Museum exchange, London, and Telephone House, Birmingham.*" [POEEJ Jan 1949.]

Additionally, a backbone radio-relay network for TV and telephone circuits across the UK, had identified *Museum* as a suitable London termination point, using a 150ft lattice mast on the roof of the exchange. The temporary mast was finally removed on 7 May 1967 as the new *Post Office Tower* took over.

Television Switching

'The opening of the first provincial B.B.C. television station at Sutton Goldfield on 17 December 1949 was made possible by the provision of an ultra-high frequency radio relay system between Museum Exchange (London) and Telephone House (Birmingham).'

Accordingly, the *London Television Network Switching Centre (NSC)* had also opened in *Museum TE* in December 1949 to allow the distribution of BBC TV to the provinces, and much later...the rest of the world.

Bloomsbury

Capacity for ITV and BBC2 channels were also planned; today the *NSC* routes the majority of TV output, satellite and terrestrial.

PO Tower

In the BBC TV series *Doctor Who*, the TARDIS lands in Bedford Square (filmed on 22 May 1966). The Doctor looks to the skyline and remarks, "So that's it." His companion Dodo replies, "What? Oh, the *Tower*, it's finished. It's great, isn't it?!" [Extract from *The War Machines* DVD.]

BT Tower in Maple Street. The re-modelled entrance following its re-launch to corporate clients mid-1990s © J. Chenery (2015)

The *Museum Radio Tower* as it was first known, was constructed adjacent to *Museum* telephone exchange to provide the London link in a chain of microwave towers across the UK.

My GPO in London: Trilogy Edition

Tower Facts

Constructed: June 1961- July 1965
Chief architect: Eric Bedford – Ministry of Works.
Main contractors: Lind and Company.
Grade II listed: 26 March 2003.
Height: 580 ft. plus 40ft. aerial mast, total 620 feet.
Opened to public: 19 May 1966.
Viewing platforms closed: 31 October 1971 due to bomb damage.
Restaurant closed: 14 June 1980 when Butlin's lease expired.

The Engineer-in-Chief's report of 1959 highlighted the question:

'The public should be permitted to view London from one of the upper platforms of the tower on payment of an admission fee?'

The report also stated that the tower would be of value for the provision of local microwave links and for the provision of v.h.f. mobile radio services in the Greater London area.

The Engineer-in-Chief's report of 1960 confirmed:

'Work on the Museum Exchange radio tower, which will be the tallest structure in London and will include two observation galleries and a restaurant for the public above the aerial galleries, is expected to start in June 1961.'

At the operational opening of the Post Office Tower, on 8 October 1965, the Prime Minister Harold Wilson telephoned the Birmingham tower which had been completed that September.

"I am going now to inaugurate this great and historic development this morning. And to inaugurate it... in a... not by cutting a tape or

Bloomsbury

any of the more traditional methods, but by speaking to the Lord Mayor of Birmingham over the microwave radio link from this new tower." [British Pathé News: Premier Opens Highest Tower.]

Horn Aerials

The tower was initially equipped with eight horn-shaped aerials to give:

"...four main microwave radio paths - from London towards Birmingham, Coventry and the North; toward Southampton, Bristol and the West and also for the satellite communication ground station at Goonhilly Downs; toward Dover, Folkestone and the Continent; and toward Norwich and the North-East of England."

"...as many as 100,000 simultaneous telephone conversations and up to 40 television channels." [Leaflet PH 1051 5/65.]

By the mid-1980s, the microwave links had been superseded by use of modern fibre-optic cable routes. Digital radio links added ever more dishes until the galleries were becoming rather cluttered! In December 2011 the remaining giant, disused and decaying horn aerials were cut up and removed together with all of the redundant older dish aerials. This left the designated aerial galleries looking very empty, although a few newer dishes have since been installed.

Design Aspects

The tower was intended purely as an operational building to ensure clear line-of-sight for its microwave signalling, up to a height of 475 feet. With a core of 22 feet (stairs and lifts), and a maximum diameter of just 52 feet, the available area per floor was restrictive. By design, the waveguides for the microwave horns needed to be

My GPO in London: Trilogy Edition

situated as close to the aerials as possible. Hence the 17 levels (B1 to B17) below the aerial galleries, which gave approximately 1500 sq. ft. for the equipment and support services.

Catering for the Public

A model of the proposed tower was shown to the press on 1 Feb 1961...

"The Post Office, believing that the design will add to London's amenities, is providing a public observation platform, about 460 feet high, which will be reached in some 40 seconds by about 8 mph, lifts." [POTJ Spring 1961.]

The design changed from inception as the revolving restaurant, wasn't initially included. As the tallest building in London during the 1960s, it was realised that the provision of an upper restaurant with additional observation galleries would be a major tourist attraction. The idea of a revolving floor on level 34 was unique!

"The restaurant floor, 65 feet in diameter and the widest part of the Tower, will seat up to 120 customers on a circular strip of floor 10 feet 6 inches wide, which will rotate once every 20 minutes so that visitors will be able to enjoy uninterrupted panoramic views of London." [POTJ Summer 1964.]

A lower-level tea bar was planned, but never came into being:

'*Refreshments at the Tower are limited to lunch and dinner only at Butlin's Restaurant (Top of the Tower).*'

[Post Office Circular DF 899 (Telephone Edition) 17th August 1966.]

Bloomsbury

Advert – *Scotsman* – April 3rd 1963

Revolving Restaurant | Cocktail Bar | With Kitchen & Cloakrooms: To be let by tender.

- The restaurant's gross area will be 3,200 sq. ft.
- The cocktail bar and cloakrooms together will also cover 3,200 sq. ft. and the kitchen and storerooms 2,400 sq. ft.
- Particulars, plans and terms of tender can be obtained by principals only on payment of £1 per set, from the Director of Lands, Ministry of Public Building and Works, Romney House, Marsham Street, London, SW1.

The lease was taken up by Butlins of holiday camp fame.

Top of the Tower

The uppermost floors of the tower were to attract and exploit the paying public:

- T36 Kitchen
- T35 Inner cocktail bar for diners only. Outer open terrace/observation platform
- T34 Revolving restaurant
- T33 Enclosed observation platform equipped with telescopes
- T32 Enclosed observation platform
- T31 Enclosed observation platform

My GPO in London: Trilogy Edition

Barbara Mower writes, *"This is a photo of the turntable base of the Post Office Tower revolving restaurant, built by Ransomes and Rapier and my Dad. When this base had been assembled it was revolving and I went to see it before it was taken apart to be transported to London. If I remember rightly, they had a threepenny bit stood on edge for some time and it never fell over."*

The special floor-carrier for the revolving restaurant being fabricated at Ransomes and Rapier's Waterside Works, Ipswich, early 1960s. Photo © Ransomes and Rapier Ltd ref 11911 from Barbara Mower's collection. Barbara's father is sitting on the beam, centre foreground.

Bloomsbury

Billy Butlin's aptly named *topofthetower* restaurant, on floor 34, was fine dining for connoisseurs; it was not for the masses of tourists who clambered over the high-level viewing platforms to sight-see London. Dining in the revolving restaurant had to be booked by telephone or via the separate reception at the base of the tower. Diners were given priority over tourists for use of the two high-speed lifts.

The revolving floor mechanism was (and still is) driven by an electric motor supplied by Radicon. Blue carpeting, matching the décor, once carried a red cog-wheel symbol:

'Patrons will notice that the emblem of the TOPOFTHETOWER is a cog-wheel and this is carried on the carpet, serviettes, and also on the jackets worn by the waiters. This emblem signifies the single cog-wheel which actually drives the revolving floor and is worked by as little as a two and a half h. p. motor.'

'The décor of the restaurant is simple, modern and yet luxurious. The main colour scheme is midnight blue highlighted with red. These colours have been specially selected to reflect the colours of the night sky, and to accentuate this, the interior walls of the restaurant are panelled with smoked glass mirrors.'

Reception

The ground floor of the tower, at the junction of Maple Street and Cleveland Mews, formed a large open platform with steps up to a wide entrance space with separate doors leading to 'viewing platforms' and 'topofthetower.' Also, within the main reception was a gift/souvenir shop and wishing well/pond, as befitted public buildings of the era.

My GPO in London: Trilogy Edition

A picturesque night view of the Post Office Tower public entrance
© BT Heritage and Archives TCB 346/T841 (1971)

Bloomsbury

Telephone Switching

Museum TE contained Strowger *Director* exchanges, but trunk units for switching Subscriber Trunk Dialling (STD) calls were housed in part of the four-storey extension, associated with the new tower complex.

- *Tower Non-Director* O/G GSC: (July 1965) with up to 22 magnetic drum type RTs.
- *Mercury Non-Director* I/C GSC: (Nov 1965) 11,000 selectors. Handled trunk traffic into London.
- *Museum Tandem*: (April 1966) 1,200 selectors. A junction tandem exchange to switch calls between local *Director* exchanges within London.

Under All-Figure Numbering, by late 1969 *Howland Street* had become the AFN unit name for *Museum* (originally code 687) giving a range of 01-636 xxxx numbers.

Howland Street 01-631 opened on 29/01/69.

A third AFN unit 01-637 opened on 23/08/69.

Additional hypothetical ranges were *Howland Street* 01-323 (parented on 01-631) and 01-632 DDI (parented on 01-637).

Langham (code 526) which started as a unit in *Mayfair TE* (circa 1934) moved into *Museum* (circa 1949) and became *Howland Street* 01-580 xxxx numbers on conversion to AFN.

My GPO in London: Trilogy Edition

A Lasting Icon

The 1960's *White Heat of Technology* optimism into which the Post Office Tower had emerged was short-lived. On 31 October 1971 at 04:30 a bomb which had been planted on the 31st floor exploded, blowing out a large section of the external structure. The restaurant re-opened on 25 November, but all other access to the public viewing galleries ended; the tourist's dream was over!

IRA bombings of mainland UK during the 1970s did little to strengthen the case for renewed tourism. And upon expiry of Butlin's lease in 1980 the restaurant too was permanently closed. The needs of an operational communications building took precedence and had to be safeguarded.

Today, more stringent fire evacuation regulations are enforced; the tower's infrastructure was never designed for masses of visitors; it had always been an afterthought in a design on a constricted site.

The tower remains an icon which many may wish to visit, but few will get an invitation, unless they have business to transact or a special event or reason to attend.

Feasibility Studies

In 1982, British Telecom commissioned the PSA (Property Services Agency – the latter-day *Office of Works*) to investigate adding an external (annular) lift to the existing structure, with the prospect of re-opening the tower to tourists.

Subsequently, in 1984, a refurbished *BT Tower Suite* opened for corporate guests only; the prospect of once again dealing with thousands of public visitors was simply impractical.

Bloomsbury

Central Headquarters (CHQ)

At the time the Post Office became a public corporation (Oct 1969) it organised functions which were common to Posts and Telecommunications into a Central HQ which was located, close to the Tower, at 23 Howland Street, on the corner of Charlotte Street.

Post Office Central Headquarters, 23 Howland St., London W1P 6HQ (01-631 2345). *Street view image capture July 2015 © Google 2018.*

These central departments reported to the Deputy Chairman and included the Radio and Broadcasting Department, the National Data Processing Department, the Statistics and Business Research Department, and the Central Personnel Department. Functions encompassed, the work of solicitors, secretaries, engineers and public relations staff.

My GPO in London: Trilogy Edition

From about 1979 CHQ functions were dispersed between PHQ and THQ as the Post Office geared up for privatisation of telecommunications.

Later, BT Radiopaging was based in room 4038.

The block 23 Howland Street and 80 Charlotte Street was demolished circa 2015 as the site was redeveloped.

References

Leaflet PH 1051 5/65
Booklets PH1676 12/70 and PHME 7378 8/91

Engineer-in-Chief's Annual Report 1949

POEEJ Vol 7 1914 – *New Exchanges: Museum.*
POEEJ Vol 25 Pt 4 Jan 1933 *Mayfair Building.*
POEEJ Vol 41 Part 4 Jan 1949 – *The London-Birmingham Television Cable.*
POEEJ Vol 55 Part 2 July 1962 – *Museum Radio Tower.*

www.samhallas.co.uk/telecomms.htm

BT Archives:
Museum lattice tower demolition 7 May 1967 Film 1231.
Butlin's pamphlet (1968) ref: TCB 325/EHA2047

Outlet 25: On His Majesty's Service

O.H.M.S.

The letters O.H.M.S. were once regularly used on postal envelopes sent by departments of HM Government. As part of the Civic Service, the Post Office was effectively 'in the service of his/her majesty.' [An official explanation of this term is unknown.]

Accordingly, conditions of employment in the Post Office were onerous, and staff were expected to strictly perform their duties in the correct manner.

Probationer telegraphist George Stow explains the working conditions in 1927 at the Central Telegraph Office:

"The manners and dress of some of the supervision and staff that I first encountered in the gallery was very formal. And a subsequent perusal of the Staff Rule Book showed that we were expected to wear dark suits and ties. I have a memory of a superintendent, at a desk, raised on a dias, and dressed in a frock coat with a winged or butterfly collar. He was wearing pince-nez spectacles with a gold safety chain attached to his ear. And to complete the picture, a golden watch chain stretched across his ample waistcoat, with a sovereign dangling from it...I do not think even in those days that a wage of seventeen shillings and fivepence would have bought me much in the way of a black coat, and striped trousers...but I was proud of my new job."

In 1952, the Post Office still employed probationer grades, as noted on the poster (next page).

My GPO in London: Trilogy Edition

GIRL PROBATIONERS WANTED

LONDON POST OFFICE DEPARTMENTS NEED GIRLS OF 14 TO 15 FOR INDOOR MESSENGER DUTIES

GIRL PROBATIONER SERVICE LEADS ON TO A PERMANENT CAREER IN THE POST OFFICE.

MEAL VOUCHERS ARE PROVIDED AND FREE EDUCATIONAL CLASSES IN OFFICIAL TIME ARE AVAILABLE.

FOR FURTHER INFORMATION APPLY TO:-
   THE STAFF CONTROLLER (REF SA/2A)
   LONDON TLECOMMUNICATIONS REGION
   WATERLOO BRIDGE HOUSE, S.E.1

PRD 428

GPO Poster (1952) © BT Heritage & Archives TCB 473/P5596